ANTHOLOGY
for
SIGHT SINGING

ANTHOLOGY
for
SIGHT SINGING

Gary S. Karpinski

Richard Kram

W. W. NORTON

NEW YORK   LONDON

W. W. Norton & Company has been independent since its founding in 1923, when William Warder Norton and Margaret D. Herter Norton first published lectures delivered at the People's Institute, the adult education division of New York City's Cooper Union. The Nortons soon expanded their program beyond the Institute, publishing books by celebrated academics from America and abroad. By mid-century, the two major pillars of Norton's publishing program—trade books and college texts—were firmly established. In the 1950s, the Norton family transferred control of the company to its employees, and today—with a staff of 400 and a comparable number of trade, college, and professional titles published each year—W. W. Norton & Company stands as the largest and oldest publishing house owned wholly by its employees.

Manufacturing by Quad/Graphics
Composition by A-R Editions
Book design by Chris Welch

Editor: Maribeth Anderson Payne
Project Editor: Allison Courtney Fitch
Associate Editor: Allison Benter
Managing Editor—College: Marian Johnson
Production Manager: JoAnn Simony

ISBN-10: 0-393-97382-4
ISBN-13: 978-0-393-97382-2

W. W. Norton & Company, Inc., 500 Fifth Avenue, New York, N.Y. 10110
    www.wwnorton.com
W. W. Norton & Company Ltd., Castle House, 75/76 Wells Street, London W1T 3QT

4 5 6 7 8 9 0

To Julia and Alex—
thanks for your patience and understanding
—G.S.K.

To my parents
—R.K.

CONTENTS

PREFACE

Purpose

The purpose of this *Anthology* is to provide excerpts for sight singing and for preparation and study. These excerpts are taken from both composed works and folk sources. No method (solfège, conducting, rhythm syllables, etc.) is advocated, nor does any single approach to sight singing shape the *Anthology*. Indeed, one of the main goals of this book is to make these materials available to and usable by all instructors and students. (For a step-by-step approach to sight singing, see Karpinski's *Manual for Ear Training and Sight Singing,* which is coordinated with this *Anthology*.)

Scope

The excerpts offer a wide variety of music to support a multi-year curriculum in aural skills training. The main focus of this *Anthology* is on tonal music, but there is also a group of modal selections and several dozen others that stretch the limits of tonality and explore some non-diatonic pitch collections.* Although the lion's share of the excerpts come from Western European art music of the common-practice period, many are drawn from Medieval, Renaissance, twentieth-century, and popular repertoires and over a hundred excerpts come from folk sources. A significant number of excerpts were composed by women and by American composers. Vocal and instrumental genres are both well represented by selections from operas, oratorios, masses, motets, songs, symphonies, concertos, sonatas, chamber music, and various other genres.

While reaching far and wide to provide an extensive variety of excerpts from many eras, regions, and genres, we have sought to include both the obscure and the renowned. Thus, for example, readers will find both the Bizzarria in C major by Bernardo Pasquini and sections from Handel's *Messiah*. We have intentionally included a fair number of excerpts from well-known compositions from the Western canon—"warhorses," if you will—for two important reasons. First, students can more readily associate new concepts and skills with music that is already familiar to them. For example, students who know the second theme from the overture to Rossini's *William Tell* already have a solid foundation on which to build the labels for the tonic and dominant triads. Second, these excerpts also afford ample opportunity for students to learn themes from many of the canonic works of Western music. Still, there are plenty of less familiar excerpts in each section for instructors who wish to avoid the warhorses altogether.

---

*Readers looking for more post-tonal aural-skills materials should consult books entirely devoted to this repertoire, such as Lars Edlund, *Modus Novus: Studies in Reading Atonal Melodies* (Stockholm: Nordiska Musikförlaget, 1964) and Michael Friedmann, *Ear Training for Twentieth-Century Music* (New Haven: Yale University Press, 1990).

Organization

The *Anthology* is arranged in sequence from easy to difficult in general accordance with the learning sequence used in the *Manual for Ear Training and Sight Singing*. The earliest excerpts feature basic rhythms in simple meters and skip only to scale degrees $\hat{1}$, $\hat{3}$, and $\hat{5}$ in the major mode. Thereafter, each new element is clearly announced with a heading (for example, "Compound Meters") followed by excerpts that introduce that element first in simple, relatively isolated contexts followed by more complex excerpts. In this way, this book provides progressively graded excerpts that allow instructors and students to focus on very specific musical elements while dealing entirely with real music.

Despite the fact that the excerpts appear in a particular pedagogical order, instructors will be able to use the *Anthology* as a sourcebook for excerpts to match many different learning sequences, especially through consulting the Useful Lists at the end of this book and using the accompanying software (see "Software," below). For example, although the *Anthology* begins with excerpts that skip to members of the tonic triad, instructors who wish to begin with stepwise materials can find dozens of such melodies using either the appropriate list or the software.

Maintenance of Original Appearance

One of the goals of studying sight singing is to enable students to read the variety of music from the many sources they will encounter as musicians. Readers should be able to take a score from the library shelf, read from an orchestral part, play an etude, study an excerpt in a harmony textbook, examine a work in a history anthology, consider a composition for sale in a music store, or look at any music and apply the skills they learn through studying sight singing. To that end, this *Anthology* strives to maintain the original "look" of all excerpts as one of its guiding principles. All excerpts retain their original tempo marks, dynamics, articulation, phrasing, beaming (where possible), lyrics, and so forth. (Alert readers may note the necessary exceptions to this principle, such as when a single line is extracted from a crowded staff, the "correction" of stem directions when such lines are isolated, the reprinting of tempo and dynamic markings established earlier, and so on.) Double barlines appear at the ends of only those excerpts that originally end with double barlines; other excerpts end with single barlines or none at all (for those that end mid-bar). All excerpts are printed at their original pitch (but see "Vocal Range and Transposition," below). In addition, all inconsistencies in orthography have been maintained. No attempt has been made to standardize such features as beaming, text extensions, double bars, and triplet symbols. Every excerpt appears as it does in its original context.

Because such care has been taken to preserve the original look of these excerpts, students will find little difference between reading melodies in the *Anthology* and reading from the scores and parts they encounter in their other musical endeavors.

Sources

An important principle guiding the collection of excerpts for this *Anthology* is authenticity. In order to provide the most authentic versions possible, we obtained excerpts from Urtext editions, editions overseen or approved by the composer, and other such authoritative sources. At times, this principle conflicts with the effort to maintain the appearance of excerpts as readers might come across them in other contexts. For example, an orchestral player might be given a part to a Mozart symphony from an edition that contains markings different from those in the *Neue Mozart*

Ausgabe. These discrepancies are generally slight, and in those cases we have adhered to the most authoritative source. Musicians encounter some works so frequently in other editions that we opted to reproduce them as they appear in those settings (Carissimi's cantata "Vittoria, mio core!" as it appears in *Twenty-Four Italian Songs and Arias* is one such case).

Attributions

All excerpts are identified as completely as possible so that readers with access to a well-stocked music library will be able to find them in their original contexts. Excerpts from composed literature are labeled with the composer's name, the title of the work (including movement number, section title, or other divisional label), measure numbers, and the date, when it is known. If a work was composed over a number of years, the date of completion is used, and if a work was substantially revised at a later date, we list the date of the version used for this *Anthology.* Questionable and approximate dates are noted (1790? or c. 1790).

Opus numbers and catalog numbers (such as Köchel numbers for Mozart's works) are included when they are available and useful. J. S. Bach's cantatas do not include catalog numbers because the customary numbers correspond to the BWV numbering scheme (Cantata no. 212 is catalogued as BWV 212). His chorales are labeled with the numbering scheme developed by C. P. E. Bach and still used widely in the teaching of music theory. Titles are printed in their original language unless the work is pervasively known in English-speaking countries by a translated title or widely recognized subtitle.

Each excerpt taken from folk sources is labeled with a tune name and country or region of origin. However, some folk melodies have been sung in a variety of regions and some exist in a variety of versions. No systematic attempt has been made to identify various versions of individual melodies. We chose one version from one area for each folk melody. Readers should not infer any sense of authenticity or primacy from our labels.

Vocal Range and Transposition

There are two primary principles that affect the vocal practicality of excerpts in this *Anthology.* First, each excerpt is printed in its original key. (Even parts for transposing instruments—with the exception of those in the section devoted to transposition—are shown at concert pitch. Maintaining the original key takes precedence over maintaining the original look in these cases.) Second, each excerpt should be sung in its original key, if possible. In this way, all excerpts look and sound as they do in the settings in which students will find them outside the aural skills classroom. (For example, the subject at the beginning of the C minor fugue from Book II of Bach's *Well-Tempered Clavier* will indeed appear in C minor.)

We recognize, of course, that some excerpts in their original keys contain pitches too high or low for many sight-singing students. We presuppose a *practical vocal range* of an octave and a 5th for all students of sight singing. Specifically, this range spans the following pitches:

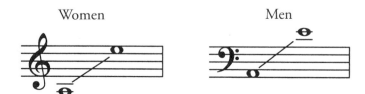

Women   Men

No matter what type of singing voice a music student possesses—soprano, alto, tenor, bass, or some variation of these—he or she will need to be able to sing the pitches within this range to accommodate all the excerpts in this *Anthology*. Not all students will be able to sing the highest or lowest pitches with effortless grace (particularly those who do not have much singing experience), but everyone's goal should be to sing them in the service of producing correct pitches and rhythms with musicality.

For those who find a range of an octave and a 5th to be too wide, nearly two-thirds of the excerpts in this *Anthology* have a range of an octave or smaller. Excerpts with such narrower ranges can be found easily using the accompanying software (see "Software," below).

Excerpts are printed at their original octaves. Therefore, excerpts that are an octave or more above or below the practical vocal range should be adjusted accordingly (no special instructions are given when only octave transposition is necessary). This includes the singing of treble-clef parts by men and bass-clef parts by women. However, special care should be taken when singing multiple-part excerpts in ensemble so that the parts retain their relative positions above and below one another.

When an excerpt exceeds the bounds of the practical vocal range (regardless of octave transposition), a simple indication is printed before the excerpt giving a transposition (for example, "down 5th") or range of transpositions (for example, "down 3rd–6th") that will bring the excerpt within the practical vocal range. These transpositions are given in terms of *number* but not *quality*, so that—for example—a 3rd is indicated but not a major or minor 3rd. This allows instructors to choose particular transpositions (to F♯, for example, instead of F) without straining too far beyond the bounds of the practical vocal range.

Regardless of our suggested transpositions, readers are under no obligation to make any transposition if their vocal ranges can accommodate an excerpt at concert pitch. In addition, nothing should prevent readers from transposing any of these excerpts to better accommodate their own particularly high, low, or restricted ranges.

Occasionally, excerpts are printed with octave signs indicating the original register of certain pitches. To accommodate vocal ranges, readers should sing these excerpts without regard to the octave signs.

Ledger Lines

Most sight-singing books transcribe excerpts so that they all appear within the staff, changing the octave placement of those excerpts that originally appear on ledger lines. In keeping with the principle of maintaining the original appearance of excerpts, this *Anthology* reproduces excerpts at their original octaves, even when they include many ledger lines (see, for example, the two violin parts in No. 43). It is important for music students to develop a familiarity and facility with scores and parts printed on ledger lines.

Vocal Notation

All musicians encounter both instrumental and vocal notation in their musical lives. In general, instrumental notation uses beams to join notes into logical rhythmic and metric groups—beaming, for example, four sixteenth notes together in $\frac{3}{4}$ meter. In contrast, most vocal notation uses beams to show the division of syllables in the text. This makes rhythmic and metric groups more difficult to read, but students must become accustomed to reading vocal as well as instrumental notation. This *Anthology* reproduces each vocal excerpt using the beaming found in the original score. We encourage students unfamiliar with vocal beaming to spend extra time with those excerpts that use vocal beaming so that they may become more accustomed to this widespread notational practice.

Most vocal works are reproduced with their original texts, with the exception of most folk melodies (which usually sport a wide variety of text variants) and excerpts from Bach's chorales (which are reproduced without text, as in Riemenschneider and most theory texts).

Ornaments

Grace notes, trills, and other such ornaments that appear in the original notation are reproduced here without comment. It is well beyond the scope of this (or any) sight-singing book to provide a comprehensive treatment of how to execute these signs. Some sight-singing instructors might choose to omit all ornaments, while others might require students to perform some or all of them. Readers wishing to pursue the subject further can consult the excellent article "Ornaments" in *The New Grove Dictionary of Music and Musicians,* 2nd edition (New York: Oxford University Press, 2001).

Multiple-Part Excerpts

Duets, trios, and excerpts for larger ensembles are printed alongside single-part excerpts (not isolated at the ends of sections or in separate sections of the book). All excerpts appear where pedagogically appropriate according to their musical contents, regardless of the number of parts. Instructors are under no obligation to have students sing all multiple-part excerpts in ensemble at all times. Indeed, individual parts may be sung in isolation to focus profitably on the topics at hand.

Software

The software that accompanies the *Anthology* treats the excerpts as a database, so that instructors will be able to select excerpts appropriate for any level or topic of study. For example, consider the following requests:

- Find all minor-mode excerpts in simple meters with skips only to scale degrees $\hat{1}$, $\hat{3}$, and $\hat{5}$.
- Find all excerpts containing syncopation.
- Find all excerpts that outline V/V in the major mode.
- Find all excerpts in the bass clef containing notes of one beat or longer.
- Find all excerpts with a range of a fifth or smaller.

Using the software, instructors will be able to search the *Anthology* for excerpts to fit many different criteria. In this way, the *Anthology* is flexible enough to meet the needs of a wide variety of approaches to teaching sight singing. For example, one instructor might teach major and minor modes from the first day but remain on very simple rhythms until later in the curriculum, whereas another might teach only major mode for many weeks or months while introducing many rhythmic complexities during that same time period. Both instructors will be able to retrieve ample materials for each class meeting by using the software. Many instructors will find the software to be an invaluable tool for discovering music literature appropriate for a wide variety of sight-singing needs.

ACKNOWLEDGMENTS

Many wonderful people played a part in the conception and creation of this anthology and the accompanying software. At W. W. Norton, Suzanne LaPlante, former music editor, was deeply involved in the earliest stages of envisioning how this collection would take shape. When Maribeth Payne took over as music editor, she helped shepherd this project along. Allison Benter, former associate music editor, spent many hours helping with the manuscript. Courtney Fitch, assistant music editor, worked tirelessly to see the book through copy editing and production; her common sense and sunny disposition made so much of this process a pleasure. JoAnn Simony, senior production manager, was instrumental in overseeing production. Claire McCabe, former assistant music editor, and Katie Hannah, college sales representative, were of great assistance early in the process. Steve Hoge, emedia editor for music, was an important resource in developing and producing the software.

It was a joy to surround ourselves with such great music as we searched for the right excerpts to fill this volume. In this endeavor, three music librarians were especially helpful: at the University of Massachusetts, Amherst, music librarian Pamela Juengling gave generous assistance on numerous occasions, and at Amherst College, music librarian Jane Beebe and music library assistant Ann Maggs provided valuable help. In addition, Sigrun Heinzelmann, Jane Hanson, and Andrew Davis brought several excellent excerpts to our attention. David Butler and Rene van Egmond provided indispensable melodic search tools. Diane Luchese and Rob Haskins were particularly helpful in tracking down sources.

Christa Kober assisted skillfully and professionally in setting some of the excerpts. Her painstaking thoroughness proved beneficial in many ways. Sarah Marlowe provided invaluable assistance checking the data for the software. Her meticulous attention to detail saved us from our own carelessness on countless occasions.

In addition to the many years of classroom testing we carried out on the materials in this book, Sigrun Heinzelmann, Jane Hanson, Mark McFarland, and Brent Auerbach have used these excerpts in their own teaching and offered valuable feedback, providing many helpful suggestions and corrections over the years.

Finally, none of this would have been possible without the loving support of our families. Hongnim, Peter, Jean, Julie, and Alex—we owe you our deepest gratitude. Thank you.

You must learn by heart a fair number of melodies so that by the memory of these . . . notes you will recognize all sounds, of whatever sort. For it is indeed quite another thing to recall something with understanding than it is to sing something by rote; only the wise can do the former while persons without foresight can often do the latter.

—GUIDO OF AREZZO
C. 1030

BASIC RHYTHMS IN SIMPLE METERS; SKIPS TO 1̂, 3̂, AND 5̂ IN C MAJOR

Pierre Francisque Caroubel, *Terpsichore,* No. 4, Bransle double no. 1, mm. 1–4 (1612)

1

J. S. Bach, Cantata No. 61, "Nun komm, der Heiden Heiland," Overture, mm. 33–36 (1714)

2 gai.

"John Dory," British sea song, mm. 9–16

3

J. S. Bach, Chorale No. 348, "Meinen Jesum laß ich nicht," mm. 10–13

4

"Watt's Cradle Hymn," North American Christmas hymn, mm. 1–4

5 Sleep, my——— babe; thy food and——— rai - ment,

Orlando di Lasso, *Magnificat octavi toni,* "Et exsultavit spiritus meus," mm. 12–16 (1567)

6 spi - ri - tus me - us, spi - ri - tus me - - - us

Allegro

Béla Bartók, *For Children*, Part II, No. 6, "There Is an Old Witch," mm. 9–22 (1909)

7

Ruhige, nicht zu langsame Bewegung.

Engelbert Humperdinck, *Hänsel und Gretel*, Prelude, mm. 1–4 (1893)

8

Poco Allegretto

Béla Bartók, *For Children*, Part I, No. 5, "Kitty, Kitty," mm. 1–18 (1909)

9

W. A. Mozart, German Dance K. 605, No. 3, mm. 1–8 (1791)

10

Corresponding Chapter in *Manual for Ear Training and Sight Singing*: 9

Vocal transposition: down 2nd–7th

Modest Mussorgsky, *Boris Godunov*, Prologue, Scene 2 (Coronation scene), mm. 50–61 (1872)

Moderato cantabile

11

Like the sun in the skies,___ su - preme in its glo - ry, glo -

ry, O - ver Rus - sia our Tsar Bo -ris now reigns___ in glo - ry, glo - ry!

Allegro

Domenico Scarlatti, Sonata K. 487, mm. 1–8

12

Vocal transposition: up 2nd–6th

Béla Bartók, *For Children*, Part II, No. 21, "Funny Story
[She flew down and was in tears]," mm. 1–8 (1909)

Allegro moderato

13

f umoristico

Vocal transposition: down 2nd–7th

Jean Sibelius, Symphony No. 3, Op. 52, mvt. 3, mm. 246–257 (1907)

Allegro (ma non tanto), con energia

14

f   poco f

Corresponding Chapter in *Manual for Ear Training and Sight Singing:* **9**

THE FIFTEEN MAJOR KEYS

W. A. Mozart, Minuet K. 65ᵃ (61ᵇ), No. 6, Trio, mm. 1–8 (1769)

15

Vocal transposition: down 3rd–7th

J. S. Bach, Cantata No. 61, "Nun komm, der Heiden Heiland," No. 6, mm. 8–14 (1714)

16

Dei - ner wart' ich mit Ver - lan - gen._____

J. S. Bach, Chorale No. 247, "Wenn wir in höchsten Nöten sein," mm. 1–2 [melody: Loys Bourgeois (1547)]

17

Johannes Brahms, *49 deutsche Volkslieder*, WoO 33, No. 11,
"Jungfräulein, soll ich mit euch gehn," mm. 1–16 (1894)

Lebhaft, doch zart

18

Jung - fräu - lein, soll ich mit euch gehn in eu - ren Ro - sen - gar - ten, da

wo die ro - ten Rös - lein stehn, die fei - nen und die zar - ten, und

auch ein Baum der blü - het und sei - ne Läub - lein wiegt, und

auch ein küh - ler Brun - nen, der grad da - run - ter liegt.

Vocal transposition: down 4th–7th

Muzio Clementi, Sonatina Op. 36, No. 2, mvt. 3, mm. 1–8 (1797)

19

George Frideric Handel, Cantata *Cor fedele, in vano speri (Clori, Tirsi, e Fileno)*,
HWV 96, "Senza occhi e senza accenti," mm. 1–8 (1707)

20

Vocal transposition: down 3rd–6th

Béla Bartók, *First Term at the Piano,* No. 13, "Hungarian Folk Song
[Where have you been, my lambkin?]," mm. 1–4 (1913)

21

Vincenzo Bellini, *Norma,* Act I, "Ah! bello a me ritorna," mm. 30–42 (1831)

22

Sei len-to, dì, sei len-to o gior-no di ven-det-ta; ma i-ra-to il Dio t'af-

fret-ta che il Te-bro con-dan-nò, ma i-ra-to il Dio t'af-fret-ta che il Te-bro con-dan-nò.

Corresponding Chapter in *Manual for Ear Training and Sight Singing*: 11

Vocal transposition: Transpose the upper part down an octave.

W. A. Mozart, *A Musical Joke*, K. 522, mvt. 1, mm. 1–7 (1787)

Allegro.

23

Joseph Haydn, String Quartet Op. 74, No. 2 (Hob III:73), mvt. 4, mm. 1–4 (1793)

Presto

24

Antonín Dvořák, "Scherzo Capriccioso," Op. 66, mm. 355–362 (1883)

355   **Poco tranquillo**

25

mf espressivo   *f*

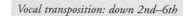*Vocal transposition: down 2nd–6th*

Jean-Philippe Rameau, *Hippolyte et Aricie*, Act II, mm. 49–56 (1733)

Vite

49

26

Non,   dans   le   sé - jour   té - né - breux,   C'est   en

53

vain   qu'on   gé - mit,   c'est   en   vain   que   l'on   cri -   e,

"Brave News from Admiral Vernon," British sea song, mm. 1–4

27

Corresponding Chapter in *Manual for Ear Training and Sight Singing*: 11

National anthem of Austria, mm. 1–8
[possibly attributable to W. A. Mozart, Johann Holzer, or Joseph Baurnjöpel]

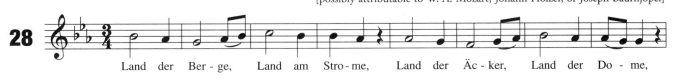

What can you do before you sing to hear the first note of the top voice in the following excerpt?

Vocal transposition: up 2nd–4th

Ludwig van Beethoven, Piano Concerto No. 5, Op. 73 ("Emperor"), mvt. 1, mm. 48–56 (1809)

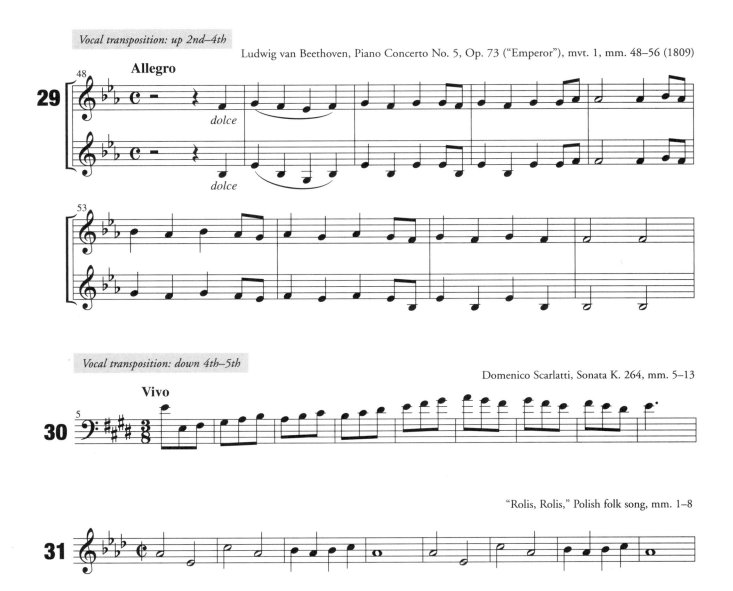

Vocal transposition: down 4th–5th

Domenico Scarlatti, Sonata K. 264, mm. 5–13

"Rolis, Rolis," Polish folk song, mm. 1–8

Joseph Haydn, String Quartet Op. 77, No. 1 (Hob III:81), mvt. 3, mm. 82–86 (1799)

41 Andantino M. M. ♩ = 66 — *rubato*

Alexander Scriabin, Prelude Op. 11, No. 9, mm. 1–8 (1899)

Conduct the following two excerpts in a fast 3. Look ahead to "Conducting Pulse Levels Other Than the Notated Beat" in this *Anthology* and in the *Manual for Sight Singing and Ear Training* (Chapter 23) for other ways of performing them.

What can you do before you sing to hear the first note in the following excerpt?

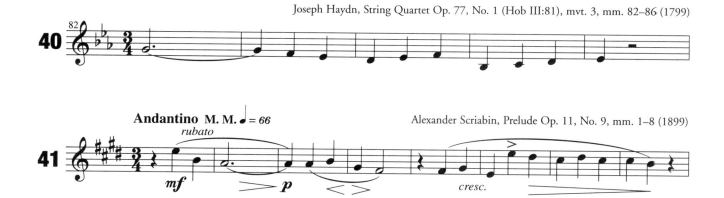

42 Mit Humor M. M. ♩ = 192

Robert Schumann, *Fantasiestücke*, Op. 12, No. 4, "Grillen," mm. 9–16 (1837)

Vocal transposition: down 4th–5th

Antonín Dvořák, Violin Concerto, Op. 53, mvt. 3 , mm. 11–2C (1879)

Allegro giocoso, ma non troppo

Allegretto ♩ = 76.

Ludwig van Beethoven, Symphony No. 7, Op. 92, mvt. 2, mm. 101–109 (1812)

44

Conduct the following excerpt in a fast 3. Look ahead to "Conducting Pulse Levels Other Than the Notated Beat" for other ways of performing it.

Ludwig van Beethoven, Symphony No. 6, Op. 68 ("Pastoral"), mvt. 3, mm. 91–98 (1808)

Allegro. ♩. = 108.

45

Ludwig van Beethoven, Piano Concerto No. 4, Op. 58, mvt. 1, mm. 147–154 (1807)

Allegro moderato

46

Jacob Arcadelt, "Il bianco e dolce cigno," mm. 1–5 (1539)

47

Il   bian   -   co e dol - ce   ci   -   gno can - tan - do mo   -   re.

Corresponding Chapter in *Manual for Ear Training and Sight Singing*: 12

Conduct the following excerpt in a slow 4. Look ahead to "Conducting Pulse Levels Other Than the Notated Beat" for other ways of performing it.

Ernest Chausson, Symphony Op. 20, mvt. 1, mm. 1–3 (1890)

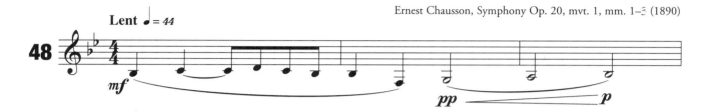

Conduct the following excerpt in a fast 3. Look ahead to "Conducting Pulse Levels Other Than the Notated Beat" for other ways of performing it.

When singing all parts together in the following excerpt, sopranos with high ranges should sing the top part.

Ludwig van Beethoven, Symphony No. 7, Op. 92, mvt. 3, mm. 149–155 (1812)

J. S. Bach, Chorale No. 68, "Wenn wir in höchsten Nöten sein," mm. 1–3 [melody: Loys Bourgeois (1547)]

Corresponding Chapter in *Manual for Ear Training and Sight Singing*: 12

Frederick Field Bullard, "From Age to Age They Gather," Unitarian hymn, mm. 1–4 (1902)

51

From age to age they gath - er, all the brave of heart and strong,

Charles Ives, "Slow March," mm. 8–16 (1887?)

Largo

p

52

One eve - ning just at sun - set we laid him in the

grave; Al - though a hum - ble an - i - mal his heart was true and brave.

Robert Schumann, *Blumenstück,* Op. 19, mm. 1–8 (1839)

Leise bewegt. M.M. ♩ = 69.

53

p

Ludwig van Beethoven, "Der Jüngling in der Fremde," WoO 138, mm. 1–4 (1809)

Etwas lebhaft, jedoch in einer mäßig geschwinden Bewegung

54

Der Früh - ling ent - blü - het dem Schoß____ der Na - tur,____

W. A. Mozart, Concerto for Flute and Harp,
K. 299 (297ᶜ), mvt. 1, mm. 262–265 (1778)

Allegro

55

f

f

Corresponding Chapter in *Manual for Ear Training and Sight Singing:* **12**

Vocal transposition: down 6th–7th

Allegro molto

Joseph Haydn, Symphony No. 32, mvt. 1, mm. 1–5 (c. 1760?)

56

Moderate march tempo

Panapasa Balekana, national anthem of the Solomon Islands, mm. 1–8 (1978)

mf

57

God   save   our   Sol - o - mon   Is - lands   from   shore   to   shore.

Bless   all   our   peo - ple   and   all   our   lands

Moderate march tempo

Panapasa Balekana, national anthem of the Solomon Islands, mm. 21–28 (1978)

p   *cresc.*   *ff*

58

Our   So - lo - mon   Is - lands,   Our   So - lo - mon   Is - lands,   Our

na - tion,   So - lo - mon   Is - lands,   Stands   for   e - ver - more.

"On Earth There Is a Lamb So Small," North American hymn tune, mm. 5–9

59

The   im - age   of   poor   sin - ners   all,   The   whole world's   guilt   it   car - ries.

"While by My Sheep I Watched at Night," Christmas carol, mm. 1–4

60

Corresponding Chapter in *Manual for Ear Training and Sight Singing*: 12

Joseph Haydn, *The Creation,* "The Heavens are Telling the Glory of God," mm. 109–113 (1798)

61 The won-der of his works dis - plays the fir - ma - ment,

Vocal transposition: up 2nd–6th

Orlando di Lasso, *Missa super Benedicam Dominum,* Sanctus, mm. 1–9 (1570)

62 San - - - - - ctus,

San - - - - ctus, San - - - - ctus

Vocal transposition: down 3rd–7th

Ludwig van Beethoven, Piano Sonata No. 21, Op. 53 ("Waldstein"), mvt. 2, Rondo, mm. 1–8 (1804)

Allegretto moderato

63 *sempre pp*

Ottorino Respighi, *Ancient Airs and Dances,* First Suite, mvt. 1, Balletto detto "Il conte Orlando," mm. 1–4 (1917)

Allegretto moderato ♩ = 126

64 *pp stacc. e legg.*

Michael Praetorius, *Terpsichore,* No. 46, Courante, mm. 6–15 (1612)

65

Corresponding Chapter in *Manual for Ear Training and Sight Singing*: 12

Vocal transposition: Sing the following excerpt in E♭ major by transposing the top two parts down a 5th while transposing the lower part up a 4th.

Arcangelo Corelli, Sonata da chiesa Op. 1, No. 5, mvt. 1, mm. 1–4

66 Grave

W. A. Mozart, Clarinet Concerto, K. 622, mvt. 2, mm. 1–4 (1791)

67 Adagio

Vocal transposition: Sing the following excerpt in D major by transposing the top part down a 4th while transposing the lower part up a 5th.

François Couperin, *Concert dans le gout théâtral,* Sarabande grave et tendre, mm. 1–4 (1724)

68

Ludwig van Beethoven, Symphony No. 7, Op. 92, mvt. 4, mm. 24–28 (1812)

69 Allegro con brio. ♩ = 72.

Corresponding Chapter in *Manual for Ear Training and Sight Singing*: 12

Ludwig van Beethoven, Symphony No. 9, Op. 125, mvt. 4, mm. 92–107 (1824)

Hans Leo Hassler, *Missa II*, Credo, mm. 98–102

et vi - tam ven - tu - ri sae - cu - li. A - - - men,

"Hurricane Wind," Anglo-American folk song, mm. 1–8

Corresponding Chapter in *Manual for Ear Training and Sight Singing*: 12

SKIPS TO 7̂ AND 2̂
AS PREFIX NEIGHBORS

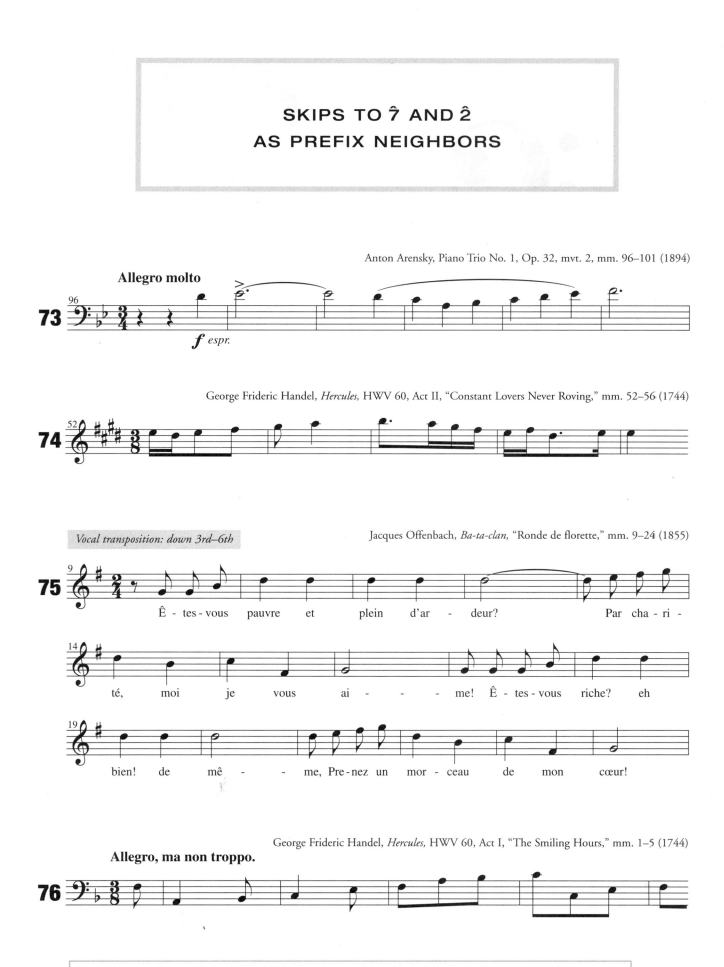

Anton Arensky, Piano Trio No. 1, Op. 32, mvt. 2, mm. 96–101 (1894)

George Frideric Handel, *Hercules,* HWV 60, Act II, "Constant Lovers Never Roving," mm. 52–56 (1744)

Vocal transposition: down 3rd–6th

Jacques Offenbach, *Ba-ta-clan,* "Ronde de florette," mm. 9–24 (1855)

Ê - tes - vous pauvre et plein d'ar - deur? Par cha - ri -

té, moi je vous ai - - me! Ê - tes - vous riche? eh

bien! de mê - - me, Pre - nez un mor - ceau de mon cœur!

George Frideric Handel, *Hercules,* HWV 60, Act I, "The Smiling Hours," mm. 1–5 (1744)

Allegro, ma non troppo.

"d'Ou viens-tu, Bergère," French Canadian carol, mm. 1–16

Franz Schubert, Trio D. 471, mvt. 1, mm. 1–9 (1816)

78 Allegro

Christoph Willibald von Gluck, *Orfeo ed Euridice,* Act II, "Vieni a regni del riposo," mm. 1–10 (1792)

79 Andantino.

Thomas Morley, "Hard by a Crystal Fountain," mm. 1–7, from *The Triumphs of Oriana* (1601)

80

Hard by a Crys - tal fount - - - - - - - - ain,

Corresponding Chapter in *Manual for Ear Training and Sight Singing:* 14

What do you think Schubert intended by using such an unorthodox meter sign in the following excerpt?

Franz Schubert, *Four Impromptus,* D. 899 [Op. 90], No. 3, mm. 5–8 (1827)

"Who's That Tapping at the Window?," North American folk song

"Fais do-do," French lullaby

Vocal transposition: down 3rd–7th

W. A. Mozart, Variations on "Lison dormait" from N. Dezède:
Julie, K. 264 (315ᵈ), Theme, mm. 1–8 (1778)

"Old King Cole," Nova Scotia folk song, mm. 1–8

Franz Schubert, Violin Sonata D. 408 [Op. 137, No. 3], mvt. 3, Trio, mm. 1–8 (1816)

Jean-Philippe Rameau, *Pièces de clavécin,* "Musette en Rondeau," mm. 1–8 (1724)

Tendrement

Corresponding Chapter in *Manual for Ear Training and Sight Singing:* **14**

COMPOUND METERS

COMPOUND DUPLE METER

"En roulant ma boule," Canadian folk song

88 a

"En roulant ma boule," Canadian folk song

b

"Voici venu le mois de mai," French folk song

89 a

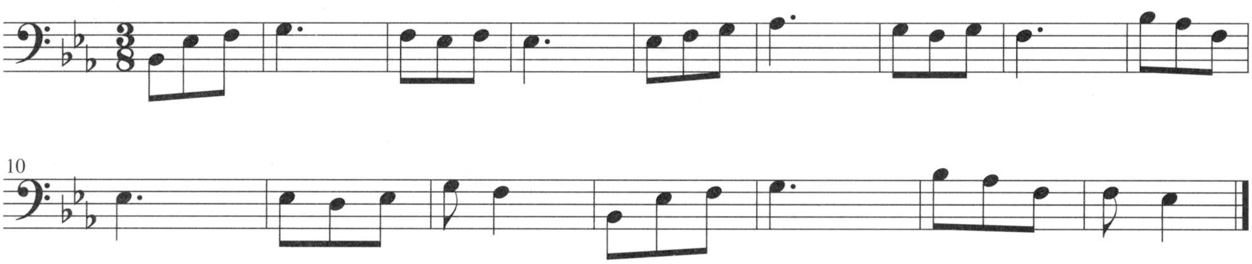

"Voici venu le mois de mai," French folk song

b

Corresponding Chapter in *Manual for Ear Training and Sight Singing*: 16

"Ich spring an diesem Ringe," German folk song

90
a

"Ich spring an diesem Ringe," German folk song

b

Georges Bizet, *Carmen,* Act II, Quintet,
"Nous avons en tête une affaire," mm. 3–6 (1874)

Allegro vivo. ♪· = *152*.

91

Nous a-vons en tê - te une af - fai - re.

Maria Szymanowska, "Sérénade," mm. 1–4 (1821)

Andante

92

Vocal transposition: Sing the following excerpt in D major by transposing the top part down a minor 3rd while transposing the bottom part up a major 6th.

John Philip Sousa, "Semper Fidelis," mm. 49–64 (c. 1888)

Moderato, quasi Andante.

Charles Gounod, "Jésus de Nazareth," mm. 5–8 (1856)

Né   dans u - ne   crê - che,   Di - vin   Ré - demp - teur___

Richard Wagner, *The Flying Dutchman*, Overture, mm. 2–6 (1841)

Allegro con brio

Corresponding Chapter in *Manual for Ear Training and Sight Singing:* **16**

COMPOUND TRIPLE METER

"Ça, dit le pigeon," French folk song

"Ça, dit le pigeon," French folk song

"Le petit oiselet," French folk song

"Le petit oiselet," French folk song

"Mon amie est bien malade," French folk song

"Mon amie est bien malade," French folk song

Corresponding Chapter in *Manual for Ear Training and Sight Singing*: 16

Think of the D in measure 1 of the following excerpt as part of the C–D–E line in measures 1–3.

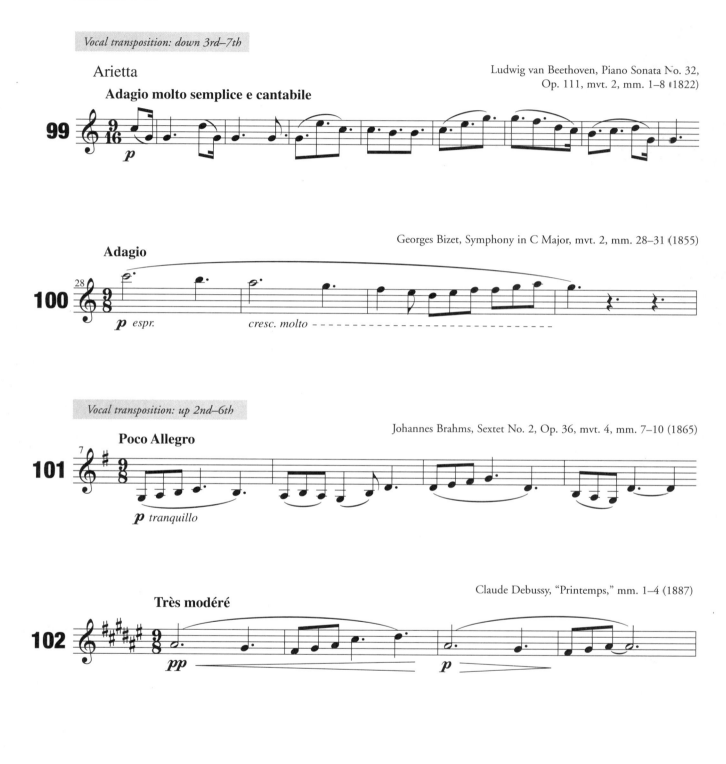

Vocal transposition: down 3rd–7th

Arietta

Ludwig van Beethoven, Piano Sonata No. 32, Op. 111, mvt. 2, mm. 1–8 (1822)

Adagio molto semplice e cantabile

99

Georges Bizet, Symphony in C Major, mvt. 2, mm. 28–31 (1855)

Adagio

100

Vocal transposition: up 2nd–6th

Johannes Brahms, Sextet No. 2, Op. 36, mvt. 4, mm. 7–10 (1865)

Poco Allegro

101

Claude Debussy, "Printemps," mm. 1–4 (1887)

Très modéré

102

Corresponding Chapter in *Manual for Ear Training and Sight Singing: 16*

COMPOUND QUADRUPLE METER

"Los enanos," Mexican folk song

"Los enanos," Mexican folk song

"Los enanos," Mexican folk song

"Kuckuck, Kuckuck," Austrian folk song

"Kuckuck, Kuckuck," Austrian folk song

"Kuckuck, Kuckuck," Austrian folk song

Corresponding Chapter in *Manual for Ear Training and Sight Singing*: 16

"Freut euch des Lebens," German folk song

105
a

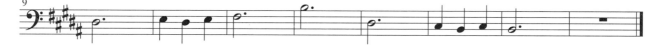

"Freut euch des Lebens," German folk song

b

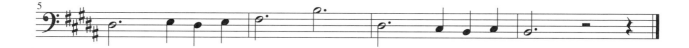

"Freut euch des Lebens," German folk song

c

J. S. Bach, French Suite No. 5, BWV 816, Gigue, mm. 7–9 (c. 1725)

106

Peter Ilich Tchaikovsky, Symphony No. 5, Op. 64, mvt. 2, mm. 8–12 (1888)

Andante cantabile, con alcuna licenza ♪. = 54

107

dolce con molto espress.

Corresponding Chapter in *Manual for Ear Training and Sight Singing*: 16

Vocal transposition: up 3rd–4th

François Couperin, *Pièces de clavecin,* Book II, "Le moucheron," mm. 1–4 (1717)

Légérement.

Corresponding Chapter in *Manual for Ear Training and Sight Singing:* 16

DIATONIC MINOR

Marie Jaëll, "Les jours pluvieux, Petite pluie fine," mm. 18–21 (1894)

109 Vite

Gustav Mahler, Symphony No. 1, mvt. 3, mm. 11–14 (1888)

110 Feierlich und gemessen, ohne zu schleppen

"Job," Welsh carol, mm. 1–4

111

National anthem of Slovakia [music traditional]

112

"Ma mère et mon père," French folk song

113

Corresponding Chapter in _Manual for Ear Training and Sight Singing:_ 17

Hector Berlioz, *Grande messe des morts* (Requiem) Op. 5, "Lacrimosa," mm. 3–5 (1837)

Andante non troppo lento (♩. = 60)

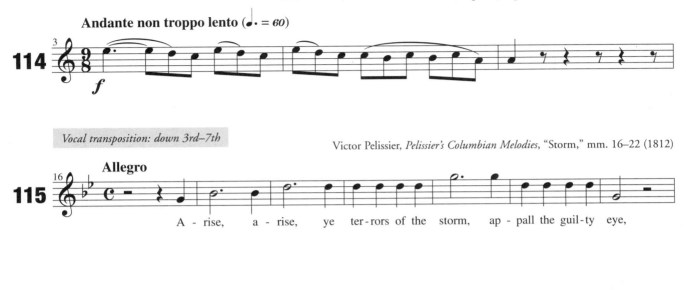

Vocal transposition: down 3rd–7th

Victor Pelissier, *Pelissier's Columbian Melodies*, "Storm," mm. 16–22 (1812)

Allegro

A - rise,   a - rise,   ye ter-rors of the storm,   ap - pall the guil-ty eye,

J. S. Bach, Cantata No. 212, "Mer hahn en neue Oberkeet," ("Peasant Cantata"), No. 1, mm. 43–46 (1742)

Adagio

"My Uncle Itsche," Yiddish folk song

"Est-il permis dans c'te maison?," French folk song

Corresponding Chapter in *Manual for Ear Training and Sight Singing:* 17

"Jésus-Christ s'habille en pauvre," French folk song

"Tarantella," Italian folk melody

Jean Sibelius, Symphony No. 2, Op. 43, mvt. 2, mm. 40–46 (1902)

Tempo Andante, ma rubato.

lugubre

mf

dim.

mf

dimin.

pp

Langsam

Johannes Brahms, *Sechs Gesänge,* Op. 7, No. 5, "Die Trauernde," mm. 1–8 (1852)

p   *espressivo*

Mei   Mue - ter   mag   mi   net,   und   kei   Schatz   han   i   net,

ei   wa - rum   sterb   i   net,   was   tu   i   do?

Corresponding Chapter in *Manual for Ear Training and Sight Singing:* 17

Anton Bruckner, Symphony No. 7, mvt. 3, mm. 1–9 (1883)

Sehr schnell

123

Vocal transposition: up 2nd–6th

Peter Ilich Tchaikovsky, Symphony No. 1, Op. 13, mvt. 4, mm. 17–24 (1874)

Andante lugubre (♩ = 76)

124

Corresponding Chapter in *Manual for Ear Training and Sight Singing:* **17**

LOWER CHROMATIC NEIGHBORS

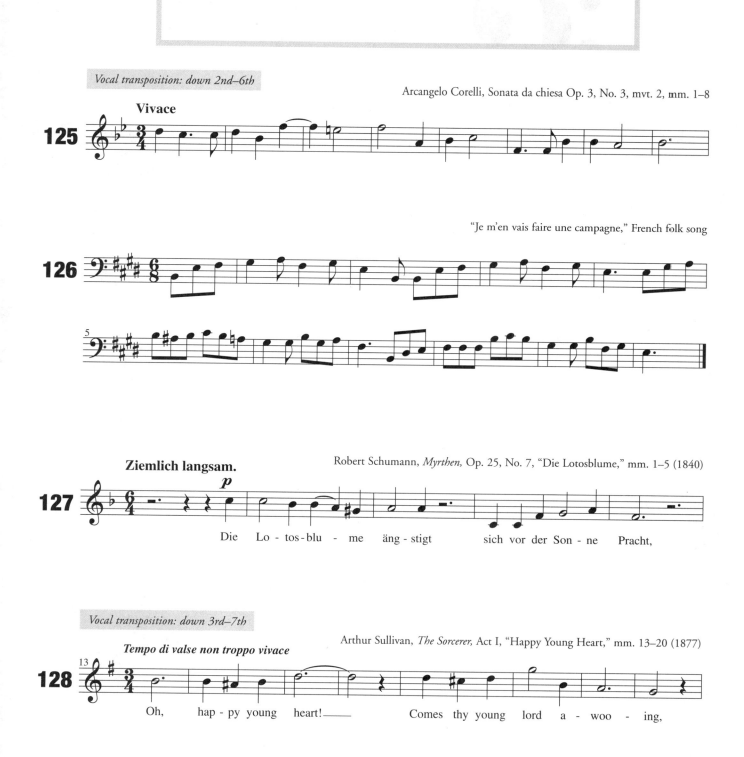

Arcangelo Corelli, Sonata da chiesa Op. 3, No. 3, mvt. 2, mm. 1–8

125 Vivace

"Je m'en vais faire une campagne," French folk song

126

Robert Schumann, *Myrthen*, Op. 25, No. 7, "Die Lotosblume," mm. 1–5 (1840)

Ziemlich langsam.

127

Die Lo - tos - blu - me äng - stigt sich vor der Son - ne Pracht,

Vocal transposition: down 3rd–7th

Arthur Sullivan, *The Sorcerer,* Act I, "Happy Young Heart," mm. 13–20 (1877)

Tempo di valse non troppo vivace

128

Oh, hap - py young heart!___ Comes thy young lord a - woo - ing,

Corresponding Chapter in *Manual for Ear Training and Sight Singing:* **18**

Vocal transposition: down 3rd–7th

Franz Schubert, German Dance D. 89, No. 5, Trio II, mm. 1–8 (1813)

129

Vocal transposition: down 2nd–7th

Louise Reichardt, *Sei canzoni di Metastasio,* Op. 4, No. 3, mm. 1–12 (1811)

Scherzando.

130

Sem - pli - cet - ta tor - to - rel - la, che non ve - de il suo pe -

ri - glio, non ve - de, non ve - de il suo pe - ri - glio per fug - gir da

cru - do arti - glio, vo - la in grem - bo al cac - cia - tor.

Gustav Mahler, Symphony No. 1, mvt. 4, mm. 175–179 (1888)

Sehr gesangvoll

131

pp   *sempre pp*

Corresponding Chapter in *Manual for Ear Training and Sight Singing:* 18

Vocal transposition: Sing the following excerpt in ensemble by transposing all parts down an octave.

Franz Schubert, Ländler D. 980b [formerly 679], No. 1, mm. 1–8

132

"Paddling Song," Lummi Native American song

133

Jean-Philippe Rameau, *Pièces de clavécin*, "Tambourin," mm. 24–28 (1724)

Vif

134

Corresponding Chapter in *Manual for Ear Training and Sight Singing*: 18

CHROMATIC 6̂ AND 7̂
IN THE MINOR MODE

"You'll Climb the Mountain," Polish folk song

135

Vocal transposition: down 2nd–5th

W. A. Mozart, German Dance K. 509, No. 5, mm. 171–178 (1787)

136

J. S. Bach, Sinfonia No. 15, BWV 801, mm. 1–3 (c. 1720)

137

Arcangelo Corelli, Sonata da chiesa Op. 1, No. 6, mvt. 3, mm. 1–6

Adagio

138

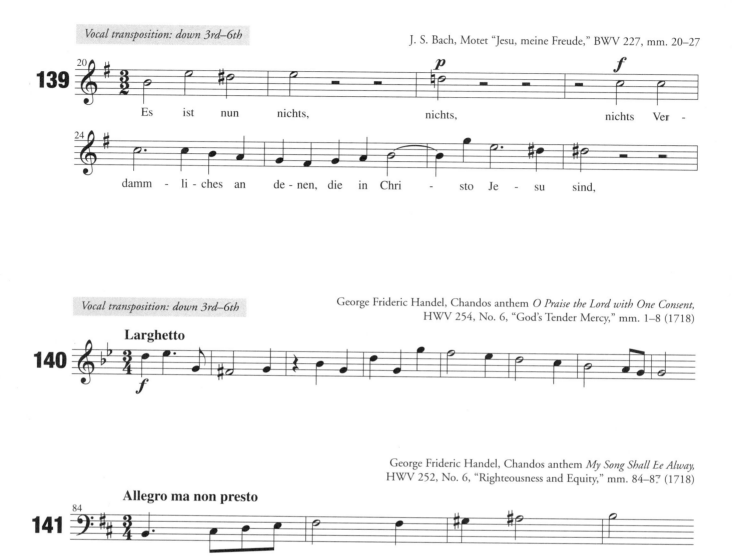

Vocal transposition: down 3rd–6th

J. S. Bach, Motet "Jesu, meine Freude," BWV 227, mm. 20–27

139

Es ist nun nichts, nichts, nichts Ver -

damm - li - ches an de - nen, die in Chri - sto Je - su sind,

Vocal transposition: down 3rd–6th

George Frideric Handel, Chandos anthem *O Praise the Lord with One Consent,* HWV 254, No. 6, "God's Tender Mercy," mm. 1–8 (1718)

Larghetto

140

George Frideric Handel, Chandos anthem *My Song Shall Ee Alway,* HWV 252, No. 6, "Righteousness and Equity," mm. 84–87 (1718)

Allegro ma non presto

141

How can you reconcile Couperin's use of accidentals in the following excerpt with the three forms of the minor scale?

François Couperin, "Air serieux," mm. 4–7 (1697)

142

Qu'on   ne   me   di - se   plus   que c'est   la   seule   ab - sen - ce

Corresponding Chapter in *Manual for Ear Training and Sight Singing*: 19

Béla Bartók, *First Term at the Piano,* No. 3, "Dialogue" (1913)

143

J. S. Bach, *Well-Tempered Clavier,* Book II, Fugue in B minor (No. 24), BWV 875, mm. 95–99 (c. 1740)

144

"Hier J'ai rencontré," French folk song

145

Corresponding Chapter in *Manual for Ear Training and Sight Singing:* 19

What is unusual about the use of scale degree $\hat{7}$ in the following folk song?

"Là-bas, là-bas," French folk song

146

Ludwig van Beethoven, String Quartet Op. 131, mvt. 7, mm. 21–29 (1826)

147

Louise Farrenc, Trio Op. 45, mvt. 1, mm. 192–199 (1862)

148

Ludwig van Beethoven, String Quartet Op. 59, No. 3, mvt. 2, mm. 1–5 (1806)

149

Corresponding Chapter in *Manual for Ear Training and Sight Singing*: 19

TRIPLETS; DUPLETS

Antonín Dvořák, Cello Concerto Op. 104, mvt. 3, rehearsal 13, mm. 25–37 (1895)

150

Johannes Brahms, Piano Concerto No. 2, Op. 83, mvt. 1, mm. 1–5 (1881)

Allegro non troppo (M.M. ♩ = 92)

151

Vocal transposition: down 3rd–7th

Johannes Brahms, Symphony No. 3, Op. 90, mvt. 4, mm. 52–56 (1883)

Allegro

152

Johannes Brahms, Symphony No. 3, Op. 90, mvt. 2, mm. 40–44 (1883)

Andante

153

Ludwig van Beethoven, Symphony No. 2, Op. 36, mvt. 2, mm. 90–93 (1802)

Larghetto. ♪_92.

154

Corresponding Chapter in *Manual for Ear Training and Sight Singing*: 20

Why do you suppose Saint-Saëns (or his publisher) notated measure 13 this way?

Camille Saint-Saëns, "Havanaise," Op. 83, mm. 11–14 (1887)

"La Paloma," Puerto Rican folk song

Joseph Haydn[?], Piano Sonata in A (Hob XVI:5), mvt. 3, mm. 1–5 (c. 1755?)

"Arrullo del Niño Dios," Mexican folk song

Vocal transposition: down 3rd–6th

Carlos Chávez, *Sinfonia India*, rehearsal 73, mm. 1–8 (1936)

Corresponding Chapter in *Manual for Ear Training and Sight Singing*: 20

Vocal transposition: down 2nd–3rd

Carlos Chávez, *Sinfonia India*, rehearsal 88, mm. 1–6 (1936)

Poco Più Vivo ♪. = *138*, **sempre giusto**

160

ff sempre

Reynaldo Hahn, *Chansons grises,* No. 5, "L'heure exquise," mm. 4–12 (1890)

Infiniment doux et calme.

161

La lu - ne blan - che Luit dans les bois;_____ De cha - que

bran - che Part u - ne voix Sous la ra - mé - e...

Reynaldo Hahn, "Cimetière de campagne," mm. 5–12 (1893)

Andantino, sans lenteur.

très simplement.

162

J'ai re - vu le ci - me - tiè - re Du beau pa - ys d'Ambé - rieux Qui m'a

fait le coeur jo - yeux Pour la vie en - tiè - - re,

Peter Warlock, "Take, O Take Those Lips away," mm. 3–6 (1917)

Lento, con tristezza

163

Take, O take____ those lips____ a - way That so sweet - ly were____ for - sworn,

QUADRUPLE DIVISION OF THE BEAT
IN SIMPLE METERS

Camille Saint-Saëns, *The Carnival of the Animals,* "Pianists," mm. 6–8 (1886)

164 Allegro moderato

Vocal transposition: down 3rd–7th

Christoph Willibald von Gluck, Trio Sonata No. 1, mvt. 2, mm. 3–9

165 Presto

Vocal transposition: down 2nd–7th

Bianca Maria Meda, "Cari musici," (Motet), mm. 182–188 (1691)

166 Presto

George Frideric Handel, Cantata *Arresta il passo (Aminta e Fillide),* HWV 83, Overture, mm. 15–20 (1708)

167 Furioso

Corresponding Chapter in *Manual for Ear Training and Sight Singing:* 22

Vocal transposition: down 2nd–5th

Jean-Philippe Rameau, *Pièces de clavécin,* "Tambourin," mm. 1–8 (1724)

168

Franz Schubert, *Drei Klavierstücke,* D. 946, No. 2, mm. 112–115 (1828)

169

Heinrich Schütz, *Christmas Oratorio,* SWV 435, Intermedium 3, "Die Hirten auf dem Felde," mm. 1–3 (1664)

170

Frédéric Chopin, Polonaise Op. 44, mm. 35–39 (1841)

171

W. A. Mozart, Piano Concerto No. 27, K. 595 , mvt. 1, mm. 2–5 (1791)

172

Corresponding Chapter in *Manual for Ear Training and Sight Singing*: 22

Vocal transposition: down 3rd–7th

Johann Heinrich Schmelzer, *Sacro-Profanus Concentus Musicus,* Sonata No. 1, mm. 1–8 (1662)

George Frideric Handel, Chandos anthem *I Will Magnify Thee,*
HWV 250ª, No. 1, Symphony, mm. 24–29 (1718)

Allegro

J. S. Bach, *Well-Tempered Clavier,* Book I, Prelude in B♭ minor (No. 22), BWV 867, mm. 1–3 (1722)

Vocal transposition: down 2nd–7th

Joseph Haydn, *The Creation,* "The Heavens Are Telling the Glory of God," mm. 8–12 (1798)

Allegro

the   won - der   of   his   works   dis - plays   the   fir - ma - ment,

Corresponding Chapter in *Manual for Ear Training and Sight Singing:* 22

What can you do before you sing to hear the first note in the following excerpt?

W. A. Mozart, Symphony No. 40, K. 550, mvt. 1, mm. 1–9 (1788)

J. S. Bach, Cantata No. 212, "Mer hahn en neue Oberkeet" ("Peasant Cantata"), No. 2, mm. 1–8 (1742)

Mer   hahn   en   neu - e   O - ber - keet   an   un - sern   Kam - mer - herrn.   Ha

gibt   uns   Bier,   das   steigt   in's   Heet,   das   ist   der   kla - re   Kern.

Elisabeth Jacquet de la Guerre, *Pièces de clavecin* (1707), Suite No. 1 in D minor, Rigaudon No. 2, mm. 1–8 (1707)

Corresponding Chapter in *Manual for Ear Training and Sight Singing:* 22

Vocal transposition: The range of the upper part in the following excerpt is singable as is, but to sing both parts together they must both be transposed down a 2nd or 3rd.

George Frideric Handel, *Water Music* Suite No. 1, HWV 348, mvt. 5, mm. 40–46 (1717)

Vocal transposition: down 3rd

George Frideric Handel, *Judas Maccabaeus*, HWV 63, Part I, "Arm, Arm, Ye Brave," mm. 13–17 (1746)

Giacomo Meyerbeer, *Les Huguenots*, Act II, "O transport! ô démence!," mm. 1–3 (1836)

Vocal transposition: To sing the following excerpt in ensemble, transpose both parts down an octave with women singing the upper part and men singing the lower part.

Antonín Dvořák, Symphony No. 9 ("From the New World"),
Op. 95, mvt. 4, mm. 271–275 (1893)

Vocal transposition: down 3rd–7th

Henry Purcell, *The Fairy Queen,* z629, Act IV, "Hark! the Ech'in Air," mm. 1–5 (1692)

Corresponding Chapter in *Manual for Ear Training and Sight Singing*: 22

Vocal transposition: down 5th

Allegro

Alexander Reinagle, *The Philadelphia Sonatas,* No. 2, mvt. 3, mm. 9–16 (c1790)

Antonín Dvořák, Symphony No. 9 ("From the New World"), Op. 95, mvt. 2, mm. 7–10 (1893)

Largo. M.M. ♩ = 52.

Franz Schubert, Ecossaise D. 299, No. 1, mm. 1–8 (1815)

Ludwig van Beethoven, Symphony No. 1, Op. 21, mvt. 2, mm. 1–7 (1800)

Andante cantabile con moto

Johannes Brahms, *49 deutsche Volkslieder,* WoO 33, No. 42, "In stiller Nacht," mm. 1–8 (1894)

Langsam

In stil - ler Nacht, zur er - sten Wacht, ein Stimm be - gunnt zu kla - gen, der

nächt - ge Wind hat suß und lind zu mir den Klang ge - tra - gen.

Corresponding Chapter in *Manual for Ear Training and Sight Singing: 22*

190

Poco sostenuto
molto espress.

Johannes Brahms, *Romanzen*, Op. 33, No. 6, mm. 39–44 (1862)

Schla - ge, sehn - süch - ti - ge Ge - walt, in tie - fer, treu - er Brust!

Vocal transposition: The range of the following excerpt is a bit challenging. Try singing it with women on the top part in each staff and men on the bottom part in each staff. The men will have to use good support to reach the F♯ in each part at the end of m. 215.

191

Gustav Mahler, Symphony No. 1, mvt. 1, mm. 208–216 (1888)

Sehr gemächlich (♩ = 66 Metr. M.)

192

Andante
espress.

Johannes Brahms, Symphony No. 3, Op. 90, mvt. 2, mm. 1–4 (1883)

p semplice

193

Andantino

Pauline Duchambge, "Le jardin de ma fenêtre," mm. 1–16

Jar - din_____ de ma fe - nê - tre, ma seu - le

ter - re à moi! A - vril_____ t'a fait re -

naî - tre; n'est - il_____ bon que pour toi?_____

Corresponding Chapter in *Manual for Ear Training and Sight Singing*: 22

Maestoso

John Joseph Akar, national anthem of Sierra Leone, mm. 7–12

194

Sing - ing thy praise,   O   nat - ive   land.   We   raise   up   our   hearts   and   our

voic - es   on   high,   The   hills   and   the   val - leys   re - e - cho   our   cry;

Wanda Landowska, "Liberation Fanfare," mm. 1–3 (1941)

♩ = 120   *allargando*

195

Sophie Gail, "L'heure du soir," mm. 8–11

Andante

196

Heu - re   du   soir,   heu - re   pai - si - ble   et   som - bre,

W. A. Mozart, Minuet K. 105 (61ᶠ), No. 6, Trio, mm. 1–8 (1772)

197

W. A. Mozart, *Zwölf Variationen in C, über das französische Lied
"Ah, vous dirai-je Maman,"* K. 265 (300ᵉ), Theme (1778)

198

Corresponding Chapter in *Manual for Ear Training and Sight Singing*: 22

199 Moderato

Rikard Nordraak, national anthem of Norway, mm. 13–20 (1864)

200 *Vocal transposition: down 3rd*

Michael Praetorius, *Terpsichore*, No. 2, Bransle simple No. 1, mm. 7–12 (1612)

201 *Vocal transposition: down 3rd–4th*

Ottorino Respighi, "Nebbie," mm. 2–5 (1906)

Lento

Sof - fro. Lon - tan lon - ta - no Le neb - bie son - no - len - te

Sal - go - no dal ta - cen - te Pia - no.

202 Allegro con spirito

J. C. Bach, Symphony Op. 3, No. 1, mvt. 1, mm. 130–132 (1765)

203 Allegretto ♪/112

Béla Bartók, *Ten Easy Piano Pieces*, No. 6, "Hungarian Folk Song," mm. 1–6 (1908)

Corresponding Chapter in *Manual for Ear Training and Sight Singing*: 22

Henry Purcell, *King Arthur,* z628, Act I, "Woden, First to Thee," mm. 9–11 (1691)

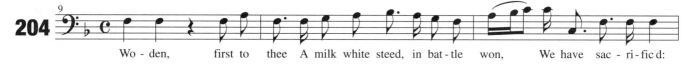

204

Wo - den,   first to   thee A milk white steed, in bat - tle   won,   We have sac - ri - fic'd:

Vocal transposition: down 6th

Antonio Vivaldi, Cantata "Par che tardo," (RV 662), mm. 5–10

205   **Larghetto**

Par che tar - do   ol - tre il co - stu - me   Og - gi___ scen - da   al mar d'At - lan - te

CONDUCTING PULSE LEVELS
OTHER THAN THE NOTATED BEAT

W. A. Mozart, *The Marriage of Figaro*, K. 492, Sinfonia, mm. 12–18 (1786)

206

Joseph Haydn, Symphony No. 87, mvt. 1, mm. 1–6 (1785)

207

Ludwig van Beethoven, Symphony No. 5, Op. 67, mvt. 4, mm. 362–369 (1808)

208

Felix Mendelssohn, Piano Trio No. 1, Op. 49, mvt.1, mm. 1–16 (1839)

209

Ludwig van Beethoven, Symphony No. 3, Op. 55,
("Eroica"), mvt. 3, Trio, mm. 1–7 (1803)

210

Corresponding Chapter in *Manual for Ear Training and Sight Singing*: 23

Ludwig van Beethoven, Symphony No. 2, Op. 36, mvt. 3, Trio, mm. 1–8 (1802)

Allegro ♩. = 100

211

Mikhail Ippolitov-Ivanov, *Caucasian Sketches,* Op. 10,
mvt. 2, "In the Village," mm. 23–40 (1894)

Allegretto grazioso. M.M. ♩. = 66

212

Vocal transposition: down 2nd–5th

Robert Schumann, String Quartet Op. 41, No. 3, mvt. 2, mm. 1–8 (1842)

Assai agitato. ♩. = 136.

213

Joseph Haydn, Symphony No. 55, mvt. 2, mm. 1–4 (1774)

Adagio ma semplicemente

214

Ludwig van Beethoven, Symphony No. 4, Op. 60, mvt. 2, mm. 2–4 (1806)

215

Joseph Haydn, Symphony No. 6 ("Le matin"), mvt. 1, mm. 1–3 (1761)

216

Johannes Brahms, Symphony No. 4, Op. 98, mvt. 2, mm. 1–3 (1885)

217

Vocal transposition: down 4th–7th

George Frideric Handel, *Messiah,* HWV 56, No. 13, Pifa (1741)

218

Corresponding Chapter in *Manual for Ear Training and Sight Singing:* 23

THE DOMINANT TRIAD

"Es steht ein Baum im Odenwald," German folk song (after Johann Friedrich Reichardt)

219

"Das Steckenpferd," German folk song

220

Franz Schubert, German Dance D. 146, No. 9, Trio, mm. 1–8 (1815)

221

Ludwig van Beethoven, Piano Sonata No. 23, Op. 57, ("Appassionata"), mvt. 3, mm. 316–321 (1805)

222

Ludwig van Beethoven, Piano Sonata No. 23, Op. 57, ("Appassionata"), mvt. 3, mm. 308–313 (1805)

223

Corresponding Chapter in *Manual for Ear Training and Sight Singing*: 25

Francesco Paolo Tosti, "Vorrei," mm. 2–7 (1885)

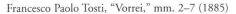

224

Vor - rei, al - lor che tu pal - lido e

mu - to pie - ghi la fron - te tra le ma - ni e pen - si,

Septimus Winner, "Der Deitcher's Dog" (after the German folk song "Lautenbach"), mm. 1–16 (1864)

225

Oh where, Oh where ish mine lit - tle dog gone; O where. Oh

where can he be_____ His ears cut short und his

tail cut long: Oh where, Oh where ish he_____

W. A. Mozart, *The Magic Flute,* K. 620, "Der Vogelfänger bin ich ja," mm. 27–30 (1791)

226

Der Vo - gel - fän - ger bin ich ja— stets lu - stig hei - ßa hop - sa - sa!

Franz Gruber, "Silent Night," Christmas carol, mm. 1–4 (1818)

227

J. S. Bach, Invention No. 10, BWV 781, mm. 27–29 (c. 1720)

228

Corresponding Chapter in *Manual for Ear Training and Sight Singing: 25*

Ludwig van Beethoven, *Coriolan* Overture, Op. 62, mm. 52–60 (1807)

229

"Red Rosy Bush," North American folk song

230

"Nun will der Lenz uns grüßen," German folk song

231

Gioachino Rossini, *William Tell*, Overture, mm. 243–259 (1829)

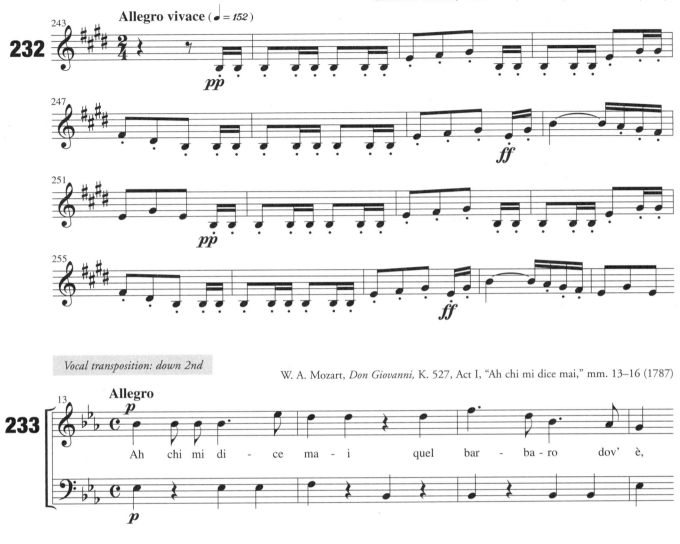

Vocal transposition: down 2nd

W. A. Mozart, *Don Giovanni*, K. 527, Act I, "Ah chi mi dice mai," mm. 13–16 (1787)

Vocal transposition: down 3rd

W. A. Mozart, Serenade K. 388 (384ª), mvt. 4, mm. 1–4 (c. 1783)

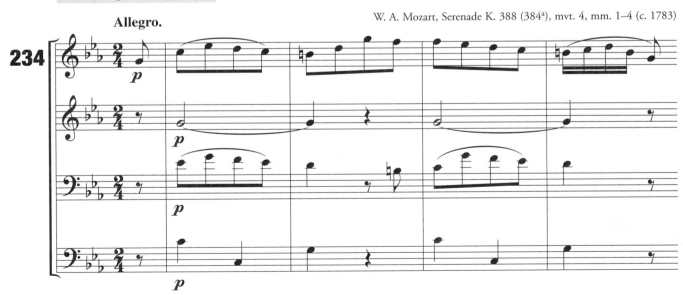

Corresponding Chapter in *Manual for Ear Training and Sight Singing*: 25

Allegro, ma non troppo.   George Frideric Handel, *Hercules,* HWV 60, Act I, "The Smiling Hours," mm. 9–13 (1744)

The smil-ing____ hours,____ a joy-ful____ train,

Antonio Vivaldi, *The Four Seasons,* Op. 8, No. 1, ("Spring"), mvt. 2, mm. 2–7

Largo e pianissimo sempre

J. S. Bach, *Well-Tempered Clavier,* Book II, Prelude in B♭ major (No. 21), BWV 890, mm. 4–6 (c. 1740)

Vocal transposition: down 2nd–6th

Edvard Grieg, *Lyrische Stücke,* Op. 43, No. 6, "An den Frühling," mm. 3–10 (1886)

Allegro appassionato.

cantabile e molto tenuta la melodia

Corresponding Chapter in *Manual for Ear Training and Sight Singing:* 25

Johannes Brahms, *49 deutsche Volkslieder,* WoO 33,
No. 40, "Ich weiß mir'n Maidlein," mm. 1–13 (1894)

Unruhig bewegt und heimlich

239

Ich weiß mir'n Maid - lein hübsch und fein. Hüt du dich! Ich weiß mir'n Maid - lein

hübsch und fein, es kann wohl falsch und freund - lich sein. Hüt du dich!

Hüt du dich! Ver - trau ihr nicht, sie nar - ret dich.

Giuseppi Verdi, *Aida,* Act II, Triumphal March, mm. 1–22 (1871)

Allº. maestoso ♩ = 100

240

Vocal transposition: down 2nd–6th

Franz Schubert, Symphony No. 2, mvt. 4, mm. 5–12 (1815)

Presto vivace

241

Corresponding Chapter in *Manual for Ear Training and Sight Singing:* **25**

THE C CLEFS: ALTO AND TENOR CLEFS

Antonín Dvořák, Slavonic Dance Op. 46, No. 1, mm. 235–243 (1878)

J. S. Bach, Cantata No. 212, "Mer hahn en neue Oberkeet" ("Peasant Cantata"), No. 1, mm. 62–69 (1742)

Antonín Dvořák, Slavonic Dance Op. 46, No. 1, mm. 2–9 (1878)

Ludwig van Beethoven, Symphony No. 9, Op. 125, mvt. 4, mm. 116–131 (1824)

Corresponding Chapter in *Manual for Ear Training and Sight Singing*: 26

Vocal transposition: down 2nd–6th

Johann Baptist Vanhal, Concerto in F for Viola, mvt. 1, mm. 1–5

Allegro moderato

246

Vocal transposition: down 3rd–7th

Peter Ilich Tchaikovsky, *The Nutcracker,* Op. 71, No. 5, mm. 187–203 (1892)

Tempo di Gross-Vater (♩. = 69)

247

Johannes Schenck, *Scherzi musicali,* Op. 6, Suite in A minor, mvt. 5, mm. 1–8 (1698)

Rondeau

248

Nicolai Rimsky-Korsakov, *The Golden Cockerel,* Act III, mm. 825–828 (1907)

Andantino. ♩. = 96

249

p dolce ed espressivo

J. C. Bach, Symphony Op. 3, No. 1, mvt. 3, mm. 13–16 (1765)

Presto

250

Corresponding Chapter in *Manual for Ear Training and Sight Singing*: 26

Andante con moto

Johannes Brahms, *Zwei Gesänge,* Op. 91, No. 2, "Geistliches Wiegenlied," mm. 1–10 (1864)

251

Jo - sef, lie - ber Jo - sef mein, hilf - mir wieg'n emin Kind - lein fein, Gott der wird dein

Loh - ner sein, im Him - mel - reich der Jung - frau Sohn, Ma - ri - a, Ma - ri - a.

Aaron Copland, *Appalachian Spring,* 59 , mm. 1–26 (1944)

252

mf cant. dolce

Carl Reinecke, *Drei Phantasiestücke,* Op. 43, No. 3, "Jahrmarkt-Szene," mm. 86–102 (1844)

Molto vivace. *Ausgelassen und mit ungebundener Laune*

253

cresc.

Corresponding Chapter in *Manual for Ear Training and Sight Singing:* 26

Johann Kuhnau, *Magnificat*, mm. 1–4

Vocal transposition: Sing the pitches in the cello (bass-clef) part up an octave in mm. 1–4.

Ludwig van Beethoven, String Quartet Op. 59, No. 3, mvt. 2, mm. 1–5 (1806)

Andante con moto quasi Allegretto

Vocal transposition: Sing all parts down an octave.

Ludwig van Beethoven, Symphony No. 5, Op. 67, mvt. 4, mm. 385–390 (1808)

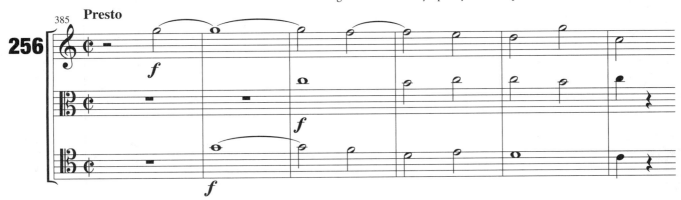

Corresponding Chapter in *Manual for Ear Training and Sight Singing*: 26

Vocal transposition: down 3rd–7th

Ludwig van Beethoven, Symphony No. 5, Op. 67, mvt. 3, mm. 169–173 (1808)

257

J. S. Bach, Cantata No. 214, "Tönet, ihr Pauken! Erschallet, Trompeten," No. 1, mm. 43–50 (1733)

258

Tö - net, ihr Pau - ken! Er - schal - let, Trom - pe - ten____!

Orlando di Lasso, *Lamentations to the Prophet Jeremiah,* "Lamentatio Secunda Primi Diei," mm. 1–7 (1585)

259

Za - - - in,____ Za - in, Za - - in.____

J. S. Bach, Cantata No. 205, "Zerreißet, zersprenget, zertrümmert die Gruft,"
No. 15, "Vivat! August, August vivat," mm. 29–33 (1725)

260

Vi - vat! vi - vat Aug - ust, Aug - ust vi - vat, sei be - glückt, ge - lehr - ter Mann!

"Sussex Carol," English Christmas carol, mm. 1–4

261

Vocal transposition: down 2nd–6th

Jean-Philippe Rameau, *Hippolyte et Aricie,* Act II, mm. 49–56 (1733)

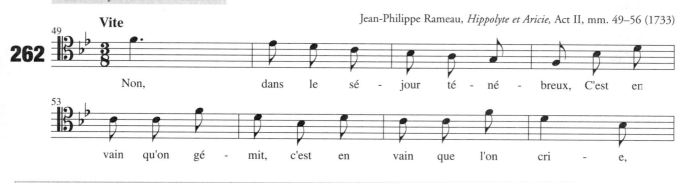

262

Non, dans le sé - jour té - né - breux, C'est en

vain qu'on gé - mit, c'est en vain que l'on cri - e,

Corresponding Chapter in *Manual for Ear Training and Sight Singing*: 26

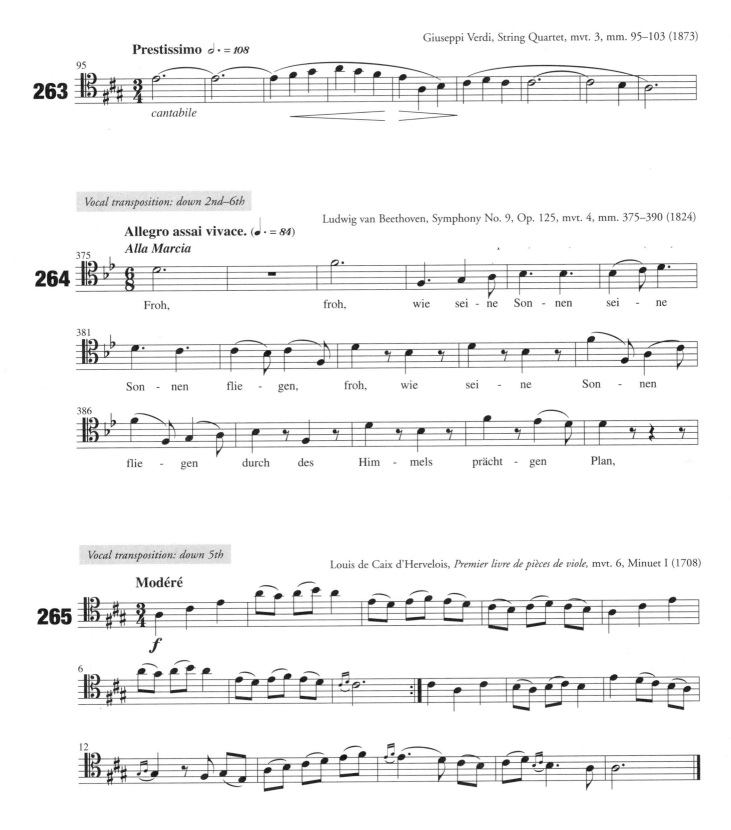

Giuseppi Verdi, String Quartet, mvt. 3, mm. 95–103 (1873)

263 Prestissimo ♩· = 108

cantabile

Vocal transposition: down 2nd–6th

Ludwig van Beethoven, Symphony No. 9, Op. 125, mvt. 4, mm. 375–390 (1824)

264 Allegro assai vivace. (♩· = 84) *Alla Marcia*

Froh, froh, wie sei - ne Son - nen sei - ne

Son - nen flie - gen, froh, wie sei - ne Son - nen

flie - gen durch des Him - mels prächt - gen Plan,

Vocal transposition: down 5th

Louis de Caix d'Hervelois, *Premier livre de pièces de viole,* mvt. 6, Minuet I (1708)

265 Modéré

f

Corresponding Chapter in *Manual for Ear Training and Sight Singing:* 26

SKIPS TO $\hat{4}$ AND $\hat{6}$ AS PREFIX NEIGHBORS

Johann Christian Rinck, "Abend wird es wieder" (1827)

266

A - bend wird es wie - der. Ü - ber Wald und Feld

säu - selt Frie - den nie - der, und es ruht die Welt.

Enoch Mankayi Sontonga, national anthem of South Africa, mm. 1–10

267

Joseph Haydn, Symphony No. 8 ("Le soir"), mvt. 1, mm. 1–8 (1761?)

Allegro molto

268

Christoph Willibald von Gluck, *L'Ivrogne corrigé,* Act I, "Ça compère Mathurin," mm. 41–48 (1760)

Allegretto

269

En dé - pit de Ma - thur - ri - ne, Co - let - te se - ra pour moi, En dé -

pit de Ma - thu - ri - ne, Co - let - te se - ra pour moi.

Corresponding Chapter in *Manual for Ear Training and Sight Singing:* **27**

Ludwig van Beethoven, Septet, Op. 20, mvt. 2, mm. 1–4 (1800)

Adagio cantabile. ♪ = 132.

270

p e dolce

Alfredo Casella, *Notturno e tarantella,* Op. 54, mvt. 1, "Notturno," mm. 6–22 (1934)

Adagio, ma non troppo

271

p

Felix Mendelssohn, *Te Deum,* No. 5, "Te gloriosus Apostolorum," mm. 3–7 (1826)

272

Te　glo - ri - o - sus　A - po - sto - lo - rum　cho - rus.

Louise Farrenc, "Air russe varié," Op. 17, mm. 214–221 (c. 1836)

Allegretto

Un poco ritenuto - *a tempo*

273

p　*f*　*ff*

Joseph Haydn, Symphony No. 12, mvt. 1, mm. 1–8 (1763)

Allegro

274

p

Corresponding Chapter in *Manual for Ear Training and Sight Singing:* 27

J. S. Bach, *Well-Tempered Clavier,* Book I, Prelude in F♯ major (No. 13), BWV 858, mm. 1–4 (1722)

275

Frédéric Chopin, Etude Op. 10, No. 3, mm. 1–5 (1832)

276

Vocal transposition: Sing the following excerpt in D major by transposing the treble-clef parts down a minor 6th while transposing the bass-clef part up a major 3rd.

Arcangelo Corelli, Sonata da chiesa, Op. 1, No. 5, mvt. 1, mm. 1–8

277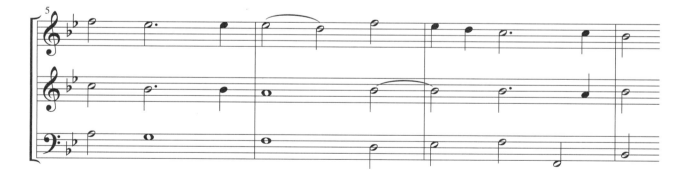

Corresponding Chapter in *Manual for Ear Training and Sight Singing*: 27

Vocal transposition: down 2nd–6th

Johann Baptist Vanhal, Concerto in F for Viola, mvt. 3, mm. 188–196

278

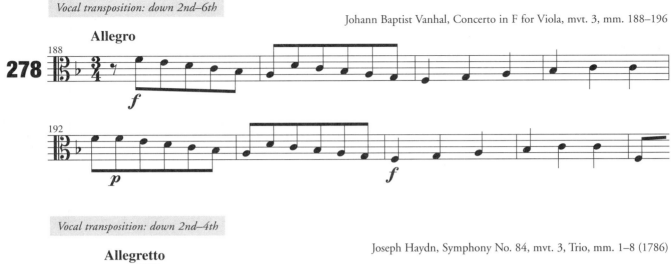

Vocal transposition: down 2nd–4th

Joseph Haydn, Symphony No. 84, mvt. 3, Trio, mm. 1–8 (1786)

279

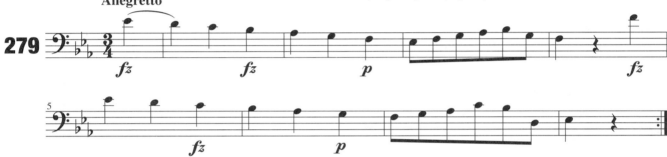

"Du, du, liegst mir im Herzen," German folk song

280

Alma Mahler, *Five Songs,* "Hymne," mm. 9–16 (1924)

Ganz ruhig beginnend, mit freiem Vortag

281

Des A - bend - mahls gött - li - che Be - deu - tung

ist den ir - di - schen Sin - nen Rät - sel.

Corresponding Chapter in *Manual for Ear Training and Sight Singing*: 27

"Weiß ich ein schönes Röselein," German folk song

282

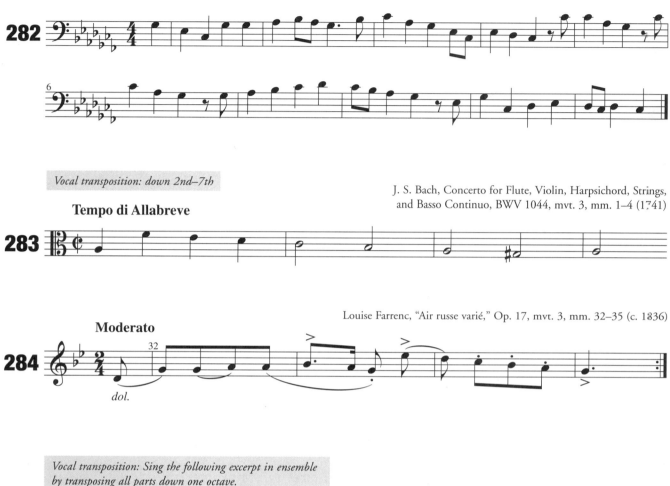

Vocal transposition: down 2nd–7th

Tempo di Allabreve

J. S. Bach, Concerto for Flute, Violin, Harpsichord, Strings, and Basso Continuo, BWV 1044, mvt. 3, mm. 1–4 (1741)

283

Louise Farrenc, "Air russe varié," Op. 17, mvt. 3, mm. 32–35 (c. 1836)

Moderato

284

dol.

Vocal transposition: Sing the following excerpt in ensemble by transposing all parts down one octave.

W. A. Mozart, Piano Sonata K. 457, mvt. 3, mm. 1–4 (1734)

Allegro assai

285

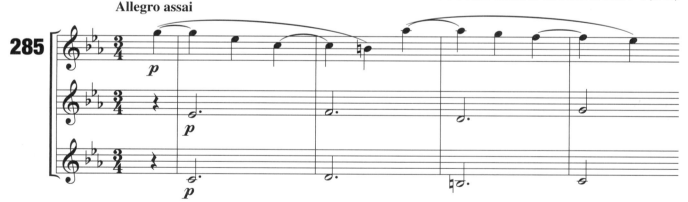

Vocal transposition: down 3rd–6th

W. A. Mozart, Minuet K. 105 (61ᶠ), No. 4, mm. 1–8 (1772)

286

f

Corresponding Chapter in *Manual for Ear Training and Sight Singing*: 27

Louise Reichardt, "Der Sänger geht," mm. 3–10

287 Langsam und getragen.

Der Säng - er geht auf rauh - en Pfad - en zer - reißt in Dor - nen sein Ge - wand; er

muss durch Fluss und Süm - pfe bad - en und keins reicht hülf - reich ihm die Hand,

Vocal transposition: down 2nd–5th

Johannes Brahms, *Neun Gesänge,* Op. 69, No. 5, "Tambourliedchen," mm. 7–11 (1877)

288 Sehr lebhaft

Den Wir - bel schlag ich gar so stark, daß euch er - zit - tert Bein und Mark,

"The Moreen," Irish air (later set as "The Minstrel Boy" by Thomas Moore), mm. 1–4

289

Harriett Abrams, "And Must We Part For Evermore," mm. 28–37

290 Largo

Each guar - dian An - gel e - ver guide for e - ver - more___ a -

Each guar - dian An - gel e - ver guide for e - ver - more___ a -

dieu,___ for e - ver - more, for e - ver - more; for

dieu,___ for e - ver - more; for

e - ver - more a - dieu! a - dieu! a - dieu!

e - ver - more a - dieu! a - dieu! a - dieu!

Corresponding Chapter in *Manual for Ear Training and Sight Singing*: 27

Vocal transposition: down 4th–7th

Mary Ann Wrighten [Pownall], "Kiss Me Now or Never," mm. 17–28 (1785)

Spiritoso

291

When Da - mon met me in the Grove, and told me I was

cle - ver   but 'stead of whisp' - ring   tales   of Love, cry'd

KISS   ME NOW   OR   NEV-ER.   KISS ME   NOW,   KISS ME

NOW,   Oh!   KISS   ME   NOW   OR   NEV - ER.

"Cousin, nous somm' le mardi gras!" French folk song

292

Vocal transposition: down 4th

Peter Ilich Tchaikovsky, Symphony No. 6, Op. 74 ("Pathétique") mvt. 1, mm. 89–101 (1893)

Andante (♩ = 69)

293

What can you do before you sing to hear the first note in the following excerpt?

Vocal transposition: down 3rd–4th

Robert Schumann, *Kreisleriana,* Op. 16, No. 8, mm. 1–8 (1838)

Schnell und spielend.

294

pp

Vocal transposition: down 2nd–6th

J. S. Bach, *Well-Tempered Clavier,* Book II,
Fugue in F♯ minor (No. 14), BWV 883, mm. 1–4 (c. 1740)

295

Vocal transposition: down 2nd–7th

Johannes Schenck, *Scherzi musicali,* Op. 6, Suite in A minor, mvt. 6, mm. 1–8 (1698)

Bourrée / Allegro

296

"Nous somm' venus vous voir," French folk song

297

Michael Praetorius, "Viva la musica" [three-voice canon]

298

Corresponding Chapter in *Manual for Ear Training and Sight Singing*: 27

Vocal transposition: up 3rd–4th

Arcangelo Corelli, Sonata da chiesa, Op. 3, No. 2, mvt. 3, mm. 1–7

299

Giacomo Carissimi, Cantata *Serenata "I Naviganti" (Sciolto havean),* "Amanti, che dite," mm. 3–6 (1653)

300

A - man - ti,   che   di - te,   che   di - te?

Vocal transposition: down 2nd

Adagio

Joseph Haydn, Canon, "Tod und Schlaf" (Hob. XXXVIIb:21) (c. 1799)

301

Tod   ist ein   lan - - ger   Schlaf,   Schlaf ist ein   kur-zer, kur-zer

Tod. Die Not, die   lin-dert der, und   je-ner tilgt die   Not. Tod ist ein   lan - ger   Schlaf.

Corresponding Chapter in *Manual for Ear Training and Sight Singing:* 27

SEXTUPLE DIVISION OF THE BEAT
IN COMPOUND METERS

"Kasienka," Polish folk song

302

François Couperin, Concert *Ritratto dell'amore,* No. 8, "L'et coetera ou menuets," mm. 13–16 (1724)
[original octaves marked on score]

303

(♩. = *42*)
Un peu lent et mélancolique.

Jules Massenet, *Le Cid,* Act II, ballet music, "Madrilène," mm. 6–8 (1885)

304

Corresponding Chapter in *Manual for Ear Training and Sight Singing:* 28

Corresponding Chapter in *Manual for Ear Training and Sight Singing*: 28

Vincent d'Indy, "Lied Maritime," Op. 43, mm. 1–5 (1896)

311 Au loin, dans la mer, s'é - teint le so - leil, et la
mer est calme et sans ri - de;

J. S. Bach, *Mass in B Minor*, BWV 232, Et in Spiritum sanctum, mm. 13–17

312 Et in Spi-ri-tum san-ctum Do - mi num et vi - vi - fi-can - - tem,

Gabriel Fauré, "Tristesse," Op. 6, No. 2, mm. 3–7 (c. 1873)

313 Av - ril est de re - tour, La pre - miè - re des
ro - ses De ses lèv-res mi-clo - ses, Rit au pre-mier beau jour,

George Frideric Handel, *Messiah*, HWV 56, No. 13, Pifa mm. 1–3 (1741)

314

Corresponding Chapter in *Manual for Ear Training and Sight Singing*: 28

Joseph Haydn, "A Pastoral Song" (Hob. XXVIa:27), mm. 9–16 (1794)

Allegretto

315

My moth - er bids me bind my hair with bands of ros - y hue, tie

up my sleeves with rib - ands rare, and lace my bod - ice blue;

"Marche de Goliath et sa femme," French folk song

316

Vocal transposition: down 2nd–6th

W. A. Mozart, Piano Sonata K. 280 (189e), mvt. 2, mm. 1–8 (1775)

Adagio

317

Jacques Offenbach, *Les contes d'Hoffmann*, Act II, "Les oiseaux dans la charmille," mm. 6–10 (1880)

Moderato

318

Les oi - seaux dans la char - mil - - - - - - le,

Michael Praetorius, *Terpsichore,* No. 98, Courante, mm. 1–8 (1612)

"Vous êtes nubile, ma mie," French folk song, mm. 1–2

Vocal transposition: down 3rd–7th

Andante

Carl Maria von Weber, *Andante e rondo ungarese,* mvt. 1, mm. 1–5 (1809)

Corresponding Chapter in *Manual for Ear Training and Sight Singing:* 28

Vocal transposition: When singing this top part alone, sing it in your own octave. When singing all the parts of the excerpt as an ensemble, sing them in the notated octave, with the deepest male voices on the bass part and the highest sopranos on the top line.

Jean Sibelius, Symphony No. 2 in D major, Op. 43, mvt. 1, mm. 7–13 (1902)

Corresponding Chapter in *Manual for Ear Training and Sight Singing*: 28

REPEAT SIGNS

"Deck the Halls," traditional Christmas carol

323

Moderato. (♩ = 52)

Béla Bartók, *First Term at the Piano,* No. 7, "Folk Song," (1913)

324

"Ein Jäger aus Kurpfalz," German folk song

325

Corresponding Chapter in *Manual for Ear Training and Sight Singing:* 29

Vocal transposition: down 2nd–6th

Franz Schubert, German Dance D. 783, No. 7 (1824)

326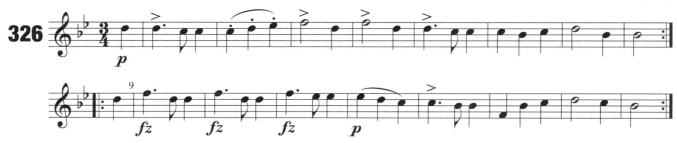

Béla Bartók, *First Term at the Piano*, No. 10, "Hungarian Folk Song"
[Erzsi Virág made her bed], mm. 5–24 (1913)

327

"A Girl Goes to the Dance," Swedish folk song

328

"Praeties," Anglo-American folk song

329

Corresponding Chapter in *Manual for Ear Training and Sight Singing*: 29

"C'était dedans un petit bois," French folk song

330

Fine

D.S. al Fine

"Sie gleicht wohl einem Rosenstock," German folk song

331

Fine

D.S. al Fine

"Old Brass Wagon," North American folk song

332

D.C. al Coda

Mässig bewegt.

(Lustig, und immer schneller und schmetternder.)

Richard Wagner, *Siegfried,* Act II, scene 2,
Siegfried's Call, mm. 29–44 (1857)

333

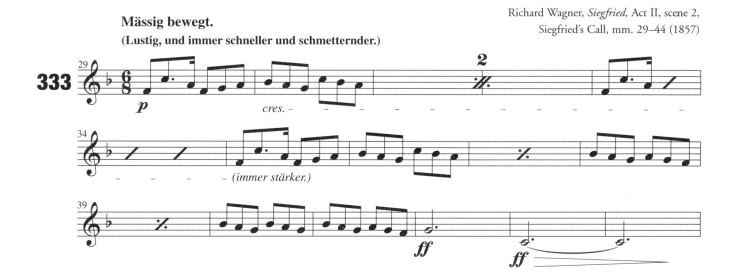

THE SUBDOMINANT TRIAD

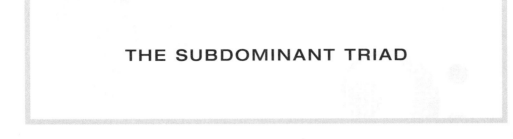

Luigi Boccherini, Symphony No. 6 (G. 506), Op. 12, No. 4, mvt. 1, mm. 30–38 (1771?)

334

Vocal transposition: down 2nd–7th

Franz Schubert, "Morgenlied," D. 685 [Op. 4, No. 2], mm. 12–18 (1820)

335

flat - tern Vög - lein da - hin und da - her,

sin - gen fröh - lich die Kreuz und die Quer ein

Lied, ein ju - beln - des Lied, ein Lied, ein ju - beln - des Lied.

"Kein Feuer, keine Kohle kann brennen so heiß," German folk song

336

"The Boar's Head Carol," English Christmas carol, mm. 1–8

337

"Vi gå över daggstänkta Berg," Swedish folk song

338

George Frideric Handel, *Saul,* HWV 53, Part II, "As Great Jehovah Lives," mm. 1–6 (1738)

Andante allegro

339

As great Je - ho - vah lives, I swear, The Youth shall not be slain:

Joseph Haydn, Symphony No. 46, mvt. 1, mm. 1–4 (1772)

Vivace

340

"Fire Down Below," sea shanty

341

Corresponding Chapter in *Manual for Ear Training and Sight Singing*: 30

"Das Lieben bringt groß Freud," German folk song

Johann Ernst Eberlin, *Te Deum,* mm. 129–131

343

In te Do - mi-ne spe - ra - vi non, non con - fun - dar in ae - ter - num,

W. A. Mozart, German Dance K. 605, No. 1, mm. 1–8 (1791)

"Wahre Freundschaft soll nicht wanken," Silesian folk song

Corresponding Chapter in *Manual for Ear Training and Sight Singing:* 30

W. A. Mozart, Minuet K. 103 (61^d), No. 5, Trio, mm. 1–8 (1772)

346

Larghetto

George Frideric Handel, *Messiah,* HWV 56, "I Know That My Redeemer Liveth," mm. 39–53 (1741)

347

I know that my Re - deem - er liv - eth, and

that He shall stand_____ at the lat - ter

day up - on the earth,_____ up - on the earth,

Andante sostenuto

Johannes Brahms, *Vier Lieder,* Op. 96, No. 4, "Meerfahrt," mm. 15–20 (c. 1885)

348

Mein Lieb - chen, wir sa-ßen bei-sam - men trau - lich im leich - ten Kahn._____

Allegro energico e fuoco. M.M. ♩ = 92.

Felix Mendelssohn, Piano Trio No. 2, Op. 66, mvt. 1, mm. 23–26 (1845)

349

Dietrich Buxtehude, *Missa brevis,* Kyrie, mm. 1–6

350

Ky - ri - e e - lei - - - - - - son,

Ky - ri - e e - lei - - - - - - son,

Corresponding Chapter in *Manual for Ear Training and Sight Singing*: 30

Vocal transposition: Sing the lower part of the following excerpt up one octave.

Johannes Brahms, *Lieder und Gesänge,* Op. 32, No. 2,
"Nicht mehr zu dir zu gehen," mm. 1–4 (1864)

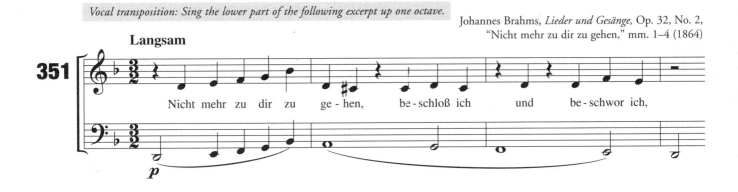

351

Nicht mehr zu dir zu ge - hen, be - schloß ich und be - schwor ich,

p

J. S. Bach, *Well-Tempered Clavier,* Book I, Fugue in A♭ major (No. 17), BWV 862, mm. 1–2 (1722)

352

J. S. Bach, Cantata No. 146, "Wir müssen durch viel Trübsal in das
Reich Gottes eingehen," No. 5, Aria, mm. 17–18 (1726? or 1728?)

353

Ich sä - - e mei - ne Zäh - - ren

James Hewitt, "Mark My Alford," mm. 9–12

Moderato

354

Vocal transposition: down 3rd–7th

Charles Gounod, *Faust,* Act V, Trio-Finale, mm. 31–34 (1859)

Moderato maestoso.

355

An - ges purs! An - ges ra - di - eux, Por - tez mon âme au sein des cieux!

Corresponding Chapter in *Manual for Ear Training and Sight Singing:* 30

In sanfter Bewegung

Johannes Brahms, Duets Op. 28, No. 3, "Es rauschet das Wasser," mm. 6–8 (1862)

356

Es rau - schet das Was - ser und blei - bet nicht stehn; gar lu - stig

Moderato. *p*

Augusta Holmès, "Noël," mm. 1–25 (1884)

357

Trois an - ges sont ve - nus ce soir M'ap - por - ter de bien bel - les

cho - ses; L'un d'eux a - vait un en - cen - soir, L'autre a - vait un cha - peau de

più f

ro - ses, Et le troi - sième a vait en main U - ne ro - be tou - te fleu -

più f

ri - e De per - les, d'or, el de jas - min, Com - me en a Ma - da - me Ma -

ri - e! No - ël! No - ël! Nous ve - nons du ciel T'ap - por -

ter ce que tu dé - si - res, Car le bon Dieu Au fond

p

du ciel bleu Est cha - grin lors - que tu sou - pi - res!

Corresponding Chapter in *Manual for Ear Training and Sight Singing*: 30

Vocal transposition: down 2nd–3rd

Peter Dodds McCormick, "Advance Australia Fair,"
national anthem of Australia (c. 1878)

358

Aus - tra - lians all, let us re - joice, For we are young and free; We've

gold - en soil and wealth for toil, Our home is girt by sea. Our

land a - bounds in Na - ture's gifts of beau - ty rich and rare; In

his - t'rys page let ev - 'ry stage Ad - vance Aus - tra - lia fair.

In joy - ful strains then let us sing, "Ad - vance Aus - tra - lia Fair."

Vocal transposition: down 2nd–6th

Jean-Jacques Rousseau, *Le devin du village,* scene 1,
"J'ai perdu tout mon bonheur," mm. 25–33 (1752)

Lent et marqué

359

J'ai per - du mon ser - vi - teur, j'ai per - du tout mon bon - heur. Co -

lin me dé - lais - se, Col - in me dé - lais - se.

Corresponding Chapter in *Manual for Ear Training and Sight Singing:* **30**

Vocal transposition: down 2nd–5th

Franz Schubert, "Frühlingsglaube," D. 686, mm. 5–13 (1822)

Ziemlich langsam

360

Die lin - den Lüf - te sind er - wacht, sie säu - seln und we - ben

Tag und Nacht, sie schaf - fen an al - len En - den, an al - len End - en.

Franz Schubert, German Dance D. 783, mm. 1–8 (1824?)

361

Franz Schubert, German Dance D. 146, No. 13, mm. 1–8 (1823)

362

Vocal transposition: down 4th–6th

Johann Strauss, Jr., "An der schönen, blauen Donau" (The Beautiful Blue Danube), Op. 314, mm. 1–16 (1867)

Walzer

363

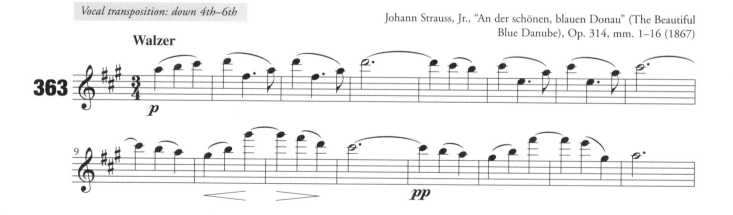

Corresponding Chapter in *Manual for Ear Training and Sight Singing*: 30

Vocal transposition: down 2nd

Ludwig van Beethoven, *Twelve Scottish Songs,* WoO 156,
No. 11, "Auld lang syne," mm. 8–15 (1818)

Vocal transposition: down 2nd

W. A. Mozart, *The Magic Flute*, K. 620, Act I, Finale, mm. 301–325 (1791)

365

Das klin - get so herr - lich, das klin - get so schön! La ra

la la la la ra la la la la ra la! Nie hab' ich so

et - was ge - hört und ge - sehn! La ra la la la la ra la la

la la ra la! Nie hab' ich so et - was ge - hört und ge -

sehn! La ra la la la la ra la la la la ra la!

Corresponding Chapter in *Manual for Ear Training and Sight Singing*: 30

Vocal transposition: down 2nd–5th

Georges Bizet, *Carmen,* Act III, Trio, "Mêlons! Coupons!" mm. 15–31 (1874)

366

SYNCOPATION

"Who's That Yonder?" North American spiritual, mm. 1–8

367

George Frideric Handel, Organ Concerto No. 6, HWV 304, mvt. 1, mm. 21–24 (c. 1746)

Andante

368

Andantino sostenuto e cantabile   W. A. Mozart, Aria "Io non chiedo, eterni Dei," K. 316 (300ᵇ), mm. 22–29 (1779)

369

Io non— chie-do, e-ter—ni De-i,   tut—to il ciel— per me— se-re-no,

Benjamin Dale, Phantasy for viola and piano, mm. 21–25 (1911)

Lento

370

p espress.

W. A. Mozart, Symphony No. 38, K. 504 ("Prague"), mvt. 3, mm. 295–303 (1786)

Presto

371

p

Vocal transposition: down 3rd–7th

Allegro   Christoph Willibald von Gluck, *Echo et Narcisse,* Act I, "Nymphes des eaux," mm. 1–9 (1779)

372

Corresponding Chapter in *Manual for Ear Training and Sight Singing: 31*

Michael J. Shea, "Notre Dame Victory March," Notre Dame fight song, mm. 17–32 (1908)

373 **Marcato**

What though the odds be great or small Old No - tre
Dame will win o - ver all While her loy - al
Sons are march - ing on - ward to Vic - to - ry._____

Louis Moreau Gottschalk, *Souvenir de Porto Rico,*
"Marche des Gibaros," Op. 31, mm. 17–32 (1858)

374 **Moderato ma con moto.**
ben rythme.

"Barbara Allen," British-American ballad

375

Vocal transposition: down 4th–7th

Allegro molto vivace. ♩ = 108.

Robert Schumann, String Quartet Op. 41, No. 3, mvt. 4, mm. 15–18 (1842)

376

Corresponding Chapter in *Manual for Ear Training and Sight Singing*: 31

Vocal transposition: down 4th–6th

Vivace e Presto

Elisabeth Jacquet de la Guerre, *Suonata* [Trio Sonata in D], mvt. 2, mm. 2–5

Vocal transposition: down 2nd–4th

Allegro

J. S. Bach, Sonata for Viola da Gamba BWV 1028, mvt. 2, mm. 5–9

Vocal transposition: down 3rd–7th

Moderate rock ♩ = *92*

Dan Wilson, "Closing Time," chorus (1998)

I know who— I want— to take me home.   I know who— I want—

— to take me home.   I know who— I   want— to take me home, take me—

— home.—

Vocal transposition: down 3rd–7th

Allegro

Gottlieb Muffat, *Componimenti musicali per il cembalo,* Suite I, Finale, mm. 1–7 (c. 1739)

Corresponding Chapter in *Manual for Ear Training and Sight Singing:* 31

Vocal transposition: down 4th–7th

Joseph Haydn, Symphony No. 45 ("Farewell"), mvt. 2, mm. 1–6 (1772)

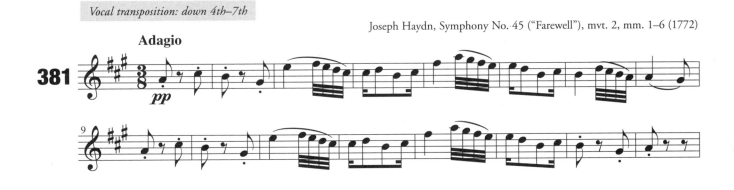

Sergei Rachmaninoff, Prelude Op. 32, No. 5, mm. 3–6 (1910)

Corresponding Chapter in *Manual for Ear Training and Sight Singing*: 31

THE DOMINANT SEVENTH CHORD

J. S. Bach, Cantata No. 197, "Gott ist unsre Zuversicht," No. 3, Aria, mm. 25–29 (1736)

383

"Drunten im Unterland," German folk song

384

Andante

Gabriel Fauré, "Les berceaux," Op. 23, No. 1, mm. 22–36 (1879)

385

Et ce jour là——— les grands——— vais - seaux, Fuy - ant le port qui di - mi - nu - e,

Sen - tent leur mas - se re - te - ne - e Par l'â - me des loin - tains——— ber -

ceaux, Par l'â - me des loin - tains——— ber - ceaux.———

Allegro spirito

James Hewitt, *Three Sonatas for the Piano Forte,* Sonata No. 1, mm. 1–7 (1796)

386

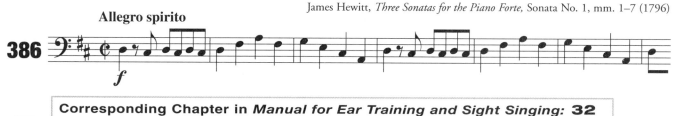

Corresponding Chapter in *Manual for Ear Training and Sight Singing:* 32

Allegro assai

W. A. Mozart, Aria "Per pietà, non ricercate," K. 420, mm. 78–84 (1783)

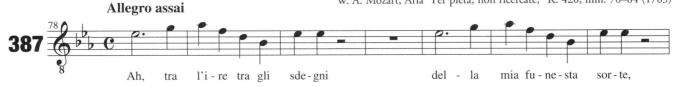

387

Ah,   tra   l'i - re   tra gli sde - gni   del - la   mia fu - ne - sta sor - te,

W. A. Mozart, March K. 215 (213ᵇ) [also with Serenade K. 204 (213ᵃ)], mm. 1–6 (1775)

388

Vocal transposition: down 6th–7th

Franz Schubert, Ecossaise D. 299, No. 8, mm. 1–8 (1815)

389

Amélie Julie Candeille, Piano Concerto, Op. 2, mvt. 1, mm. 1–7 (1784)

Allegro Maestoso

390

Malinconico. ♩ = 92

Louis Moreau Gottschalk, "Le mancenillier," Op. 11, mm. 26–33 (c. 1850)

ben cantato ma molto simplice.

391

Corresponding Chapter in *Manual for Ear Training and Sight Singing*: 32

Vocal transposition: Sing in E♭ major by transposing the top part down a major 6th while transposing the lower two parts up a minor third.

Joseph Haydn, Divertimento in C major, (Hob V:16), mvt. 2, mm. 1–4 (c. 1764)

392

Vocal transposition: Sing both parts an octave lower.

Joseph Haydn, Symphony No. 56, mvt. 3, Trio, mm. 1–8 (1774)

393

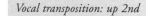
Vocal transposition: up 2nd

Joseph Haydn, *The Creation,* "Rolling in Foaming Billows" mm. 75–93 (1798)

394

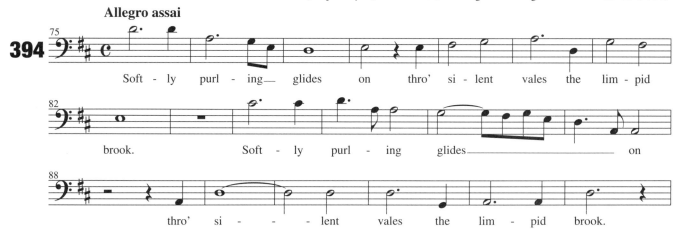

Soft - ly purl - ing— glides on thro' si - lent vales the lim - pid

brook.   Soft - ly purl - ing glides_____ on

thro' si - - - lent vales the lim - pid brook.

Corresponding Chapter in *Manual for Ear Training and Sight Singing:* 32

Vocal transposition: down 3rd–5th

Felix Mendelssohn, Sonata for Viola and Piano, mvt. 2, mm. 18–34 (1824)

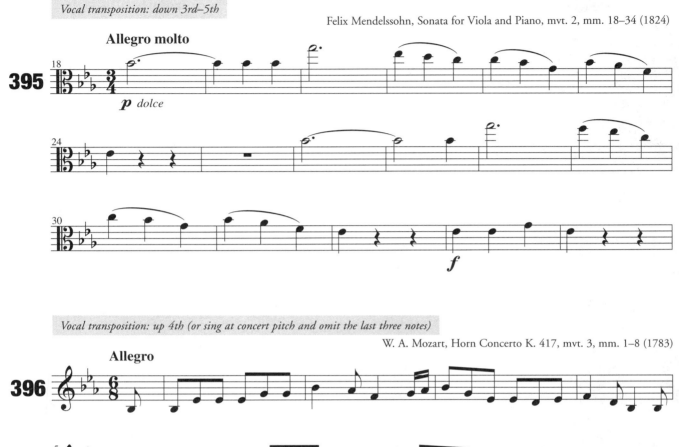

395

Allegro molto

p dolce

f

Vocal transposition: up 4th (or sing at concert pitch and omit the last three notes)

W. A. Mozart, Horn Concerto K. 417, mvt. 3, mm. 1–8 (1783)

396

Allegro

Vocal transposition: up 4th (or sing at concert pitch and omit the last three notes)

W. A. Mozart, Horn Concerto K. 495, mvt. 3, mm. 1–8 (1786)

397

Allegro vivace

Corresponding Chapter in *Manual for Ear Training and Sight Singing:* **32**

Vocal transposition: down 3rd–4th

Joseph Haydn, Symphony No. 104, mvt. 1, mm. 17–32 (1795)

Louise Reichardt, "Herbstlied"

399

Feld - ein - wärts flog ein Vö - ge - lein und sang im mun - tern Son - nen
Doch als ich Blät - ter fal - len sah, da sagt' ich: ach der Herbst ist

schein mit süs - sen wun - der - ba - ren Ton: A - de! ich flie - ge
da! der Som - mer gast, die Schwal - be zieht, viel - leicht so Lieb und

nun da - von, Weit, weit, reis' ich noch heut.
Sehn - sucht flieht! Weit, weit, rasch mit der Zeit!

Christoph Willibald von Gluck, *L'Ivrogne corrigé,* Act II, "Allons, morbleu!" mm. 16–56 (1760)

400

Al - lons, mor - bleu! Point de cha - grin, Mon mé - tier est de fai - re du

vin, Et mon plai - sir d'en boi - re, à boire, à boire, à boi - re! Char -

mant Bac - chus tes en - fants sont heu - reux, Les vrais plai - sirs ne sont faits que pour eux, Al -

lons, mor - bleu! Mont de cha - grin, Mon mé - tier est de fai - re du vin,

et mon plai - sir d'en boi - re, à boire, à boire, à boi - re!

Corresponding Chapter in *Manual for Ear Training and Sight Singing: 32*

401 Allegro assai

Ludwig van Beethoven, Symphony No. 9, Op. 125, mvt. 4, mm. 241–256 (1824)

Freu - de, schö - ner Göt - ter - fun - ken, Toch - ter aus E - ly - si - um,

wir be - tre - ten feu - er - trun - ken, Himm - li - sche, dein Hei - lig - tum!

Dei - ne Zau - ber bin - den wie - der, was die Mo - de streng ge - teilt; al -

- le Men - schen wer - den Brü - der, wo dein sanf - ter Flü - gel weilt.

Vocal transposition: down 3rd–7th

Anne Home Hunter, Arietta No. 4, (1783)

402 Adagio

Bright Orb whose pure coe - les - tial light beams mild - ly o'er my

pen - sive head, as wand' - ring thro' the Dews of Night I

seek the glim' - ring in the shade ah! in thy Jour - ney

thro' the Sky, bear to my Love this ten - der Sigh.

Corresponding Chapter in *Manual for Ear Training and Sight Singing: 32*

Camille Saint-Saëns, *The Carnival of the Animals,* "Tortoises"
(after Jacques Offenbach, *Orpheus in Hades*), mm. 3–10 (1886)

403

Vocal transposition: up 2nd–6th

Gustav Mahler, Symphony No. 9, mvt. 2, mm. 9–13 (1909)

404

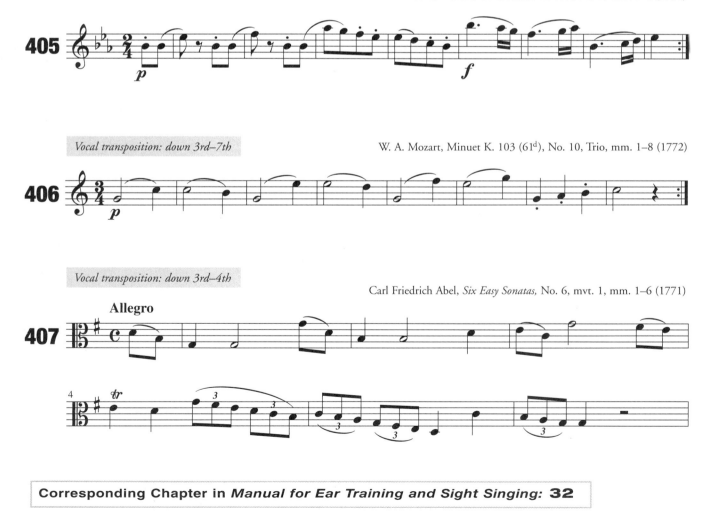

W. A. Mozart, Contredanse K. 609, No. 2, mm. 1–8 (1791)

405

Vocal transposition: down 3rd–7th

W. A. Mozart, Minuet K. 103 (61d), No. 10, Trio, mm. 1–8 (1772)

406

Vocal transposition: down 3rd–4th

Carl Friedrich Abel, *Six Easy Sonatas,* No. 6, mvt. 1, mm. 1–6 (1771)

407

Corresponding Chapter in *Manual for Ear Training and Sight Singing:* 32

Joseph Haydn, Symphony No. 28, mvt. 1, mm. 14–22 (1765)

408

W. A. Mozart, Minuet K. 105 (61^f), No. 1, mm. 1–8 (1772)

409

W. A. Mozart, Minuet K. 105 (61^f), No. 2, Trio, mm. 1–8 (1772)

410

Corresponding Chapter in *Manual for Ear Training and Sight Singing*: 32

"Shoo, Fly," North American folk song

411

J. S. Bach, Suite No. 3 for Unaccompanied Cello, BWV 1009, Bourée I, mm. 1–4 (c. 1720)

412

Vocal transposition: up 2nd–6th

J. S. Bach, *Well-Tempered Clavier*, Book II, Fugue in C♯ minor (No. 4), BWV 873, mm. 1–2 (c. 1740)

413

Joseph Haydn, Symphony No. 13, mvt. 1, mm. 1–7 (1763)

Allegro molto

414

Vocal transposition: down 2nd–3rd

J. S. Bach, *Well-Tempered Clavier*, Book I, Prelude in A minor (No. 20), BWV 865, mm. 13–16 (1722)

415

Corresponding Chapter in *Manual for Ear Training and Sight Singing*: 32

Giacomo Puccini, *La rondine,* Act I, "Chi il bel sogno di Doretta," mm. 1–4 (1917)

Andantino (♩ = 52)

416

Chi il bel so - gno di Do - ret - ta po - te in - so - vi - nar? Il suo mi

ste - ro nes - sun, nes - sun mai sco - prì!

What can you do before you sing to hear the first note of the top voice in the following excerpt?

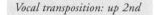

Vocal transposition: up 2nd

Ludwig van Beethoven, Violin Sonata Op. 30, No. 3, mvt. 2, mm. 1–3 (1802)

Tempo di Minuetto
ma molto moderato e grazioso

417

Vocal transposition: down 3rd–6th

Joseph Haydn, Symphony No. 77, mvt. 4, mm. 1–16 (1782?)

Allegro spiritoso

418

Corresponding Chapter in *Manual for Ear Training and Sight Singing:* 32

W. A. Mozart, Minuet K. 103 (61ᵈ), No. 3, Trio, mm. 1–8 (1772)

419

Joseph Haydn, Symphony No. 94, mvt. 4, mm. 1–16 (1791)

420   **Allegro di molto**

How does the dominant seventh chord arise in the following excerpt?

Sopranos with higher ranges should sing the top part of the following excerpt. Alternatively, transpose down a 3rd and singers with the lowest ranges should sing the lowest part.

Felix Mendelssohn, *Te Deum,* No. 4, "Tibi Cherubim," mm. 1–5 (1826)

421

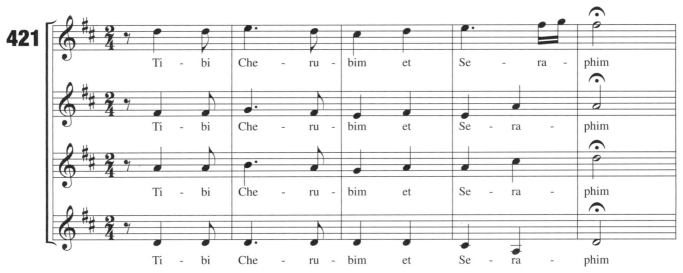

Ti - bi Che - ru - bim et   Se - ra - phim

Ti - bi Che - ru - bim et   Se - ra - phim

Ti - bi Che - ru - bim et   Se - ra - phim

Ti - bi Che - ru - bim et   Se - ra - phim

Corresponding Chapter in *Manual for Ear Training and Sight Singing*: 32

In what places is the dominant seventh chord stated melodically in the following excerpt? Where else is it implied by the interaction between the parts?

Vocal transposition: down 2nd–4th

Allegretto moderato

Arthur Sullivan, *The Gondoliers,* Act I, "List and Learn," mm. 16–24 (1889)

422

List and learn, list and learn, list and

List and learn, list and learn, list and

learn, ye dain - ty ros - es, Ros - es white and ros - es red,

learn, ye dain - ty ros - es, Ros - es white and ros - es red,

W. A. Mozart, Minuet K. 103 (61ᵈ), No. 4, mm. 1–8 (1772)

423

W. A. Mozart (?), Minuet K. 61ʰ, No. 5, Trio, mm. 1–8 (1772)

424

Corresponding Chapter in *Manual for Ear Training and Sight Singing*: 32

Franz Schubert, Ecossaise D. 781, No. 2 (1823)

How will you conceive of the A in m. 2, beat 2 to make it as easy as possible to sing?

Vocal transposition: down 4th–5th

Guiseppe Tartini, Violin Sonata Op. 2, No. 4 [Brainard e7], mvt. 1, mm. 1–2 (1743)

Grave

BASS LINES

Sing the bass voice while playing the upper three voices on the piano.

"Lord, I Am Thine," Presbyterian hymn, mm. 1–4 (18th century)

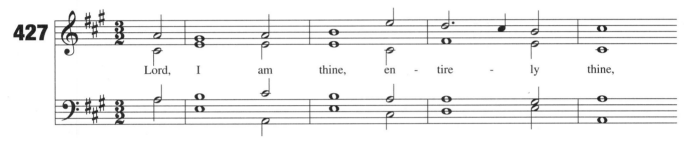

427

Lord,   I   am   thine,   en - tire - ly   thine,

Sing the bass voice while playing the upper three voices on the piano.

William Selby, "Thus Spake the Saviour," Universalist hymn (1762)

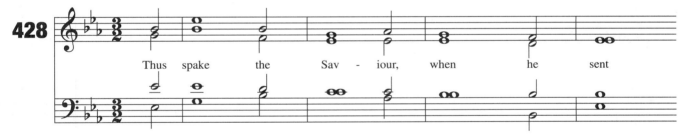

428

Thus   spake   the   Sav - iour,   when   he   sent

Sing the bass voice while playing the upper voices on the piano.

Jean Sibelius, *Finlandia*, Op. 26, No. 7, mm. 132–139 (1900)

429

Allegro

mf espress

Sing the bass voice while playing the upper voices on the piano.

George Frideric Handel, *Rinaldo,* HWV 7, Act II, "Lascia ch'io pianga mia cruda sorte," mm. 1–8 (1711)

Sing the bass voice while playing the upper voices on the piano.

Robert Schumann, *Album for the Young,* Op. 68, No. 4, "Chorale," mm. 17–32 (1348)

Corresponding Chapter in *Manual for Ear Training and Sight Singing:* 36

INTRODUCTION TO VOICE LEADING

Luigi Boccherini, Symphony No. 6 (G. 506), Op. 12, No. 4, mvt. 1, mm. 30–36 (1771?)

432

Allegro assai

Vocal transposition: down 2nd–3rd

Alexander Reinagle, *The Philadelphia Sonatas,* No. 3, mvt. 4, mm. 1–6 (c. 1790)

433

Allegro

J. S. Bach, Sinfonia No. 15, BWV 801, mm. 1–3 (c. 1720)

434

Vocal transposition: down 4th–7th

Domenico Scarlatti, Sonata K. 295, mm. 5–13

435

Allegro

James Hewitt, "Advice to the Ladies," mm. 1–6

436

Allegretto

Corresponding Chapter in *Manual for Ear Training and Sight Singing:* 38

Vocal transposition: down 3rd–4th

George Frideric Handel, Cantata, *Ah! crudel, nel pianto mio*, HWV 78,
No. 4, "Per trofei di mia costanza," mm. 96–108 (c. 1707)

437

Vocal transposition: down 2nd–3rd

J. S. Bach, *Well-Tempered Clavier*, Book I,
Fugue in C♯ major (No. 3), BWV 848, mm. 5–7 (1722)

438

Vocal transposition: down 3rd–5th

Matthias Siegmund Biechteler [von Greiffenthal], "Intonuit de coelo," mm. 39–51

Allegro assai

439

Vocal transposition: down 2nd–4th

Jean-Philippe Rameau, *Pièces de clavécin*, "Les niais de sologne," mm. 1–8 (1724)

440

Corresponding Chapter in *Manual for Ear Training and Sight Singing*: 38

Johannes Brahms, Waltzes, Op. 39, No. 9, mm. 1–4 (1865)

J. S. Bach, Suite No. 2 for Unaccompanied Cello, BWV 1008, Gigue, mm. 1–4 (c. 1720)

J. S. Bach, Invention No. 4, BWV 775, mm. 1–5 (c. 1720)

W. A. Mozart, *The Marriage of Figaro*, K. 492, Act I, scene 1, mm. 1–7 (1786)

How will you conceive of the B in measure 3 of the following excerpt as a product of voice leading?

Vocal transposition: down 3rd–4th

Joseph Haydn, Symphony No. 101, mvt. 4, mm. 1–8 (1794)

Corresponding Chapter in *Manual for Ear Training and Sight Singing*: 38

How is the G♯ in measure 2 of the following excerpt similar to the B in measure 3
of the previous one? How is it different?

J. S. Bach, *Well-Tempered Clavier*, Book II, Fugue in B major (No. 23), BWV 892, mm. 1–5 (c. 1740)

W. A. Mozart, *The Magic Flute*, Act I, "Hm! hm! hm!," mm. 3–7 (1791)

Igor Stravinsky, Violin Concerto, mvt. 4, mm. 7–12 (1931)

J. S. Bach, *Well-Tempered Clavier*, Book I, Fugue in D minor (No. 8), BWV 853, mm. 8–10 (1722)

J. S. Bach, *Well-Tempered Clavier*, Book I, Fugue in A minor (No. 20), BWV 865, mm. 1–4 (1722)

Vocal transposition: down 2nd–5th

Corresponding Chapter in *Manual for Ear Training and Sight Singing*: 38

J. S. Bach, *Well-Tempered Clavier,* Book I, Fugue in C minor (No. 2), BWV 847, mm. 7–9 (1722)

Vocal transposition: up 3rd–4th

George Frideric Handel, Organ Concerto No. 7, HWV 303, mvt. 5, mm. 1–6 (c. 1738?)

A tempo ordinario

Georg Philipp Telemann, Fantasy No. 6 for Violin, mvt. 3, mm. 1–6 (1735)

Spiritoso

Vocal transposition: down 4th–7th

George Frideric Handel, Keyboard Suite HWV 436, Menuetto, mm. 25–32 [Variation I]

Corresponding Chapter in *Manual for Ear Training and Sight Singing:* 38

Vocal transposition: Sing all parts down 4th–6th. The range of the melody part will be too extreme for some singers. Can you adjust a few pitches by an octave to make the melody more singable?

W. A. Mozart, Piano Sonata K. 283 (189h), mvt. 1, mm. 1–8 (1775)

455

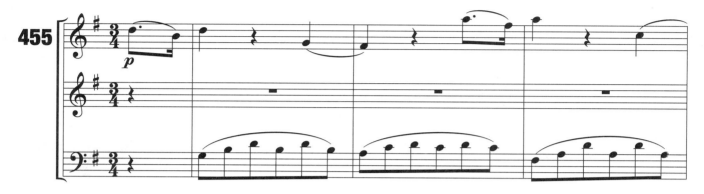

Corresponding Chapter in *Manual for Ear Training and Sight Singing:* **38**

THE LEADING-TONE TRIAD

Ludwig van Beethoven, *The Creatures of Prometheus*, Op. 43, No. 16, Finale, mm. 1–8 (1801)

456

Allegretto

George Frideric Handel, *The Triumph of Time and Truth*,
HWV 71, "Loathsome Urns," mm. 13–16 (1757)

457

Larghetto.

Loath - some urns,—— dis - close your trea - sure,

W. A. Mozart, German Dance K. 605, No. 3, Trio ("Die Schlittenfahrt"), mm. 1–8 (1791)

458

"Es hatt' ein Bauer ein schönes Weib," German folk song

459

Franz Schubert, String Quartet D. 87 [Op. 125/1], mvt. 1, mm. 49–52 (1813)

Allegro moderato

460

Igor Stravinsky, *Petrushka,* scene 3, Valse, mm. 1–5 (1911)

Lento cantabile ♩ = 72

461

Johannes Brahms, *Vier ernste Gesänge,* Op. 121, No. 4, "Wenn ich
mit Menschen- und mit Engelzungen redete," mm. 48–52 (1896)

Adagio

462

Wir se-hen   jetzt durch ei-nen   Spie - gel in   ei-nem dunk-eln   Wor - te,

J. S. Bach, Cantata No. 149, "Man Singet mit Freuden vom Sieg,"
Aria, "Sied wachsam, ihr heiligen Wachter," mm. 1–4 (1728? or 1729?)

463

Vocal transposition: down 4th–7th

Joseph Haydn, Symphony No. 87, mvt. 3, Trio, mm. 1–8 (1785)

464

Corresponding Chapter in *Manual for Ear Training and Sight Singing*: 40

George Frideric Handel, *Siroe,* HWV 24, "Gelido, in ogni vena scorrer mi sento il sangue," mm. 7–10 (1728)

465 Larghetto

Ge-li-do in o-gni ve-na scor-rer mi sen-to il san-gue: L'om - bra

Vocal transposition: up 2nd

W. A. Mozart, Minuet K. 176, No. 9, Trio, mm. 1–8 (1773)

466

Vocal transposition: down 4th–7th

Giacomo Puccini, *La rondine,* Act I, "Fanciulla è sbocciato l'amore!," mm. 1–12 (1917)

467 **Allegretto moderato** *(Tempo di Valzer)*

Fan - ciul, la è sboc-cia-to l'a - mo - re! Di -

fen - di, di - fen - di di - fen - di il tuo cuo - re!

W. A. Mozart, *The Abduction from the Seraglio,* K. 384, Act II, "Ich gehe, doch rate ich dir," mm. 2–8 (1782)

468 **Allegro**

Ich ge-he, doch ra-te ich dir, den Schur-ken Pe-dril-lo zu

mei - den, den Schur-ken Pe-dril-lo zu mei - den.

Corresponding Chapter in *Manual for Ear Training and Sight Singing: 40*

Joseph Haydn, Symphony No. 35, mvt. 1, mm. 1–8 (1767)

469 Allegro di molto
piano
f
p

W. A. Mozart, Horn Concerto K. 495, mvt. 1, mm. 36–40 (1786)

470 Allegro maestoso
p

Vocal transposition: down 2nd–5th

Joseph Haydn, *The Seasons,* Part 1 (Spring), No. 6,
"Be Now Gracious, O Kind Heaven," mm. 3–12 (1801)

471 Poco Adagio.
Be now gra - cious, o———— kind heaven   o - pen thee
o - pen thee   and let thy bles - sing   drop   on these ex - tend - ed   fields!

W. A. Mozart, Rondo K. 485, mm. 1–4 (1786)

472 Allegro

Vocal transposition: down 4th–6th

Joseph Haydn, Symphony No. 55, mvt. 1, mm. 15–22 (1774)

473 Allegro di molto
pp

Corresponding Chapter in *Manual for Ear Training and Sight Singing:* 40

Michael Praetorius, *Terpsichore*, No. 2, Bransle double No. 2, mm. 1–8 (1612)

474

Bettine von Arnim (Bettine Brentano), "Weihe an Hellas"

Con moto

475

Die du an der Kind-heit Gren - zen stan - dest mit den

tau - send Krän - zen vor dem kaum er - wach - ten Geist;

mit dem Ern - ste der Ge - schich - te, in dem Zau - ber

der Ge - dich - te leh - rend, was man wür - dig preist.

Luigi Boccherini, Symphony No. 6 (G. 506), Op. 12, No. 4, mvt. 3, mm. 30–34 (1771?)

Allegro con molto

476

Vocal transposition: down 2nd–6th

James Hewitt, *Four Quick Marches*, "Quick Step No. 3," mm. 1–8 (1791)

477

Corresponding Chapter in *Manual for Ear Training and Sight Singing*: 40

Vocal transposition: down 4th–6th

James Hewitt, "Boston Brigade March," mm. 1–6

Louis Moreau Gottschalk, "La savane, ballade créole," Op. 3, mm. 21–28 (c. 1849)

Vocal transposition: down 6th–7th

W. A. Mozart, German Dance K. 602, No. 3, mm. 1–8 (1791)

Vocal transposition: up 2nd–5th

Johannes Schenck, *Scherzi musicali,* Op. 6, Suite in A minor, mvt. 9, mm. 1–5 (1698)

Gigue

Corresponding Chapter in *Manual for Ear Training and Sight Singing*: 40

W. A. Mozart, Piano Sonata K. 533, mvt. 1, mm. 9–12 (1788)

Vocal transposition: down 4th–7th

Victor Pelissier, *Pelissier's Columbian Melodies,* Allemande, mm. 1–24 (1812)

Corresponding Chapter in *Manual for Ear Training and Sight Singing*: 40

Vocal transposition: Sing the following excerpt at concert pitch by transposing all parts down an octave. Women should sing the top part while men sing the three lower parts.

W. A. Mozart, Sinfonia Concertante K. 364 (320d), mvt. 3, mm. 80–94 (1780)

Vocal transposition: down 2nd

Joseph Haydn, String Quartet Op. 54, No. 3 (Hob. III:59), mvt. 3, mm. 39–42 (c. 1788)

Corresponding Chapter in *Manual for Ear Training and Sight Singing*: 40

THE SUPERTONIC TRIAD

Louise Reichardt, "An den Erlösser," mm. 1–6

486

Blei - be bey uns denn es will A-bend wer - den der Tag hat sich ge - nei - get

Joseph Haydn, *The Creation,* "Now heav'n in fullest glory shone," mm. 11–14 (1798)

Allegro maestoso

487

Now heav'n in full - est glo - - ry— shone;

What can you do to hear the harmony at the opening of the following excerpt more easily?

Vocal transposition: down 3rd–6th   Jules Massenet, *Hérodiade,* Act I, scene 1, "Il est doux, il est bon," mm. 1–8 (1881)

a Tempo, calme, sans lenteur, *63 =* ♩

488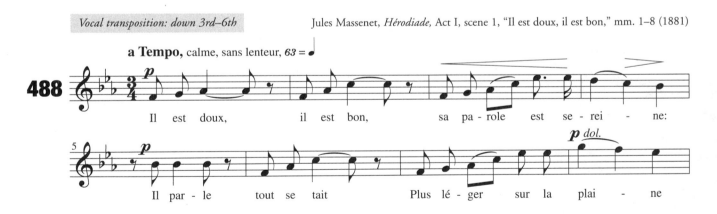

Il est doux, il est bon, sa pa - role est se - rei - ne:

Il par - le tout se tait Plus lé - ger sur la plai - ne

Joseph Haydn, Symphony No. 83, mvt. 4, mm. 1–8 (1785)

489   Vivace

Vocal transposition: down 2nd–3rd

Franz Schubert, "Im Haine," D. 738, mm. 4–8 (1822 or 1823?)

490   Mäßig

Son - nen - strah - len   durch   die   Tan - nen,   wie   sie

fal - len,   ziehn   von   dan - nen   al - le   Schmerz - en,

Vocal transposition: down 2nd–5th

Carl Stamitz, Concerto No. 2 for Cello, mvt. 3, mm. 53–60

491   Allegretto

Corresponding Chapter in *Manual for Ear Training and Sight Singing:* **41**

Jean-Philippe Rameau, *Platée,* Act II, 2nd Minuet, mm. 1–10 (1745)

Vocal transposition: down 4th

W. A. Mozart, Sinfonia Concertante K. 364 (320d), mvt. 2, mm. 1–9 (1780)

Andante

Johannes Brahms, *A German Requiem,* Op. 45, mvt. 6, mm. 208–212 (1868)

Allegro

Herr, du bist wür - dig zu neh - men Preis und Eh - re und Kraft,

James Hewitt, "Mark My Alford," mm. 84–91

Moderato

Vocal transposition: down 4th–7th

Robert Schumann, *Festival Overture,* Op. 123, mm. 9–12 (1853)

Feierlich, doch nicht zu langsam. ♩ = 58.

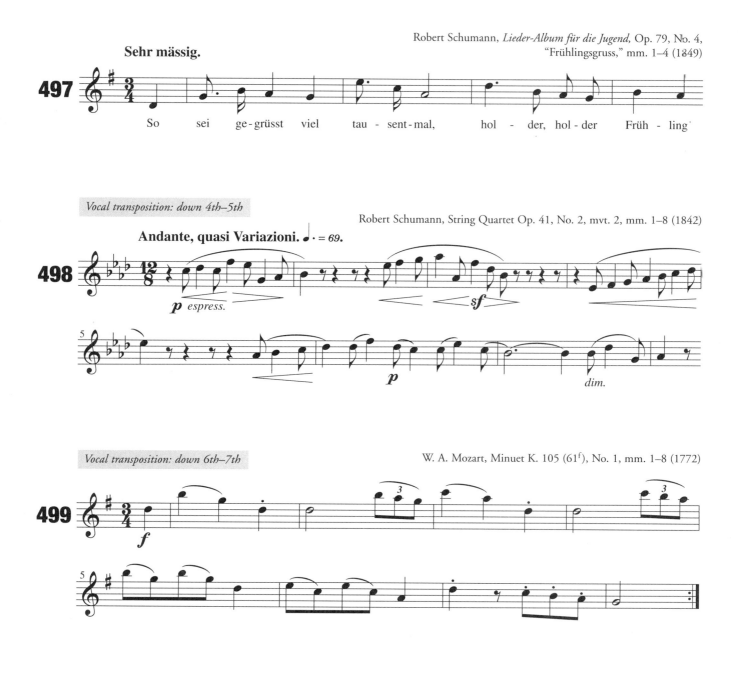

Sehr mässig.

Robert Schumann, *Lieder-Album für die Jugend,* Op. 79, No. 4, "Frühlingsgruss," mm. 1–4 (1849)

497

So   sei   ge-grüsst   viel   tau-sent-mal,   hol - der, hol - der   Früh - ling

Vocal transposition: down 4th–5th

Robert Schumann, String Quartet Op. 41, No. 2, mvt. 2, mm. 1–8 (1842)

Andante, quasi Variazioni. ♩. = 69.

498

p espress.   *sf*

p   *dim.*

Vocal transposition: down 6th–7th

W. A. Mozart, Minuet K. 105 (61f), No. 1, mm. 1–8 (1772)

499

f

J. S. Bach, *Well-Tempered Clavier,* Book II, Prelude in B♭ minor (No. 22), BWV 891, mm. 1–5 (c. 1740)

500

Corresponding Chapter in *Manual for Ear Training and Sight Singing:* 41

Vocal transposition: down 3rd–6th

Joseph Haydn, Symphony No. 85, mvt. 4, mm. 1–8 (1785?)

What is the tonic in the following excerpt? What makes that note feel like a tonic?

César Franck, *Prélude, Fugue and Variation,* Op. 18, Fugue, mm. 1–9 (1873)

Vocal transposition: down 2nd–5th

C. P. E. Bach, Sonatina No. 5, H. 452, mvt. 3, mm. 1–4 (1762)

W. A. Mozart, German Dance K. 602, No. 3, Trio, mm. 1–8 (1791)

Joseph Haydn, Symphony No. 100, mvt. 3, Trio, mm. 1–8 (1794)

Corresponding Chapter in *Manual for Ear Training and Sight Singing*: 41

"Au clair de lune," French folk song

506

Vocal transposition: down 2nd–3rd

J. S. Bach, *Mass in B Minor*, BWV 232, Confiteor, mm. 5–20

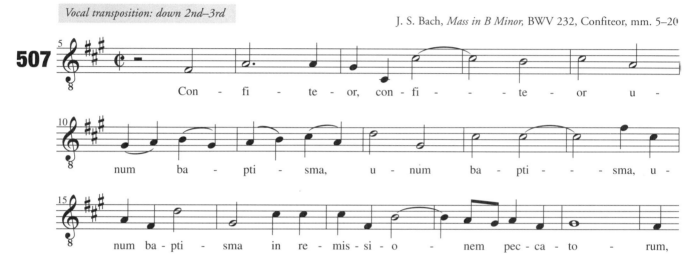

507

Con - fi - te - or, con - fi - - te - or u -

num ba - pti - sma, u - num ba - pti - - sma, u -

num ba - pti - sma in re - mis - si - o - nem pec - ca - to - rum,

Ludwig van Beethoven, Symphony No. 6, Op. 68 ("Pastoral"), mvt. 5, mm. 9–16 (1808)

Allegretto

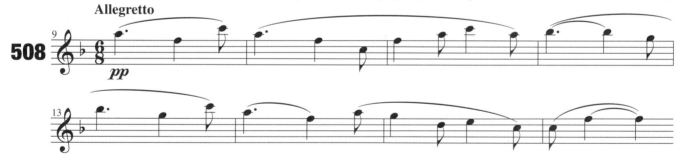

508

pp

J. S. Bach, Suite No. 4 for Unaccompanied Cello, BWV 1010, Bourrée II, mm. 1–4 (c. 1720)

Vocal transposition: up 4th–6th

509

Corresponding Chapter in *Manual for Ear Training and Sight Singing*: 41

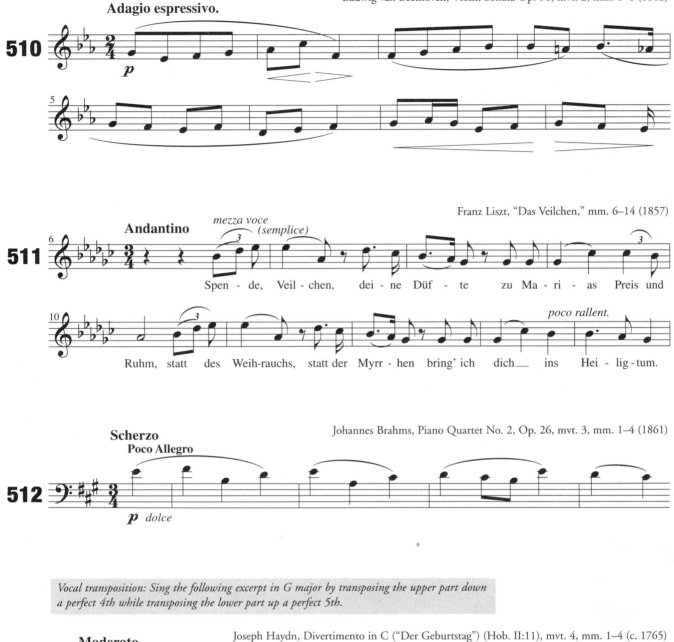

Ludwig van Beethoven, Violin Sonata Op. 96, mvt. 2, mm. 1–8 (1812)

510 Adagio espressivo.

Franz Liszt, "Das Veilchen," mm. 6–14 (1857)

511 Andantino *mezza voce (semplice)*

Spen - de, Veil - chen, dei - ne Düf - te zu Ma - ri - as Preis und

Ruhm, statt des Weih-rauchs, statt der Myr - hen bring' ich dich___ ins Hei - lig - tum.

Johannes Brahms, Piano Quartet No. 2, Op. 26, mvt. 3, mm. 1–4 (1861)

512 Scherzo Poco Allegro

p dolce

Vocal transposition: Sing the following excerpt in G major by transposing the upper part down a perfect 4th while transposing the lower part up a perfect 5th.

Joseph Haydn, Divertimento in C ("Der Geburtstag") (Hob. II:11), mvt. 4, mm. 1–4 (c. 1765)

513 Moderato

Corresponding Chapter in *Manual for Ear Training and Sight Singing*: 41

Vocal transposition: down 3rd–5th

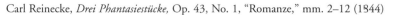

Carl Reinecke, *Drei Phantasiestücke,* Op. 43, No. 1, "Romanze," mm. 2–12 (1844)

Van Roland Edwards, national anthem of Barbados, mm. 1–16 (1966)

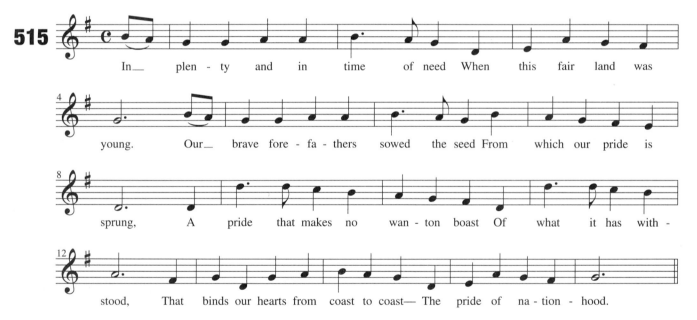

Corresponding Chapter in *Manual for Ear Training and Sight Singing:* 41

Joseph Haydn, Symphony No. 100, mvt. 4, mm. 1–8 (1794)

516

Vocal transposition: Sing the following excerpt at concert pitch by transposing both parts down an octave.

Andreas Lidl, Duet Op. 3, No. 1, mm. 23–30 (1778)

517

George Frideric Handel, Concerto Grosso Op. 6, No. 2, HWV 320, mvt. 4, mm. 1–4 (1739)

518

Corresponding Chapter in *Manual for Ear Training and Sight Singing*: 41

Vocal transposition: Sing the following excerpt in A minor by transposing the three upper parts down a perfect 4th while transposing the bass part up a perfect 5th.

George Frideric Handel, Concerto Grosso Op. 6, No. 2,
HWV 320, mvt. 4, mm. 66–69 (1739)

519

Vocal transposition: down 3rd–6th

Robert Schumann, String Quartet Op. 41, No. 3, mvt. 2, mm. 145–160 (1842)

520

Corresponding Chapter in *Manual for Ear Training and Sight Singing*: 41

What can you do to hear the harmony at the opening of the following excerpt more easily? Where does the supertonic harmony appear?

Vocal transposition: down 2nd–5th

W. A. Mozart, German Dance K. 567, No. 2, Trio (1788)

521

Vocal transposition: down 3rd–5th

W. A. Mozart, Piano Sonata K. 332 (300ᵏ), mvt. 1, mm. 1–12 (1783)

522 **Allegro**

W. A. Mozart, Symphony No. 38, K. 504 ("Prague"), mvt. 3, mm. 1–16 (1786)

523 **Presto**

Corresponding Chapter in *Manual for Ear Training and Sight Singing*: 41

THE SUBMEDIANT TRIAD

George Frideric Handel, *Saul,* HWV 53, Part I, "Birth and Fortune I Despise!," mm. 50–58 (1738)

524

Birth and For-tune I des - pise, Birth and For-tune I des - pise,

Vocal transposition: Sing the following excerpt at concert pitch by transposing all parts down one octave.

Franz Schubert, Symphony No. 5, D. 485, mvt. 1, mm. 1–5 (1816)

525

Vocal transposition: Sing the following excerpt in A major by transposing all parts up a major 3rd.

Jacobus Handl [Gallus], *Missa canonica,* Credo, mm. 1–3

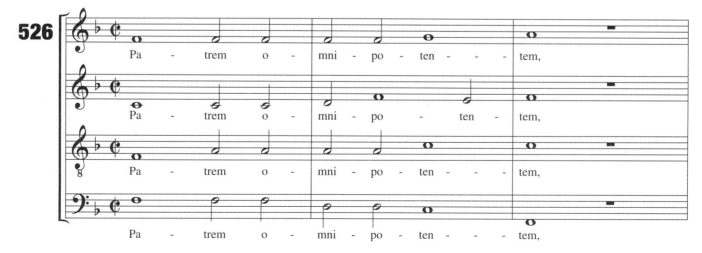

526

Pa - trem o - mni - po - ten - - tem,

Pa - trem o - mni - po - ten - tem,

Pa - trem o - mni - po - ten - - tem,

Pa - trem o - mni - po - ten - - tem,

Corresponding Chapter in *Manual for Ear Training and Sight Singing:* 42

Vocal transposition: If necessary to accommodate singers on the top part, transpose all parts down a step.

Michael Praetorius, *Terpsichore,* No. 152, Courante, mm. 1–8 (1612)

Vocal transposition: down 4th–6th

Allegro non troppo

Johannes Brahms, Violin Concerto, Op. 77, mvt. 1, mm. 1–8 (1878)

Vocal transposition: down 2nd–6th

Tempo Marche Militaire.

John Philip Sousa, "Manhattan Beach," mm. 53–68 (1893)

Corresponding Chapter in *Manual for Ear Training and Sight Singing:* 42

Ludwig van Beethoven, String Quartet Op. 135, mvt. 3, mm. 3–10 (1826)

Lento assai, cantante e tranquillo.

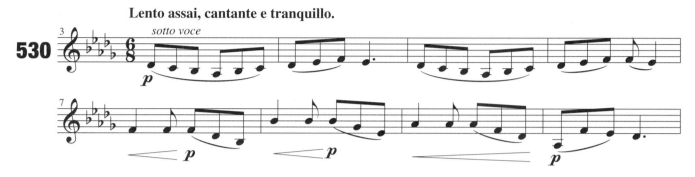

J. S. Bach, Sinfonia No. 14, BWV 800, mm. 1–5 (c. 1720)

Vocal transposition: up 2nd–3rd

Giuseppi Verdi, String Quartet, mvt. 1, mm. 1–9 (1873)

Corresponding Chapter in *Manual for Ear Training and Sight Singing*: 42

Vocal transposition: down 2nd–7th

Andante

Peter Ilich Tchaikovsky, *Swan Lake,* Op. 20, No. 9, Finale, mm. 2–9 (1876)

533

p dolce espress.

Ludwig van Beethoven, Trio Op. 1, No. 3, mvt. 4, mm. 1–7 (1795)

Prestissimo

534

ff   *sf*   *sf*

J. S. Bach[?], *Notebook for Anna Magdalena Bach,* Polonaise, mm. 1–8

Polonaise

535

Chip Davis, "Christmas Lullaby," mm. 1–8 (1995)

Simply

536

Corresponding Chapter in *Manual for Ear Training and Sight Singing*: 42

Charles A. Zimmerman, "Anchors Aweigh," U.S. Naval Academy fight song, mm. 17–32 (1907)

537 March tempo - Moderato

Roll   up the score Na - vy   An - chors A - weigh

Sail   Na - vy   down the field And sink the Ar-my, sink the Ar-my gray.

Franz Schubert, Symphony No. 4, D. 417, mvt. 3, Trio, mm. 1–8 (1816)

538

Jules Massenet, "Chant provençal," mm. 4–11 (1871)

539 Andante sostenuto

Mi - reil-le ne sait pas en - co - re Le doux char - me de sa beau - té!

C'est u - ne fleur qui vient d'é - clo - re Dans un sou - ri - re de l'é - te!

Claude Debussy, *L'enfant prodigue,* "O temps à jamais effacé," mm. 1–4 (1884)

540 Andantino
très simplement

O temps à ja - mais ef - fe - cé,   Où comme eux j'a - vais l'â - me pu - re,

Franz Schubert, Symphony No. 9, D. 944, mvt. 1, mm. 1–8 (1828)

541 Andante

Corresponding Chapter in *Manual for Ear Training and Sight Singing*: 42

W. A. Mozart, Divertimento K. 270, mvt. 2, mm. 1–8 (1777)

Antonín Dvořák, *Biblical Songs,* Op. 99, No. 9, "I Will Lift Mine Eyes," mm. 1–20 (1894)

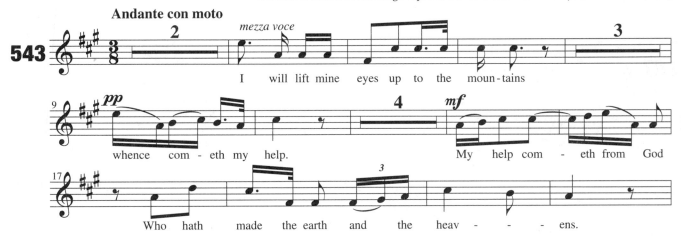

Pietro Mascagni, *Cavalleria rusticana,* Intermezzo sinfonico, mm. 20–27 (1890)

Vocal transposition: down 2nd–5th

J. S. Bach, *Well-Tempered Clavier,* Book II, Fugue in F major (No. 11), BWV 880, mm. 1–5 (c. 1740)

Corresponding Chapter in *Manual for Ear Training and Sight Singing*: 42

Mikhail Ippolitov-Ivanov, *Caucasian Sketches,* Op. 10,
mvt. 1, "In the Mountain Pass," mm. 75–82 (1894)

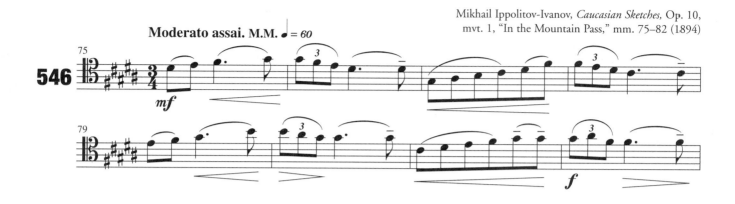

546

Pietro Mascagni, *Iris,* Act II, "Io pingo," mm. 34–39 (1898)

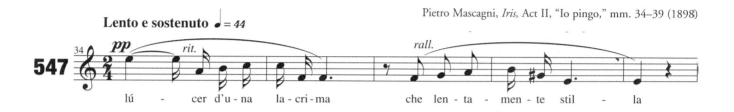

547

lú - cer d'u - na la - cri - ma   che len - ta - men - te stil - la

George Frideric Handel, *Agrippina,* HWV 6, Act III, "Io di Roma il Giove sono," mm. 11–23 (1709)

548

Vocal transposition: down 3rd–7th

Gustav Holst, *The Planets,* Op. 32, mvt. 4, "Jupiter,
the Bringer of Jollity," mm. 210–217 (1916)

549

Corresponding Chapter in *Manual for Ear Training and Sight Singing:* 42

Joseph Haydn, Symphony No. 98, mvt. 1, mm. 16–19 (1792)

Allegro

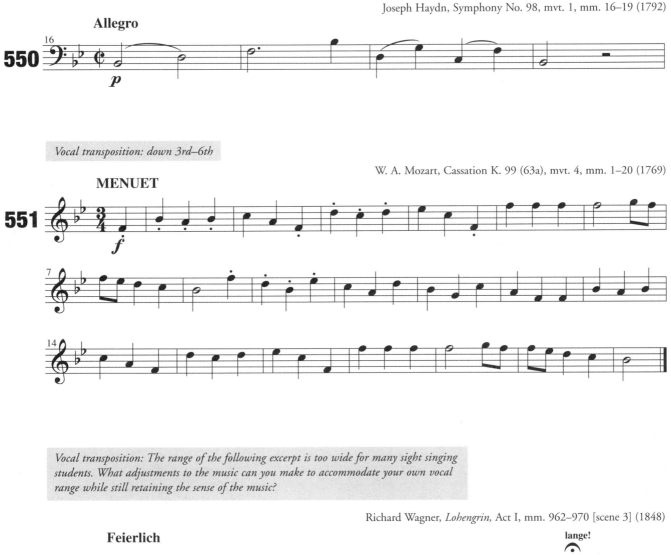

Vocal transposition: down 3rd–6th

W. A. Mozart, Cassation K. 99 (63a), mvt. 4, mm. 1–20 (1769)

MENUET

Vocal transposition: The range of the following excerpt is too wide for many sight singing students. What adjustments to the music can you make to accommodate your own vocal range while still retaining the sense of the music?

Richard Wagner, *Lohengrin,* Act I, mm. 962–970 [scene 3] (1848)

Feierlich

Vocal transposition: down 4th–5th

Johannes Brahms, Trio Op. 114, mvt. 4, mm. 1–5 (1891)

Allegro

Corresponding Chapter in *Manual for Ear Training and Sight Singing*: 42

THE MEDIANT TRIAD

Gustav Mahler, *Das Lied von der Erde,* No. 3, "Von der Jugend," mm. 39–47 (1909)

554

In dem Häus - chen sit - zen Freun - de, schön ge - klei - det,

trin - ken, plau - dern, man - che schrei - ben Ver - se nie - der.

Vocal transposition: down 3rd–7th

Sergei Rachmaninoff, "How Fair This Spot!," Op. 21, No. 7, mm. 1–5 (1902)

555

How fair this spot! I gaze to where The gold-en brook runs by. The fields are all...

Tommie Connor, "I Saw Mommy Kissing Santa Claus," mm. 1–8 (1952)

556

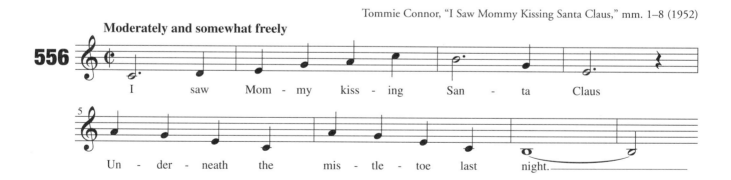

I saw Mom - my kiss - ing San - ta Claus

Un - der - neath the mis - tle - toe last night.

Lionel Bart, "As Long As He Needs Me," mm. 21–28 (1960)

557 Slowly

I won't be - tray his trust,___ Tho' peo - ple say I must.___ I've got to

stay true, just___ As Long As He Needs Me.

Freddie Mercury, "We Are the Champions," chorus, mm. 1–8 (1977)

558 Moderately Slow ♩.= 62

We___ are the cham - pions___ my friend.___ and

we'll___ keep on fight - ing___ till the end.___

Charles Gounod, "Jésus de Nazareth," mm. 5–19 (1856)

559 Moderato, quasi Andante. *p*

Né dans u - ne crê - che, Di - vin Ré - demp - teur___ I - ci bas je

prê - che, I - ci bas je prê - che Les ver - tus du coeur,

Les ver - tus du coeur,___ Les ver - tus du coeur.___

Corresponding Chapter in *Manual for Ear Training and Sight Singing:* **43**

Vocal transposition: down 5th

Camille Saint-Saëns, *The Carnival of the Animals,* "The Swan," mm. 2–5 (1386)

560

Vocal transposition: down 5th–6th

Camille Saint-Saëns, Cello Concerto No. 1, Op. 33, mm. 241–262 (1872)

561

Vocal transposition: down 5th–7th

Georg Philipp Telemann, Concerto in E♭, mvt. 1, mm. 1–11

562

Vocal transposition: down 4th–6th

Edward MacDowell, *Woodland Sketches,* Op. 51, No. 1, "To a Wild Rose," mm. 1–8 (1896)

563

Corresponding Chapter in *Manual for Ear Training and Sight Singing*: 43

Michael Palin, "Decomposing Composers" (1980)

564

Beet - ho - ven's gone but his mu - sic lives on, and

Mo - zart don't go shop - pin' no more, You'll ne - ver meet Liszt or

Brahms a - gain, And El - gar does - n't an - swer the door.

Schu - bert and Cho - pin used to chuck - le and laugh, Whilst com -

po - sing a long sym - pho - ny, But one

hun - dred and fif - ty years la - ter, There's ve - ry

lit - tle of them left to see. They're de - com - po - sing com -

po - sers, There's no - thing much a - ny - one can do,

You can still hear Beet - ho - ven, But Beet - ho - ven can - not hear you.

Corresponding Chapter in *Manual for Ear Training and Sight Singing:* **43**

Vocal transposition: down 2nd–7th

Martin Luther, chorale melody, "Vom Himmel kam der Engel Schar" (1543)

565

Vocal transposition: Sing the following excerpt at concert pitch by transposing the top part down an octave while transposing the bottom part up an octave.

Sergei Rachmaninoff, Suite No. 2 for Two Pianos, Op. 17, mvt. 4, "Tarantelle," mm. 22–26 (1901)

566

Henry Purcell, *Ten Sonatas of Four Parts,* Sonata No. 3, z804, mvt. 5, mm. 1–2 (c. 1679)

567

Vocal transposition: down 2nd–4th

Richard Wagner, *Parsifal,* Act III, mm. 940–945 ["Amfortas's Prayer"] (1881)

568

Corresponding Chapter in *Manual for Ear Training and Sight Singing:* 43

Henry Purcell, *Ten Sonatas of Four Parts,* Sonata No. 3, z804, mvt. 4, Canzona, mm. 1–3 (c. 1679)

Allegro ma non troppo

Antonín Dvořák, Symphony No. 9, Op. 95 ("From the New World"), mvt. 4, mm. 10–17 (1893)

Allegro con fuoco. M.M. ♩ = *152*

Vocal transposition: down 2nd–6th

Johannes Brahms, *Fünf Lieder,* Op. 107, No. 5, "Mädchenlied," mm. 1–9 (c. 1888)

Leise bewegt

571

Auf die Nacht in den Spinn-stubn, da__ sing-en die Mäd-chen, da__

lach-en die Dorf-bubn, wie flink gehn die Räd - chen!

Vocal transposition: Sing the following excerpt in D minor by transposing all parts down a perfect 5th.

Robert Schumann, *Album for the Young,* Op. 68, No. 6, "Poor Orphan Child," mm. 13–20 (1848)

Langsam.

Corresponding Chapter in *Manual for Ear Training and Sight Singing*: 43

OTHER SEVENTH CHORDS

Vocal transposition: The range of the following excerpt is a bit wide. Try transposing it down a 2nd or 3rd, and use good support to reach the high notes in m. 5 and the lowest note in m. 8.

Maria Szymanowska, "Caprice sur la romance de Joconde," mm. 1–8 (1819)

573

Joseph Haydn, String Quartet Op. 77, No. 1 (Hob. III:81), mvt. 2, mm. 1–8 (1799)

574

Joseph Haydn, Symphony No. 91, mvt. 4, mm. 181–187, (1788)

575

Corresponding Chapter in *Manual for Ear Training and Sight Singing:* **47**

"Sing a Song of Sixpence," English folk song

J. S. Bach, Keyboard Partita No. 5, BWV 829, Gigue, mm. 1–3

Gigue

George Frideric Handel, *Rinaldo*, HWV 7, Act I, scene 7, "Cara sposa," mm. 12–24 (1711)

Largo.

Ca - - ra spo - sa, a - man - te ca - ra, do - ve
se - i?____ do - ve se - i? deh! ri - tor - na a pian - ti mie - i!

Vocal transposition: down 2nd–5th

Frédéric Chopin, Waltz Op. 34, No. 2, mm. 16–20 (c. 1834)

Lento

p

J. S. Bach, Cantata No. 211, "Schweigt stille, plaudert nicht" ("Coffee Cantata"), No. 6, mm. 7–10 (c. 1734)

Aria

Mäd - chen, die von har - ten Sin - nen, die von har - ten Sin - nen, sind nicht leich - te zu ge - win - nen,

Corresponding Chapter in *Manual for Ear Training and Sight Singing*: 47

J. S. Bach, Cantata No. 76, "Die Himmel erzählen die Ehre Gottes,"
No. 12, "Liebt, ihr Christen, in der Tat," mm. 13–15 (1723)

Liebt___ ihr Chri - sten, in der Tat,

Corrente

J. S. Bach, Violin Partita No. 2, BWV 1004, Courante, mm. 1–3 (1723)

Vocal transposition: down 2nd–7th

J. S. Bach, *Well-Tempered Clavier*, Book II, Fugue in A minor
(No. 20), BWV 889, mm. 1–3 (c. 1740)

[**Allegro moderato** ♩ = *112*]

Poco più mosso

Sergei Prokofiev, Piano Sonata No. 6, Op. 82, mvt. 1, mm. 40–43 (1940)

Vocal transposition: down 4th–7th

Adagio sostenuto

Ludwig van Beethoven, Violin Sonata Op. 47 ("Kreutzer"), mvt. 1, mm. 1–4 (1803)

Corresponding Chapter in *Manual for Ear Training and Sight Singing*: 47

Alexander Borodin, String Quartet No. 1, mvt. 3, Trio, mm. 21–29 (1879)

Moderato. (♩ = *92.*)

586

Giuseppi Verdi, *Un ballo in maschera,* Act I, "Alla vita che t'arride," mm. 3–10 (1859)

Andante ♩ = *40*

espress.

587

Al - la vi - ta che t'ar - ri de   di spe - ran - ze   e gau - dio pie - na,   d'al - tre

mil - le e mil - le   vi - te   li de - sti - no   s'in - ca - te - na!

On what chord does the following excerpt seem to begin? What can you do to make
it easier to sing this opening?

Vocal transposition: down 2nd–6th

Richard Wagner, *Götterdämmerung,* Prelude, mm. 362–365 (1874)

Sehr ruhig, ohne zu schleppen

588

Zu neu - en Ta - ten,   teu - rer Hel - de,

Gustav Mahler, Symphony No. 2, mvt. 1, mm. 18–22 (1894)

Allegro maestoso. Mit durchaus ernstem und feierlichem Ausdruck.

589

Corresponding Chapter in *Manual for Ear Training and Sight Singing: 47*

Vocal transposition: down 2nd–3rd

Giuseppi Verdi, *Otello*, Act IV, "Piangea cantando nell'erma landa," mm. 1–9 (1837)

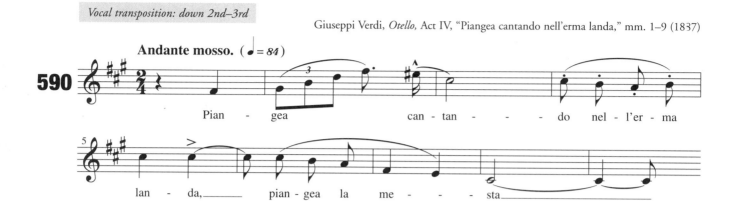

Johannes Brahms, *Fünf Lieder,* Op. 94, No. 2, "Steig auf, geliebter Schatten," mm. 2–5 (1883)

George Frideric Handel, Concerto Op. 4, No. 6, HWV 294, mvt. 1, mm. 1–6 (c. 1736)

Corresponding Chapter in *Manual for Ear Training and Sight Singing*: 47

Omit the grace notes when singing the following excerpt (they're printed in brackets).

Vocal transposition: Take the first two notes in the cello part up an octave.

W. A. Mozart, String Quartet K. 428 (421^b), mvt. 3, mm. 1–6 (1783)

593

Vocal transposition: Sing the following excerpt in F major by transposing all parts up a perfect 4th.

Richard Wagner, *Die Meistersinger von Nürnberg*, Act III, mm. 2771–2777 (1867)

tranquillo

Alexander Glazunov, Violin Concerto, Op. 82, mm. 37–41 (1904)

595

dolce

Joseph Haydn, *Missa in angustiis* ("Nelson" Mass), Agnus Dei, mm. 43–45 (1798)

Vivace

596

f

Vocal transposition: down 2nd–3rd

J. S. Bach, Sinfonia No. 2, BWV 788, mm. 1–3 (c. 1720)

597

Jean-Philippe Rameau, *Thétis,* "Partez, volez, brillants éclairs," mm. 28–50 (1718)

598

Par - tez   vo - lez, bril - lants   é - clairs! Si - gna - lez,   si - gna-

lez,   le   maî - tre   du   mon - de,   Si - gna - lez   le   maî - tre   du

mon - de!   Por - tez   vos   feux   jus - que dans   l'on - de,   Por - tez   vos

feux   jus - que dans   l'on - de,   Em - bra - sez   l'em - pi - re   des   mers!

Corresponding Chapter in *Manual for Ear Training and Sight Singing: 47*

George Frideric Handel, Sonata Op. 1, No. 7, HWV 365, mvt. 1, mm. 1–2

Larghetto

Ambroise Thomas, *Hamlet,* Act IV, "Pâle et blonde," mm. 1–4 (1868)

Vocal transposition: down 3rd–5th

Andantino. (52 = ♪)

Pâle et blon - de Dort sous l'eau pro - fon - de La Wil - lis au re - gard de feu!

Christoph Willibald von Gluck, *Ezio,* Act II, "Quel fingere affetto," mm. 25–34 (1750)

Tempo giusto

Quel fin - ge - re af - fet - to, al - lor__ che__ non__

s'a - ma, per mol - ti, per mol - ti è__ di - let - - to;

Johannes Brahms, Piano Sonata No. 3, Op. 5, mvt. 2, mm. 1–4 (1853)

Andante espressivo

Joseph Haydn, Symphony No. 86, mvt. 4, mm. 1–5 (1786)

Allegro con spirito

Corresponding Chapter in *Manual for Ear Training and Sight Singing:* 47

Virgil Thomson, *The Mother of us all*, Act I, "Hush," mm. 1–8 (1947)

Vocal transposition: down 3rd–5th

Benjamin Britten, *Serenade for Tenor, Horn, and Strings,* Op. 31, Nocturne, mm. 2–10 (1943)

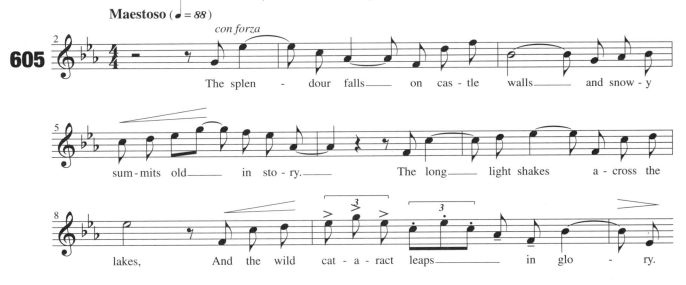

Corresponding Chapter in *Manual for Ear Training and Sight Singing*: 47

"Dis Long Time, Gal," Jamaican folk song

606

Vocal transposition: down 3rd–6th

Alexander Scriabin, Symphony No. 3, "Le poème divin," Op. 43, mvt. 3, mm. 3–4 (1904)

Allegro M.M. ♩ = 116

Avec une joie éclatante

607

Corresponding Chapter in *Manual for Ear Training and Sight Singing*: 47

Vocal transposition: The range of the following excerpt is a bit wide. Try transposing it down a 3rd, and use good support to reach the low note in mm. 1 and 3 and the high note in m. 10.

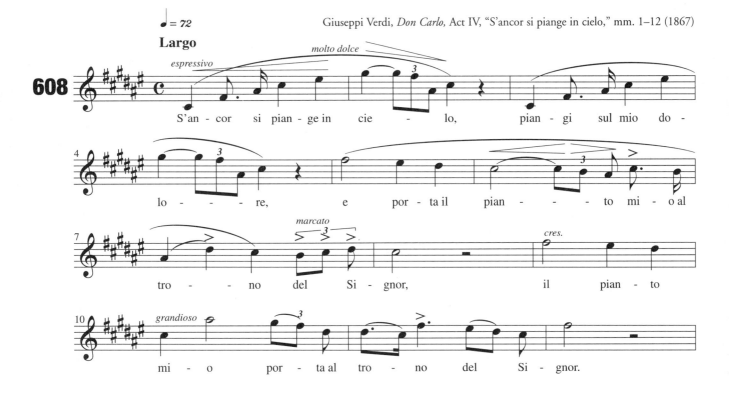

♩ = 72

Giuseppi Verdi, *Don Carlo,* Act IV, "S'ancor si piange in cielo," mm. 1–12 (1867)

Largo

608

S'an - cor si pian - ge in cie - lo, pian - gi sul mio do -

lo - - - re, e por - ta il pian - - - to mi - o al

tro - - no del Si - gnor, il pian - to

mi - o por - ta al tro - no del Si - gnor.

Corresponding Chapter in *Manual for Ear Training and Sight Singing:* 47

TRANSPOSITION

Sing the following excerpt on letter names in the key of E.

Béla Bartók, *For Children,* Part I, No. 7, "Look For the Needle," mm. 1–8 (1909)

Play the following excerpt on piano a minor 3rd lower than written.

Clara Schumann, Six Songs, Op. 13, No. 1, "Ich stand in dunklen Träumen," mm. 28–31 (1843)

Play the following excerpt on piano at concert pitch.

Ludwig van Beethoven, Symphony No. 2, Op. 36, mvt. 2, mm. 8–16 (1802)

Sing, on letter names, the pitches an English horn player would need to play in order to produce the following excerpt at concert pitch.

Hector Berlioz, *Symphonie fantastique,* Op. 14, mvt. 3, "Scène aux champs," mm. 20–23 (1830)

Sing, on letter names, the pitches an alto sax player would need to play in order to read the following part in unison with a French horn player. (Tip: Could you renotate this part with a key signature?)

Aaron Copland, *Appalachian Spring,* rehearsal 60, mm. 1–16 (1944)

Play the following excerpt at concert pitch on any instrument.

Henry Bishop, "Copenhagen" (Bohemian Waltz), mm. 1–8 (1813)

Corresponding Chapter in *Manual for Ear Training and Sight Singing:* 48

Sing the following excerpt on letter names in ensemble; make octave adjustments as necessary. Also try playing all parts at concert pitch on instruments in C.

Joseph Haydn, Symphony No. 103, mvt. 4, mm. 1–12 (1795)

THE MODES

Dorian exemplar

Béla Bartók, *For Children,* Part II, No. 24, "I Passed through the Forest," mm. 1–5 (1909)

616

Phrygian exemplar

J. S. Bach, Chorale No. 10, "Aus tiefer Not schrei ich zu dir," mm. 1–5 [melody: Martin Luther (1524)]

617

Lydian exemplar

Béla Bartók, *For Children,* Part II, No. 20, "Frisky"
["Don't go down at dawn, Hanulienka"], mm. 1–16 (1909)

618

Mixolydian exemplar

"The Three Butchers," English folk song

619

Aeolian exemplar

"Margoton sous un pommier," French folk song

620

"The Bonny Labouring Boy," English folk song

621

Béla Bartók, *Mikrokosmos*, No. 34, "In Phrygian Mode," mm. 1–9 (1939)

Calmo, ♩ = 80

622

p, legato

mf

"The Rocky Road to Dublin," Irish folk song, chorus

623

Corresponding Chapter in *Manual for Ear Training and Sight Singing*: 49

Konrad von Würzburg, Meistersinger song, "Des soltu clein geniessen," mm. 1–7

J. S. Bach, Chorale No. 81, "Christus, der selig macht," mm. 1–8 [melody: anonymous (1531)]

Vocal transposition: down 2nd–6th

Michel Behaim, Meistersinger song, "Gekronte Weist," mm. 14–22

"Nous avons trois bell' filles," French folk song

Richard de Semilli, Trouvère song, "L'autrier tout seus chevauchoie mon chemin"

"The Cunning Cobbler," British folk song

Hector Berlioz, *Symphonie fantastique*, Op. 14, mvt. 5
("Songe d'une nuite du Sabbat"), mm. 127–147 ["Dies irae"] (1830)

Corresponding Chapter in *Manual for Ear Training and Sight Singing*: 49

Béla Bartók, *Mikrokosmos,* No. 55, "Triplets in Lydian Mode," mm. 1–8 (1939)

Tempo di marcia, ♩= 106

631

"The Months of the Year," British folk song

632

Vocal transposition: down 3rd–7th

Béla Bartók, *For Children,* Part I, No. 42, "Swineherd Dance," mm. 36–51 (1909)

Allegro vivace

633

Corresponding Chapter in *Manual for Ear Training and Sight Singing*: 49

Johannes Brahms, *28 deutsche Volkslieder,* WoO 32 posth., No. 15, "Die beiden Königskinder" (1858)

634

Ach El - se - lein, lie - bes El - se - lein mein, wie gern wär ich bei dir, wie

gern wär ich bei dir; so sind zwei tie - fe Was - ser wohl zwi-schen

dir und mir, so sind zwei tie - fe Was - ser wohl zwi-schen dir und mir.

Ludwig van Beethoven, *Twelve Scottish Songs,* WoO 156, No. 6, "Highland Harry," mm. 8–15 (1815)

Allegretto spiritoso

635

My Harry was a gal - lant gay, Fu' state - ly strade he on the plain; But

now he's ban - ish'd far a - wa, I'll nev - er see him back a–gain.

Arnaut Daniel, Troubadour song, "Lo ferm voler qu'el cor," mm. 1–7 (late 12th century)

636

"Fillettes de Champagne," French folk song

637

"Le noël des oiseaux," French folk song

"Old Joe Clark," North American folk song

Vocal transposition: down 3rd–7th

Béla Bartók, *First Term at the Piano,* No. 16, "Peasant's Dance" (1913)

Jacob Arcadelt, "Il bianco e dolce cigno," mm. 6–10 (1539)

641

Et io pian - gen - do giung' al fin del vi - ver mi - o,

Et io pian - gen - do giung' al fin del vi - ver mi - o,

Et io pian - gen - do giung' al fin del vi - ver mi - o,

Et io pian - gen - do giung' al fin del vi - ver mi - o,

Luys Milán, Fantasia No. 8 for Vihuela, mm. 1–7 (16th century)

642

ADVANCED TRIPLETS

Michael Haydn, Symphony in G, P16, mvt. 2, mm. 33–38 (1783)

Andante sostenuto.

643

Vocal transposition: Sing the following excerpt at concert pitch by transposing both parts down an octave.

Domenico Scarlatti, Sonata K. 206, mm. 1–4

Andante

644

Ludwig van Beethoven, Symphony No. 8, Op. 93, mvt. 4, mm. 1–4 (1812)

Allegro vivace

645

Isaac Albéniz, *Suite española,* Op. 47, No. 3, "Sevilla," mm. 3–5 (1886)

Allegro moderato

646

Peter Ilich Tchaikovsky, Symphony No. 4, Op. 36, mvt. 1, mm. 1–4 (1378)

Ludwig van Beethoven, Piano Concerto No. 5, Op. 73 ("Emperor"), mvt. 1, mm. 11–17 (1809)

Vocal transposition: When singing the top part (Violin I) of the following excerpt alone, transpose down a 3rd or 4th. When singing all parts together, either (1) transpose all parts down a 2nd and use good support for the highest notes in Violin I in m. 1, or (2) transpose all parts down a 3rd and use good support for the lowest notes in Violin II in m. 6.

Joseph Haydn, String Quartet Op. 1, No. 1 (Hob. III:1), mvt. 5, mm. 1–6 (c. 1759)

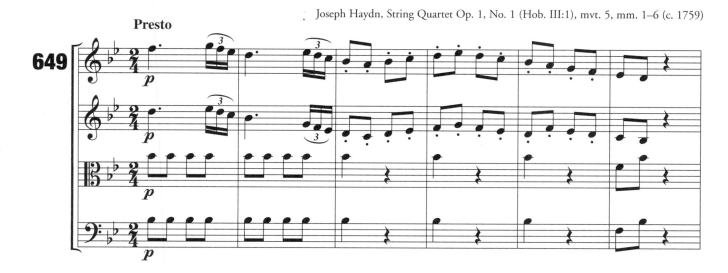

Corresponding Chapter in *Manual for Ear Training and Sight Singing*: 51

Virgil Thomson, *The Mother of us all,* Act I, scene 4, "We Are the Chorus of the V. I. P.," mm. 1–8 (1947)

650

We are the cho-rus of the V. I. P. Ver-y im-por-tant per-sons to ev-ry one

We are the cho-rus of the V. I. P. Ver-y im-por-tant per-sons to ev-ry one

We are the cho-rus of the V. I. P. Ver-y im-por-tant per-sons to ev-ry one

who can hear and see, we are the cho-rus of the V. I. P.

who can hear and see, we are the cho-rus of the V. I. P.

who can hear and see, we are the cho-rus of the V. I. P.

Langsam, aber nicht zu schleppend

Hugo Wolf, "Harfenspieler II," mm. 5–8 (1888)

651

An die Tü - ren will___ ich schlei - chen, still und sitt - sam will ich stehn;

Virgil Thomson, *Four Saints in Three Acts,* Act III, "He Asked For a Distant Magpie," mm. 1–4 (1928)

Allegro militare (♩ = 120)

652

He asked for a dis - tant mag - pie as if they made a dif - fer-ence.

Corresponding Chapter in *Manual for Ear Training and Sight Singing: 51*

Richard Strauss, *Capriccio,* Op. 85, "Du Spiegel bild der verliebten Madeleine," mm. 1–6 (1941)

Arthur Sullivan, *The Yeomen of the Guard,* Act I, "This the Autumn of Our Life," mm. 72–77 (1888)

Corresponding Chapter in *Manual for Ear Training and Sight Singing:* 51

Vocal transposition: The range of the following excerpt is a bit wide for many sight-singing students. Sing in one of the following ways: (1) Transpose down a 3rd and use good support for the high note in mm. 7–8; or (2) Transpose down a 4th and use good support for the low note in m. 3.

Virgil Thomson, *The Mother of us all*, Act I, scene 4, "My Constantly Recurring Thought," mm. 1–15 (1947)

Charles Ives, Symphony No. 4, mvt. 3, mm. 111–117 (1925)

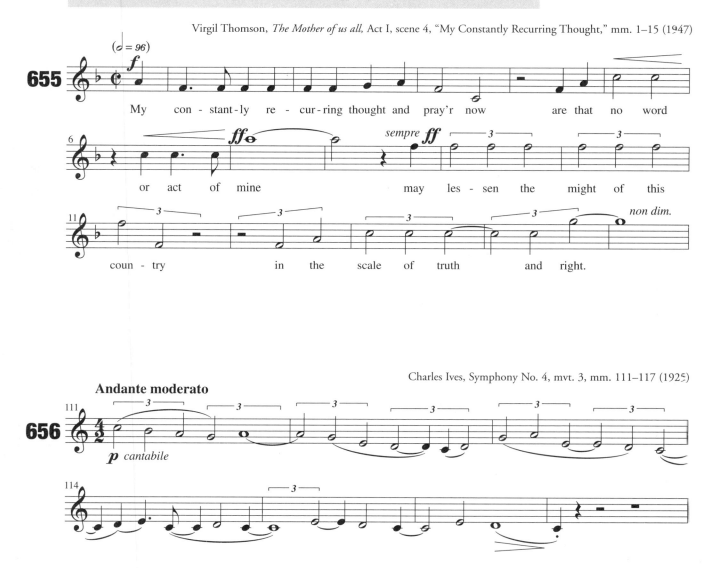

Corresponding Chapter in *Manual for Ear Training and Sight Singing*: 51

CHROMATIC PASSING TONES

W. A. Mozart, *The Magic Flute,* K. 620, Act II, Finale, mm. 584–591 (1791)

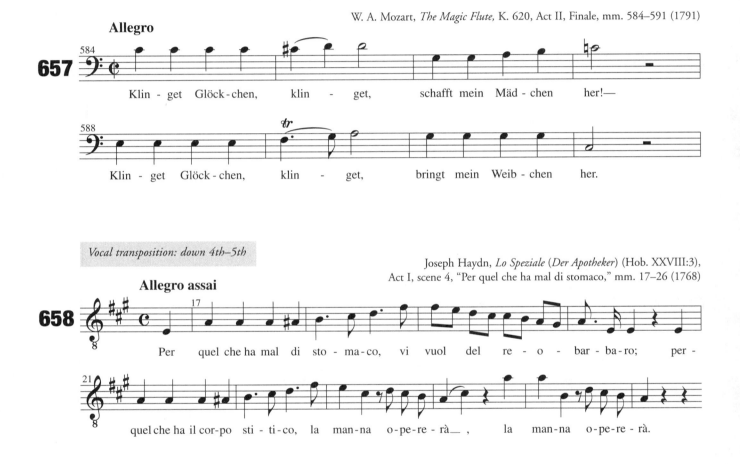

Vocal transposition: down 4th–5th

Joseph Haydn, *Lo Speziale* (*Der Apotheker*) (Hob. XXVIII:3),
Act I, scene 4, "Per quel che ha mal di stomaco," mm. 17–26 (1768)

W. A. Mozart, *Don Giovanni,* K. 527, Overture, mm. 32–38 (1787)

Corresponding Chapter in *Manual for Ear Training and Sight Singing:* **52**

Vocal transposition: down 3rd–6th

Maria Szymanowska, Nocturne No. 2, mm. 1–4 (1831)

660

Joseph Haydn, Cello Concerto in D (Hob. VIIb:2), mvt. 3, mm. 1–8 (1783)

661

Vocal transposition: down 2nd–3rd

Ludwig van Beethoven, Symphony No. 9, Op. 125, mvt. 3, mm. 43–46 (1824)

662

George Frederick Bristow, *The Oratorio of Daniel*, Op. 42,
"Now I Praise and Extol the King of Heaven," mm. 28–35

663
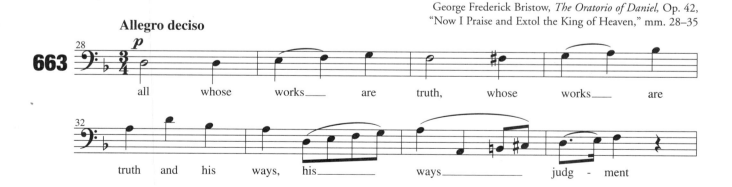

Corresponding Chapter in *Manual for Ear Training and Sight Singing*: 52

Franz Schubert, Viennese German Dance D. 128, No. 5, mm. 1–8 (1812?)

664

Johannes Brahms, Symphony No. 4, Op. 98, mvt. 4, mm. 1–8 (1885)

Allegro energico e passionato

665

Vocal transposition: down 4th–5th

W. A. Mozart, Horn Concerto K. 447, mvt. 2, mm. 9–16 (1787)

Larghetto

666

Max Reger, Suite for Solo Viola, Op. 131d, mvt. 2, mm. 47–50 (1915)

667

Corresponding Chapter in *Manual for Ear Training and Sight Singing*: 52

Ludwig van Beethoven, Symphony No. 3, Op. 55
("Eroica"), mvt. 4, mm. 381–396 (1303)

668 Poco Andante ♪ = 108

Johann Strauss, Jr., *Der Zigeunerbaron* (*The Gypsy Baron*),
Act II, "Ha, seht es winkt," mm. 1–8 (1885)

669 Tempo di Valse

Ha, seht es winkt, es blinkt, es klingt
ach, un - sern Blik - ken welch ein Ent - zük - ken,

Joseph Haydn, Symphony No. 85, mvt. 3, mm. 1–8 (1785?)

670 Allegretto

W. A. Mozart, *The Marriage of Figaro,* K. 492, Sinfonia, mm. 1–7 (1786)

671 Presto

Corresponding Chapter in *Manual for Ear Training and Sight Singing*: 52

"Casey Jones," North American folk song [in a variant as a union anthem], mm. 1–8

672

Vocal transposition: down 3rd

Robert Schumann, *Kinderscenen,* Op. 15, No. 8, "Am Camin," mm. 1–8 (1838)

673

Vocal transposition: The octave sign in the following excerpt indicates the range of the original. To keep this excerpt within a singable range, ignore the octave sign.

J. S. Bach, Invention No. 6, BWV 777, mm. 1–9 (c. 1720)

674

Corresponding Chapter in *Manual for Ear Training and Sight Singing*: 52

Sanft   Hugo Wolf, "Als ich auf dem Euphrat schiffte," mm. 1–2 (1889)

675

Als ich auf dem Eu - phrat__ schiff - te,

Franz Schubert, German Dance, D. 146, No. 4, Trio, mm. 1–8 (1815)

676

Vocal transposition: down 2nd–4th

Tempo di Valse   Will Marion Cook, "Molly Green," mm. 43–74 (1902)

677

Mol - ly,   Mol - ly,   Dear lit - tle dark eyed Mol - ly,

Al - ways so gay and so jol - ly   Who can help lov - ing you

Mol - ly,   Mol - ly   My heart is pledged to Mol - ly   If

molto rit.

Chol - ly loves Mol - ly   I don't think it fol - ly   to love   her   too.

Feierlich und gemessen   Hugo Wolf, "Wächterlied auf der Wartburg," mm. 1–8 (1887)

678

Schwingt Euch auf, Po - sau - nen - chö - re,   daß in ster - nen - kla - rer Nacht

Gott der Herr ein Lob - lied hö - re   von__ der Tür - me ho - her Wacht;

Corresponding Chapter in *Manual for Ear Training and Sight Singing:* **52**

Vocal transposition: down 3rd–4th

Mässig mit Empfindung
Etwas geschwinder und froher

Sophie Westenholz, *Zwölf deutsche Lieder,* Op. 4,
"Trost der Hoffnung," mm. 21–30 (1806)

W. A. Mozart, "Ave verum corpus," K. 618, mm. 3–6 (1791)

W. A. Mozart, Symphony No. 41, K. 551 ("Jupiter"), mvt. 3, mm. 1–8 (1788)

679

dann reichst du aus_ lich ter_ Fer - ne, hol - de Kö - ni - gin der Ster - ne, Hoff - nung! mu - thig, hehr und kühn, mir___ den Kranz von Im - - mer___ grün, mir den Kranz von Im - mer grün.

680

Adagio

sotto voce

A - ve, a - ve ve - rum Cor - pus
A - ve, a - ve ve - rum Cor - pus
A - ve, a - ve ve - rum Cor - pus
A - ve, a - ve ve - rum Cor - pus

681

Allegretto.

Corresponding Chapter in *Manual for Ear Training and Sight Singing:* **52**

Vocal transposition: down 2nd–6th

Andante

Jacques Offenbach, *La chanson de fortunio,* "Chanson de fortunio," mm. 3–10 (1861)

con anima.

682

Si vous cro - yez que je vais di - re   Qui j'ose ai - mer, Je ne sau -

dim.

rais pour un em - pi - re   Vous la nom - mer;

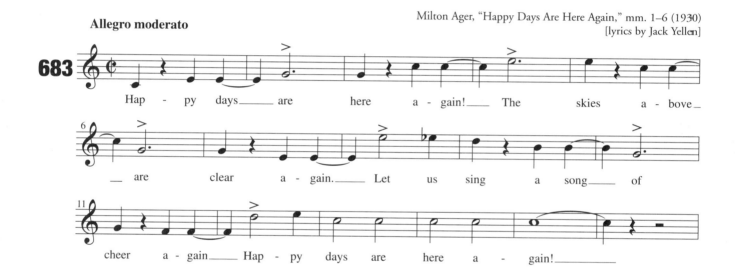

Allegro moderato

Milton Ager, "Happy Days Are Here Again," mm. 1–6 (1930)
[lyrics by Jack Yellen]

683

Hap - py days____ are   here a - gain!____ The   skies a - bove____

____ are   clear a - gain.____ Let   us   sing   a   song____ of

cheer a - gain____ Hap - py days are   here a - gain!_____

Larghetto (♩ = 116)

Frédéric Chopin, Nocturne Op. 9, No. 1, mm. 19–22 (1832)

sotto voce

684

pp

Corresponding Chapter in *Manual for Ear Training and Sight Singing:* **52**

Vocal transposition: Sing the following excerpt at concert pitch by transposing the bass-clef part up an octave.

Sergei Rachmaninoff, *Morceaux de fantasie,* Op. 3, No. 2, Prélude, mm. 14–17 (1892)

685
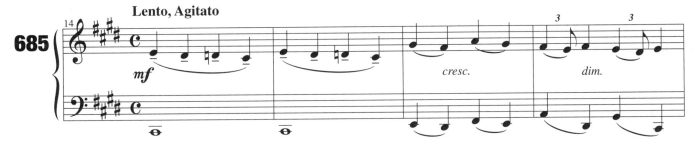

Franz Schubert, Ecossaise D. 299, No. 3 (1815)

686

W. A. Mozart, Horn Concerto K. 447, mvt. 3, mm. 1–8 (1787)

687

Corresponding Chapter in *Manual for Ear Training and Sight Singing:* 52

Vocal transposition: down 2nd–3rd. The octave signs indicate the range of the original. To keep this excerpt in a singable range, ignore the octave signs.

Joseph Haydn, String Quartet Op. 54, No. 2 (Hob. III:57), mvt. 4, mm. 80–88 (c. 1788)

688

W. A. Mozart, Serenade K. 525, "Eine kleine Nachtmusik," mvt. 3, Trio, mm. 1–8 (1787)

689

Vocal transposition: down 2nd–5th

W. A. Mozart, Piano Concerto No. 23, K. 488, mvt. 1, mm. 38–46 (1786)

690

Theodore C. van Etten, "Go U Northwestern," Northwestern University fight song, mm. 1–32 (1914)

691

Go U North - west - ern, Break right through that line.____

With our col - ors fly - ing, We will cheer you all the time, U Rah! Rah!

Go U North - west - ern, Fight for vic - tor - y____

Spread far the fame of our fair name,___ Go North-west-ern, win that game!____

Corresponding Chapter in *Manual for Ear Training and Sight Singing*: 52

W. A. Mozart, Contredanse K. 267 (271ᶜ), No. 2, Gavotte, mm. 1–8 (1777)

692

MINUETTO

W. A. Mozart, Divertimento K. 287, Minuet, mm. 1–8 (1777)

693

Trio

Ludwig van Beethoven, Duet for Viola and Cello WoO 32, mvt. 2, mm. 66–75 (1797)

694

Vocal transposition: down 2nd–3rd

W. A. Mozart, "Ave Maria," K. 554 (1788)

Andante

695

A - ve Ma - ri - a, a - - ve Ma - ri - a, a -

ve,___ a - ve Ma - ri - a, a - ve Ma - ri - a, Ma -

ri - a, a - ve, a - ve Ma - ri - a, a - ve, a - ve.

Corresponding Chapter in *Manual for Ear Training and Sight Singing*: 52

Vocal transposition: down 4th–5th

Felix Mendelssohn, *Songs Without Words* Op. 62, No. 6, mm. 1–15 (1842)

696

Henry Purcell, *The Fairy Queen,* z629, Act III, "Next, Winter Comes Slowly," mm. 16–21 (1629)

697

Next, Win - ter comes slow - ly, pale, mea - ger and old,_____

Vocal transposition: up 2nd–6th

Henry Purcell, *Dido and Aeneas,* z626, Act III, "When I Am Laid in Earth," mm. 1–5 (1689?)

Larghetto

698

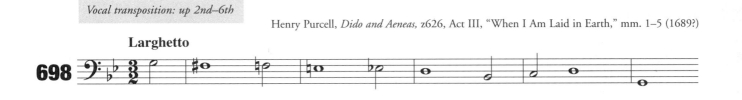

J. S. Bach, *Mass in B Minor,* BWV 232, Crucifixus, mm. 1–5

699

Vocal transposition: up 6th–7th

J. S. Bach, Sinfonia No. 9, BWV 795, mm. 1–3 (c. 1720)

700

Corresponding Chapter in *Manual for Ear Training and Sight Singing:* 52

W. A. Mozart, Symphony No. 34, K. 338, mvt. 1, mm. 176–180 (1780)

Allegro vivace

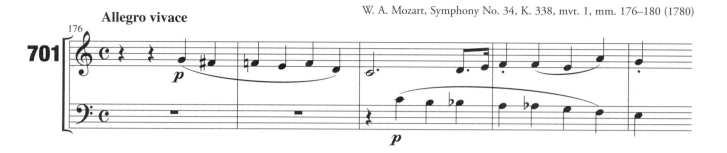

701

Francesco Paolo Tosti, "Addio!," mm. 9–24

Andantino

702

Lan - gue è - spol - to è - l'ar - bo - siel, Sol - can Na - vi il te - tro Mar,

D'om - bra noi cir - con da un vel. D'om - bra noi cir con - da un vel,

What can you do before you sing to hear the first note in the following excerpt?

Christoph Willibald von Gluck, *Iphigenie auf Tauris,* Act II, "Laßt die Natur uns rächen," mm. 1–8 (1781)

Animato

703

Laßt die Na - tur uns rä - chen, laßt die Na - tur uns

rä - chen und die Gott - heit, wel - che zürnt!

Vocal transposition: up 2nd–6th

Felix Mendelssohn, Piano Concerto No. 1, Op. 25, mvt. 1, mm. 1–4 (1831)

Molto Allegro con fuoco.

704

Corresponding Chapter in *Manual for Ear Training and Sight Singing:* 52

Vocal transposition: down 6th–7th

W. A. Mozart, Variations on "Lison dormait" from N. Dezède:
Julie, K. 264 (315d), Variation 5, mm. 1–8 (1778)

705

César Franck, Symphony in D minor, Op. 48, mvt. 1, mm. 129–145 (1888)

Allegro non troppo

706

Vocal transposition: down 3rd–7th

Peter Ilich Tchaikovsky, Symphony No. 1, Op. 13, mvt. 1, mm. 49–58 (1874)

Allegro Tranquillo (♩ = 132)

707

Corresponding Chapter in *Manual for Ear Training and Sight Singing: 52*

SKIPS TO CHROMATIC PITCHES
AS PREFIX NEIGHBORS

Franz Schubert, German Dance D. 146, No. 4, Trio, mm. 1–8 (1815)

708

Vocal transposition: down 2nd–6th

Franz Schubert, *Die schöne Müllerin*, D. 795 [Op. 25],
No. 7, "Der Neugierige," mm. 4–8 (1823)

709

Langsam

Ich fra - ge kei - ne Blu - me, ich fra - ge kei - nen Stern,

W. A. Mozart, Piano Concerto No. 27, K. 595, mvt. 3, mm. 9–16 (1791)

710

Allegro

Carl Maria von Weber, *Abu Hassan,* Overture, mm. 72–79 (1811)

711

Presto.

Corresponding Chapter in *Manual for Ear Training and Sight Singing:* 53

Vocal transposition: down 2nd–6th

W. A. Mozart, "Sehnsucht nach dem Frühlinge," K. 596 (1791)

712 **Fröhlich**

Komm, lie - ber Mai, und ma - che die Bäu - me wie - der grün, und
laß mir an dem Ba - che die klei - nen Veil - chen blüh'n! Wie möcht' ich doch so
ger - ne ein Veil - chen wie - der seh'n! Ach, lie - ber Mai, wie
ger - ne ein - mal spa - zie - ren geh'n!

Gustav Mahler, Symphony No. 5, mvt. 4, Adagietto, mm. 2–12 (1902)

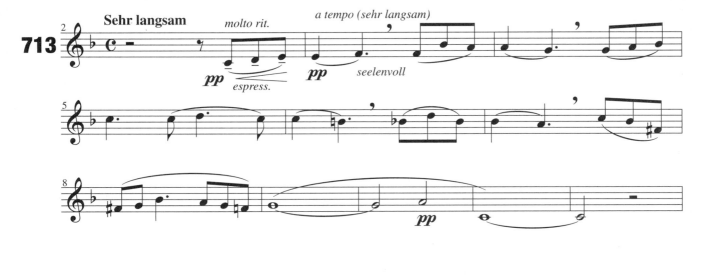

713 **Sehr langsam**

Edward Elgar, Serenade for String Orchestra, Op. 20, mvt. 1, mm. 46–50 (1892)

714 **Allegro piacevole.**

Corresponding Chapter in *Manual for Ear Training and Sight Singing*: 53

Vocal transposition: down 3rd–5th

Corona Schröter, *Die Fischerin*, "Für Männer uns zu plagen," mm. 9–32 (1782)

719

Für Män - ner uns zu pla - gen__ uns__ zu__ pla - gen Sind lei - der__

lei - der wir be - stimmt. Wir las - sen sie ge -

wä - ren, wir fol - gen ihr - em Wil - len: und wä - ren sie nur dank - bar, so

wär__ noch__ al - les__ gut, so wär__ noch__ al - les__ gut.

Ludwig van Beethoven, Duet for Viola and Cello WoO 32, mvt. 2, mm. 1–8 (1797)

720

Vocal transposition: down 2nd–6th

Giuseppi Verdi, *Un ballo in maschera*, Act II,
"Non sai tu che se l'anima mia," mm. 1–9 (1859)

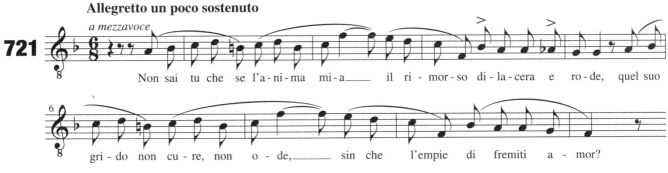

721

Non sai tu che se l'a - ni - ma mi - a_____ il ri - mor - so di - la - cera e ro - de, quel suo

gri - do non cu - re, non o - de,_____ sin che l'empie di fremiti a - mor?

Corresponding Chapter in *Manual for Ear Training and Sight Singing*: 53

Gesangvoll, mit innigster Empfindung

Andante molto cantabile ed espressivo

mezza voce

Ludwig van Beethoven, Piano Sonata No. 30,
Op. 109, mvt. 3, mm. 1–4 (1820)

722

W. A. Mozart, Minuet K. 461 (448ª), No. 5, Trio, mm. 1–8 (1784)

723

Vocal transposition: up 2nd–3rd

Joseph Haydn, Symphony No. 94, mvt. 2, mm. 1–8 (1791)

Andante

724

Vocal transposition: down 2nd–6th

Carl Stamitz, Duo in F major for Viola and Cello, mvt. 1, mm. 111–114

Allegro moderato

725

Corresponding Chapter in *Manual for Ear Training and Sight Singing*: 53

Vocal transposition: down 4th–5th

Hélène Riese Liebmann, *Grande sonate,* Op. 15, mvt. 2, Trio, mm. 1–32 (1815)

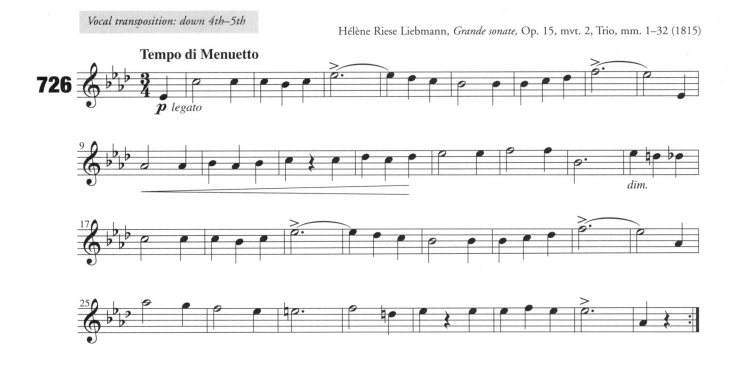

726

Vocal transposition: The range of the following excerpt is a bit wide for most sight-singing students. Transpose it down a 7th and use good support for the high D and low F♯.

Georg Philipp Telemann, *Continuation des sonates méthodiques,* No. 4, mvt. 3, mm. 1–14 (1732)

727

Arthur Sullivan, *The Sorcerer,* Act I, Incantation, mm. 15–22 (1877)

728

Corresponding Chapter in *Manual for Ear Training and Sight Singing*: 53

Vocal transposition: up 2nd–3rd

Andantino (♪ = 120)

Camille Saint-Saëns, "Le rouet d'omphale," Op. 31, mm. 91–106 (1871)

729

Vocal transposition: The range of the bass-clef part in the following excerpt is a bit wide for most sight-singing students. Sing it at concert pitch or transpose it up a 2nd, and use good support for the low G and high E♭.

Ludwig van Beethoven, Symphony No. 5, Op. 67, mvt. 3, mm. 1–8 (1808)

Allegro. ♩. = 96.

730

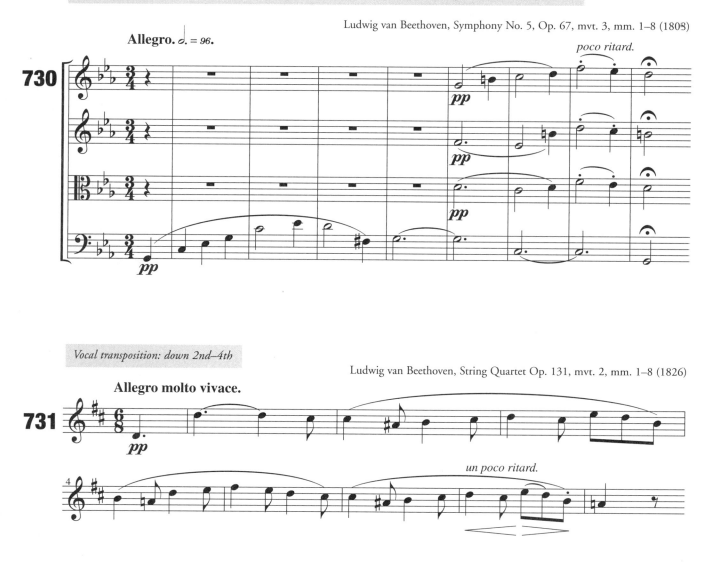

Vocal transposition: down 2nd–4th

Ludwig van Beethoven, String Quartet Op. 131, mvt. 2, mm. 1–8 (1826)

Allegro molto vivace.

731

Corresponding Chapter in *Manual for Ear Training and Sight Singing*: 53

Felix Mendelssohn, String Quartet Op. 44, No. 2, mvt. 3, mm. 3–6

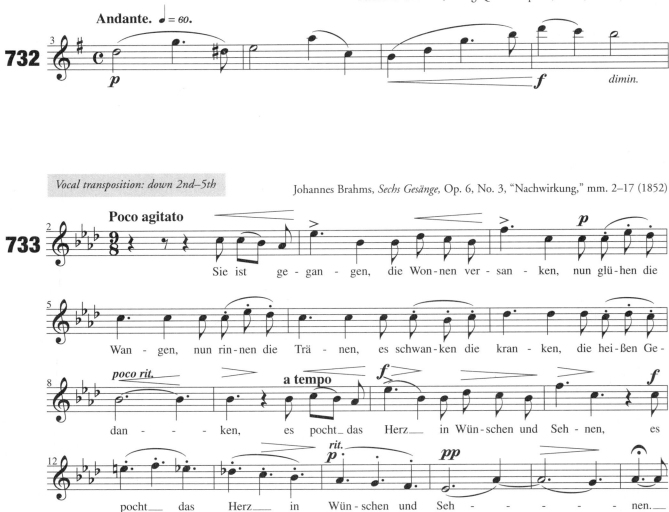

Vocal transposition: down 2nd–5th

Johannes Brahms, *Sechs Gesänge,* Op. 6, No. 3, "Nachwirkung," mm. 2–17 (1852)

Sie ist ge - gan - gen, die Won - nen ver - san - ken, nun glü - hen die

Wan - gen, nun rin - nen die Trä - nen, es schwan - ken die kran - ken, die hei - ßen Ge -

dan - - ken, es pocht das Herz in Wün - schen und Seh - nen, es

pocht das Herz in Wün - schen und Seh - - - - nen.

Joseph Haydn, Symphony No. 103, mvt. 1, mm. 2–13 (1795)

Corresponding Chapter in *Manual for Ear Training and Sight Singing:* 53

Vocal transposition: down 2nd–7th

J. S. Bach, Sinfonia No. 3, BWV 789, mm. 1–3 (c. 1720)

Vocal transposition: The range of the following excerpt is too wide for many sight-singing students. Sing it in one of the following manners: (1) transpose down a 3rd or 4th and use good support at the extremes (mm. 154 and 160); or (2) transpose down a 4th, 5th, or 6th and end with the first note in m. 160.

Arnold Bax, Sonata for Viola and Piano, mvt. 2, mm. 155–162 (1922)

Allegro energico ma non troppo presto. (♩ = 128)

Vocal transposition: down 4th–7th

Henri Vieuxtemps, *Ballade et Polonaise,* Op. 38, mm. 318–321 (c. 1860)

Largamente, ma in tempo.

Aaron Copland, *Passacaglia,* mm. 1–2 (1922)

Assez lent

Sergei Rachmaninoff, Prelude Op. 23, No. 7, mm. 12–17 (1903)

Allegro. (♩ = 80)

Corresponding Chapter in *Manual for Ear Training and Sight Singing:* **53**

Menuetto

Johannes Brahms, Serenade No. 1, Op. 11, Minuet I, mm. 1–8 (1858)

piano e dolce

Vocal transposition: down 4th–7th

W. A. Mozart, Violin Concerto K. 218, mvt. 2, mm. 1–4 (1775)

Andante cantabile

Allegro non troppo

W. A. Mozart, String Quartet K. 428 (421^b), mvt. 1, mm. 1–4 (1783)

W. A. Mozart, Contredanse K. 609, No. 4, mm. 1–8 (1791)

743

What have you learned in the preceding excerpts that will help you hear the first note in the following excerpt?

Joseph Haydn, Symphony No. 99, mvt. 1, mm. 157–162 (1793)

Vivace assai

Corresponding Chapter in *Manual for Ear Training and Sight Singing*: 53

Robert Schumann, Impromptus on a Theme by Clara Wieck, Op. 5, mm. 1–16 (1333)

Ziemlich langsam

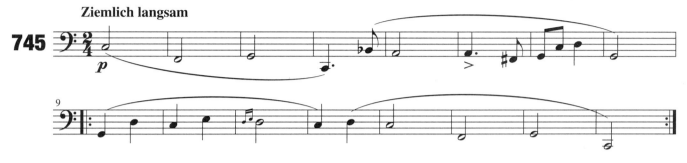

Joseph Haydn, Symphony No. 95, mvt. 1, mm. 10–13 (1791)

Allegro moderato

Corresponding Chapter in _Manual for Ear Training and Sight Singing_: 53

CHORDS APPLIED TO
THE DOMINANT

Christoph Willibald von Gluck, *Echo et Narcisse,* Act II, "O mortelles alarmes," mm. 1–6 (1779)

Lento

747

O mor - tel - les a - lar - mes, im - pi - toy - a - bles dieux!

O mor - tel - les a - lar - mes, im - pi - toy - a - bles dieux!

O mor - tel - les a - lar - mes, im - pi - toy - a - bles dieux!

O mor - tel - les a - lar - mes, im - pi - toy - a - bles dieux!

"Ereserkia," Basque folk dance, mm. 1–8

748

Vocal transposition: down 2nd–6th

Robert Schumann, *Lieder-Album für die Jugend*, Op 79,
No. 13, "Marienwürmchen," mm. 1–15 (1849)

Ma - ri - en - würm - chen, se - tze dich auf mei - ne Hand, auf mei - ne Hand, ich

thu' dir nichts zu Lei - de, nichts, nichts, zu Lei - de. Es soll dir nichts zu

Leid ge-scheh'n, will nur dei - ne bun - te Flü - gel seh'n, bun - te Flü - gel mei - ne Freu - de!

Joseph Haydn, Symphony No. 50, mvt. 1, mm. 18–25 (1773)

Muzio Clementi, Waltz Op. 39, No. 12, mm. 1–8 (1800)

Edvard Grieg, "Ausfahrt," Op. 9, No. 4, mm. 72–79 (1866)

Er - fül - lung nun ward ih-rem höch-sten Be - gehr,___ sie soll - te die Schön - heit er -

schaun,___ so zog sie da - hin___ ü - bers blau-en-de Meer, die glück - lich-ste al - ler Fraun.___

Vocal transposition: up 2nd–5th

W. A. Mozart, Minuet K. 568, No. 12, Trio, mm. 1–8 (1788)

Vocal transposition: down 3rd–7th

Jean-Baptiste Lully, *Armide,* Act II, "Laissons au tendre Amour" (1686)

Lais - sons au tendre A - mour la Jeu - nesse en par - ta - ge La Sa -

ges – se a son temps, Il ne vient que trop tôt Lais -

tôt Ce n'est pas ê - tre sa - ge D'ê - tre plus sa - ge qu'il ne

faut Ce n'est pas êt - re sa - ge D'ê - tre plus sa - ge qu'il ne faut

Corresponding Chapter in *Manual for Ear Training and Sight Singing:* 54

Vocal transposition: down 3rd–4th

Robert Schumann, *Lieder-Album für die Jugend,* Op. 79, No. 4, "Frühlingsgruss" (1849)

George Frideric Handel, *Judas Maccabaeus,* HWV 63, Part I, "Zion Now Her Head Shall Raise," mm. 17–28 (1746)

Edvard Grieg, Op. 48, No. 1, "Hilsen," mm. 5–11 (1888)

Christoph Willibald von Gluck, *Orfeo ed Euridice,* Act II, chorus, "Chi mai dell'Erebo," mm. 1–6 (1762)

Corresponding Chapter in *Manual for Ear Training and Sight Singing:* **54**

Carl Maria von Weber, *Abu Hassan*, Overture, mm. 1–4 (1811)

Corresponding Chapter in *Manual for Ear Training and Sight Singing*: 54

CHORDS APPLIED TO THE SUBDOMINANT

Ludwig van Beethoven, *Christus am Ölberge,* Op. 85,
"Auf, auf! ergreifet den Verräther," mm. 1–4 (1803)

Molto Allegro.

760

Auf, auf! er-greif-et den Ver-rä-ther, wei - let hier nun läu - ger nicht,

"Gestern Abend war Vetter Michel hier," German folk song

761

Corresponding Chapter in *Manual for Ear Training and Sight Singing:* 55

Vocal transposition: Basses with lower ranges should
sing the lowest part in the following excerpt.

Johannes Brahms, *Schicksalslied*, Op. 54, mm. 34–39 (1871)

762

Ludwig van Beethoven, "Ich liebe dich so wie du mich," WoO 123, mm. 21–40 (c. 1795)

763

Corresponding Chapter in *Manual for Ear Training and Sight Singing*: 55

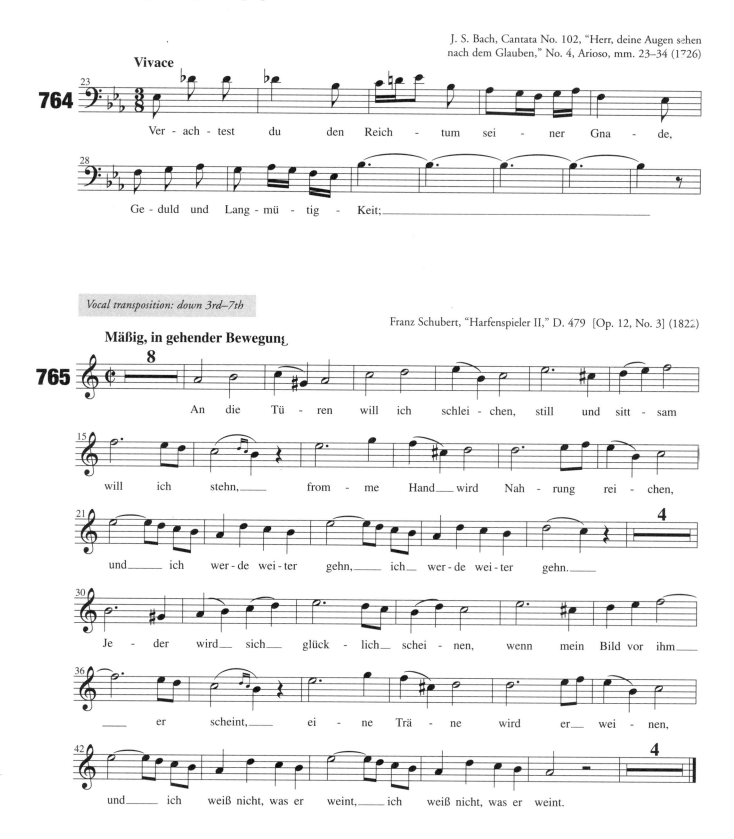

J. S. Bach, Cantata No. 102, "Herr, deine Augen sehen
nach dem Glauben," No. 4, Arioso, mm. 23–34 (1726)

764

Ver - ach - test du den Reich - tum sei - ner Gna - de,

Ge - duld und Lang - mü - tig - Keit;

Vocal transposition: down 3rd–7th

Franz Schubert, "Harfenspieler II," D. 479 [Op. 12, No. 3] (1822)

765

An die Tü - ren will ich schlei - chen, still und sitt - sam

will ich stehn, from - me Hand wird Nah - rung rei - chen,

und ich wer - de wei - ter gehn, ich wer - de wei - ter gehn.

Je - der wird sich glück - lich schei - nen, wenn mein Bild vor ihm

er scheint, ei - ne Trä - ne wird er wei - nen,

und ich weiß nicht, was er weint, ich weiß nicht, was er weint.

Corresponding Chapter in *Manual for Ear Training and Sight Singing*: 55

Vocal transposition: down 3rd–5th

W. A. Mozart, *La clemenza di Tito,* K. 621, Act I, "Del più sublime soglio," mm. 1–19 (1791)

767

Del più su-bli-me so - glio l'u-ni-co frut-to è

que-sto: tut-to è tor-men - to-il re-sto,   tut-to è tor-men-to il re-sto,   e

tut - to è ser-vi-tù,___   tor - men - to   e   ser-vi-

tù,   tut - - - to è tor-men - to___ e___ ser - vi - tù.

Vocal transposition: down 3rd–6th

Felix Mendelssohn, Overture "Ruy Blas," Op. 95, mm. 117–132 (1839)

768

Vocal transposition: down 3rd–7th

Pietro Mascagni, *Cavalleria rusticana,* "Viva il vino spumeggiante" (1890)

CHORDS APPLIED TO THE SUPERTONIC

George Frideric Handel, *Ariodante*, HWV 33, Act I, "Prendi da questa mano il pegno," mm. 17–40 (1734)

770

Corresponding Chapter in *Manual for Ear Training and Sight Singing:* **56**

Vocal transposition: down 2nd–5th

Poco Adagio

Joseph Haydn, "Dr. Harrington's Compliment" (Hob XXVIb:3), mm. 9–21 (1794)

771

What art ex - press - es and what sci - ence prais - es, Haydn the theme of both,

Haydn the theme of both to heav - en, to heav - en rais - es.

Vocal transposition: down 3rd–7th

Allegro

Franz Schubert, Symphony No. 5, D. 485, mvt. 1, mm. 231–238 (1816)

772

Robert Schumann, *Twelve Pieces for Piano Four Hands,*
Op. 85, No. 12, "Abendlied," mm. 1–6 (1849)

Ausdrucksvoll und sehr gehalten.

773

Vocal transposition: down 2nd–5th

Johannes Brahms, *Fünf Gesänge,* Op. 71, No. 5, "Minnelied," mm. 5–13 (1877)

Sehr innig, doch nicht zu langsam

774

Hol - der klingt der Vo - gel - sang, wenn die En - gel - rei - ne, die mein

Jüng - lings - herz be - zwang, wan - delt durch die___ Hai - ne.

Corresponding Chapter in *Manual for Ear Training and Sight Singing*: 56

Vocal transposition: down 2nd–5th

Andante.

Felix Mendelssohn, *Six Songs,* Op. 19a, No. 5, "Gruss," mm. 5–13 (1833)

Vocal transposition: down 2nd–3rd

Willie Nelson, "Crazy," mm. 1–16 (1961)

Carl Loewe, "Der heilige Franziskus," Op. 75, No. 3, mm. 2–6 (1837)

Adagissimo.

775

Lei - se zeit durch mein Ge - müth lieb - li - ches Ge - läu - te;

klin - ge, klei - nes Früh - lings - lied, kling' hin - aus in's Wei - te!

776

Cra - zy,___ cra - zy for feel - in' so lone - ly,___ I'm

cra - zy,___ cra - zy for feel - in' so blue.___

I knew___ you'd love me as long as you want - ed,___ And then

some - day___ you'd leave me for some - bod - y new.___

777

Fran - zis - kus einst, der Heil' - ge, sass vor sei - ner Zell' und Psal - men las.

Corresponding Chapter in *Manual for Ear Training and Sight Singing:* 56

Vocal transposition: down 3rd–6th

Robert Schumann, Impromptus on a Theme by Clara Wieck, Op. 5, mm. 17–32 (1833)

Ziemlich langsam

778

Vocal transposition: up 2nd

W. A. Mozart, Minuet K. 164 (130ª), No. 4, Trio, mm. 1–8 (1772)

779

Vocal transposition: down 3rd–6th

James Hewitt, "On the Rock Where Hangs the Willow," mm. 22–36

Andante

780

On__ the__ rock   where   hangs   the__ wil - low,   Mar - y_____

sunk   in_ sad_ de - spair.___   Cold_ and_ hard   was

Mar - y's_ pil - low,   Her___ cheek_ was   wan   with_ care.

Corresponding Chapter in *Manual for Ear Training and Sight Singing*: 56

Franz Schubert, Violin Sonata D. 574, mvt. 1, mm. 5–10 (1817)

Allegro moderato.

Vocal transposition: down 6th

W. A. Mozart, *The Abduction from the Seraglio,*
K. 384, Act II, "Martern aller Arten," mm. 61–74 (1782)

Allegro

Mar-tern al-ler Ar-ten, al-ler Ar-ten   mö-gen mei-ner war-ten. Ich ver-

la-che, ich ver-la-che, ich ver-la — — — — —

— — — — — — che Qual___ und Pein.

Vocal transposition: down 4th–6th

J. S. Bach, Cantata No. 87, "Bisher habt ihr nichts gebeten in
meinem Namen," No. 4, Aria, mm. 9–15 (1725)

Ich   will lei-den,   ich   will schwei-gen,

ich   will lei — — — den, ich   will schwei — —

— gen, Je-sus wird mir Hülf er-zei-gen,   ich   will lei-den,

Corresponding Chapter in *Manual for Ear Training and Sight Singing*: 56

CHORDS APPLIED TO
THE SUBMEDIANT

"God Save the King," national anthem of Great Britain, mm. 1–6

784

Vocal transposition: (1) down 2nd (sopranos reach high F);
or (2) down 3rd (basses and altos reach low G)

J. S. Bach, Chorale No. 108, "Valet will ich dir geben," mm. 1–4

785

Corresponding Chapter in *Manual for Ear Training and Sight Singing*: 57

Robert Schumann, "Schön Blümelein," Op. 43, No. 3, mm. 3–18 (1840)

786

Ich bin hin-aus ge-gan-gen des Mor-gens in der Früh, die

Ich bin hin-aus ge-gan-gen des Mor-gens in der Früh, die

Blüm - lein thä - ten pran-gen, ich sah so schön sie nie. Wagt'

Blüm - lein thä - ten pran-gen, ich sah so schön sie nie. Wagt'

ein's da-von zu pflü - cken, weil mir's so wohl ge - fiel. Doch

ein's da-von zu pflü - cken, weil mir's so wohl ge - fiel. Doch

als ich mich wollt' bü - cken, sah ich ein lieb-lich Spiel.

als ich mich wollt' bü - cken, sah ich ein lieb-lich Spiel.

Robert Schumann, *Waldscenen*, Op. 82, No. 1, "Eintritt," mm. 1–4 (1849)

787

Vocal transposition: The octave signs in the following excerpt indicate the range of the original. To keep this excerpt within a singable range, ignore the octave signs.

Ludwig van Beethoven, Symphony No. 5, Op. 67, mvt. 2, mm. 1–22 (1808)

788

Corresponding Chapter in *Manual for Ear Training and Sight Singing*: 57

CHORDS APPLIED TO THE MEDIANT

Vocal transposition: Sing the following excerpt in D minor by transposing the upper two parts down a perfect 5th while transposing the lower part up a perfect 4th.

Bianca Maria Meda, "Cari musici" (Motet), mm. 1–4 (1691)

Vocal transposition: down 2nd–3rd

William Billings, A Canon of 4 in 1: "When Jesus Wept"

When Je - sus wept,___ the fall - ing Tear,

In Mer - cy flow'd___ be - yond all Bound;

When Je - sus groan'd___ a trem - bling Fear,

Seiz'd all___ the guil - ty World___ a - round.

Corresponding Chapter in *Manual for Ear Training and Sight Singing*: 58

Vocal transposition: down 2nd–5th

Peter Illich Tchaikovsky, *Sixteen Children's Songs,* Op. 54, No. 5, "Legend," mm. 9–24 (1883)

791

When Je - sus was a lit - tle child He made a gar - den in the wild; There grew a rose - bush 'neath His care, Yield - ing a gar - land for His hair.

Felix Mendelssohn, Symphony No. 4, Op. 90, mvt. 2, mm. 11–27 (1833)

Andante con moto.

792

Corresponding Chapter in *Manual for Ear Training and Sight Singing*: 58

What can you do before you sing to hear the first note in the following excerpt?

Alexander Varlamov, "Snow Falls in the Street"

793

"Do Not Scold Me and Do Not Reproach Me," Russian folk song

794

Charles Gounod, *Faust,* Act IV, Romance [optional], "Si le bonheur," mm. 5–15 (1859)

795

Andante.

Si le bon - heur a sou - ri - re t'in - vi - te, Jo - yeux a - lors je sens un doux é -

moi; Si la dou - leur - t'ac - ca - ble, Mar - gue - ri - te, Ô Mar - gue -

ri - te, Ô Mar - gue - ri - te, Je pleure a - lors, je pleu - re com - me toi.

Corresponding Chapter in *Manual for Ear Training and Sight Singing*: 58

The chromaticism in the following excerpt can be somewhat disorienting. Because it seems to begin off tonic and heavily features several applied chords, you should establish a strong sense of key before beginning and retain that key sense throughout.

Robert Schumann, *Liederkreis,* Op. 39, No. 12, "Frühlingsnacht" (1840)

THE NEAPOLITAN SIXTH CHORD

Louise Farrenc, "Air russe varié," Op. 17, mm. 114–117 (c. 1836)

Andante espressivo

797

dol.

Hermann Bemberg, "Chant Hindou," mm. 7–14

Andante molto moderato

798

Brah - ma, Dieu des cro - yants, maî - tre des ci - tés sain - tes,

N'en - tends - tu pas mes longs san - glots?

Richard Wagner, *Siegfried*, Act I, scene 1, "Als zullendes Kind," mm. 1–16 (1857)

Schnell.

799

Als zul - len - des Kind zog ich dich auf, wärm - te mit Klei - den den klei - nen

Wurm: Spei - se und Trank trug ich dir zu, hü - te - te dich wie die eig' - ne Haut.

Richard Wagner, "Der Tannenbaum," WWV 50, mm. 27–47 (1838)

800 Moderato

Da rüh - ret er mit Trau - ern der dunk - len Zwei - ge Saum, und

spricht in lei - sen Schau - ern, der al - te Tan - nen - baum: daß schon die

Axt mich su - chet zu dei - nem To - ten - schrein, das macht mich

stets so trü - be, ge - denk' ich, Kna - be, dein.

Felix Mendelssohn, *Te Deum*, No. 5, "Te gloriosus Apostolorum," mm. 24–32 (1826)

801

Te per or - bem ter - ra - rum, te per or - bem ter - ra - - - - rum,

Ludwig van Beethoven, "Der Bardengeist," WoO 142, mm. 2–11 (1813)

802 **Mäßig langsam**

Dort auf dem ho - hen Fel - sen sang ein al - ter Bar - den - geist; es tönt wie Ä - ols -

har - fen - klang im ban - gen schwe - ren Trau - er - sang, der mir das Herz zer - reißt.

Joseph Haydn, Piano Sonata in C♯ minor (Hob. XVI:36), mvt. 2, mm. 4–6 (c. 1755?)

803 Moderato

p

Corresponding Chapter in *Manual for Ear Training and Sight Singing*: 59

Johannes Brahms, *Romanzen und Lieder,* Op. 84, No. 1, "Sommerabend," mm. 1–19 (1881)

Andante con moto

804

Geh schla-fen, Toch-ter, schla - fen! Schon fällt der Tau aufs Gras, und wen die

Trop-fen tra - fen, weint bald die Au-gen naß, weint bald die Au-gen naß!

Vocal transposition: down 5th–7th

W. A. Mozart, "Regina coeli," K. 108 (74^d), mvt. 3, mm. 1–8 (1771)

Adagio un poco Andante

805

Ernest Chausson, Piano Quartet, Op. 30, mvt. 3, mm. 1–5 (1897)

Simple et sans hâte

806

Corresponding Chapter in *Manual for Ear Training and Sight Singing*: 59

Vocal transposition: up 4th–7th

Ludwig van Beethoven, Piano Sonata No. 14, Op. 27,
No. 2 ("Moonlight"), mvt. 1, mm. 1–5 (1801)

807

Adagio sostenuto

Si deve suonare tutto questo pezzo delicatissimamente e senza sordino

sempre **pp** *e senza sordino*

Vocal transposition: down 2nd–6th

Franz Schubert, *Die schöne Müllerin*, D. 795 [Op. 25], No. 19,
"Der Müller und der Bach," mm. 3–27 (1823)

808

Mäßig.

(Der Müller)

Wo ein treu-es Her-ze in Lie - be ver-geht, da wel - ken die

Li - lien auf je - dem Beet. Da muß in die Wol - ken der

Voll - mond gehn, da - mit sei-ne Trä - nen die Men - schen nicht

sehn._____ Da hal - ten die Eng - lein die Au - gen sich

zu und schluch - zen und sin - gen die See - le zu Ruh.

Corresponding Chapter in *Manual for Ear Training and Sight Singing*: 59

809
J. S. Bach, *Mass in B Minor*, BWV 232, Kyrie II, mm. 1–3

Alla breve

Ky - ri - e   e - lei - - - son, e - le - i - son,

810
Felix Mendelssohn, Symphony No. 2 ("Lobgesang"), Op. 52, No. 6, mm. 5–15 (1841)

Allegro un poco agitato. M.M. ♩ = 138.

Stri - cke des To - des   hat - ten uns um - fang - en,   und Angst der

Hölle   hat - te uns ge - troff - en,   wir wan - del - ten in Fin - ster - niss,

811
Vocal transposition: down 2nd–5th

Edvard Grieg, Piano Concerto in A minor, Op. 16, mvt. 1, mm. 23–26 (1868)

Allegro molto moderato ♩ = 84

cantabile   *poco ritard.*

812
Gustav Mahler, *Des Knaben Wunderhorn*, "Das irdische Leben," mm. 7–14 (1893?)

Unheimlich bewegt (♩ = 104)

mit beängstigtem Ausdruck

"Mut - ter, ach Mut - ter, es hun - gert mich!   Gib mir Brot, sonst ster - be ich."

Corresponding Chapter in *Manual for Ear Training and Sight Singing*: 59

Vocal transposition: down 3rd–6th

Ludwig van Beethoven, Seven Variations on "God Save the King,"
WoO 78, Variation 5 (1803)

Charles Gounod, *Faust,* Act II, "Song of the Golden Calf," mm. 40–57 (1859)

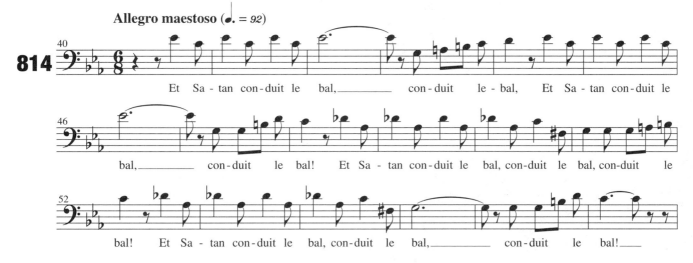

THE AUGMENTED SIXTH CHORDS

W. A. Mozart, *The Marriage of Figaro*, K. 492, Act III,
"Crudel! perchè finora," mm. 1–2 (1786)

815

Ludwig van Beethoven, Bagatelle Op. 119, No. 1, mm. 1–4 (1822)

816

Vocal transposition: down 3rd

W. A. Mozart, String Quartet K. 465, mvt. 4, mm. 13–16 (1785)

Allegro molto

817

What is unusual about Schubert's use of the augmented sixth chord in this passage?

Vocal transposition: up 4th–5th

Franz Schubert, Piano Sonata D. 845
[Op. 42], mvt. 1, mm. 3–4 (1825)

Moderato

818

Vocal transposition: up 2nd

Sergei Prokofiev, Violin Concerto No. 2, Op. 63, mvt. 1, mm. 1–6 (1935)

Franz Schubert, Violin Sonata D. 408 [Op. 137, No. 3], mvt. 1, mm. 5–12 (1816)

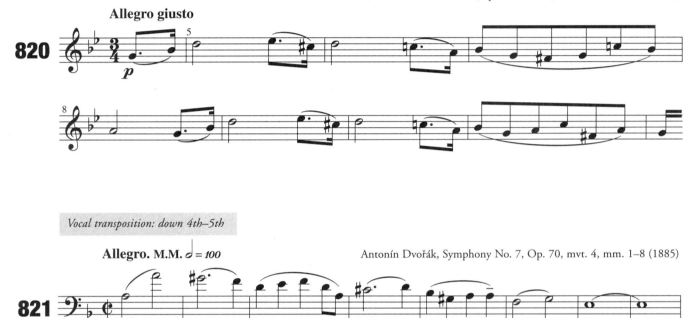

Vocal transposition: down 4th–5th

Antonín Dvořák, Symphony No. 7, Op. 70, mvt. 4, mm. 1–8 (1885)

What can you do before you sing to hear the first two notes in the following excerpt?

Giacomo Meyerbeer, *Le prophète,* Act II, No. 10, Arioso, mm. 2–15 (1849)

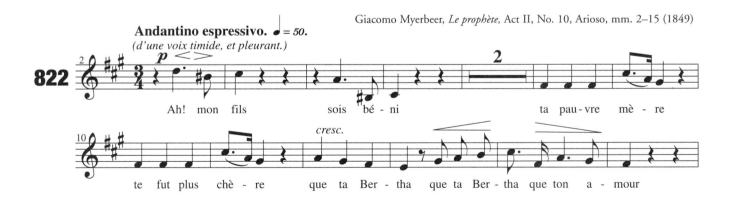

Corresponding Chapter in *Manual for Ear Training and Sight Singing:* **60**

OTHER CHORDS

Frédéric Chopin, Nocturne Op. 32, No. 2, mm. 1–2 (1837)

823

Lento

Vocal transposition: down 2nd–6th

Claude Debussy, *L'enfant prodigue,* mm. 48–51 (1884)

[Andante, très calme]

Animez un peu

824

A cha-que sai-son ra-me-né - e, Leurs jeux et leurs é - bats m'at-tris - tent mal-gré moi:

Antonín Dvořák, *Gypsy Songs,* Op. 55, No. 3, "All Round About the Woods Are Still," mm. 3–6 (1880)

Moderato

825

A les je ti - chy ko - lem kol,

Corresponding Chapter in *Manual for Ear Training and Sight Singing: 61*

Vocal transposition: up 4th (women sing the upper three parts; basses will have to sing the second note in m. 219 up an octave)

Johannes Brahms, Violin Sonata No. 3, Op. 108, mvt. 4, mm. 218–222 (1888)

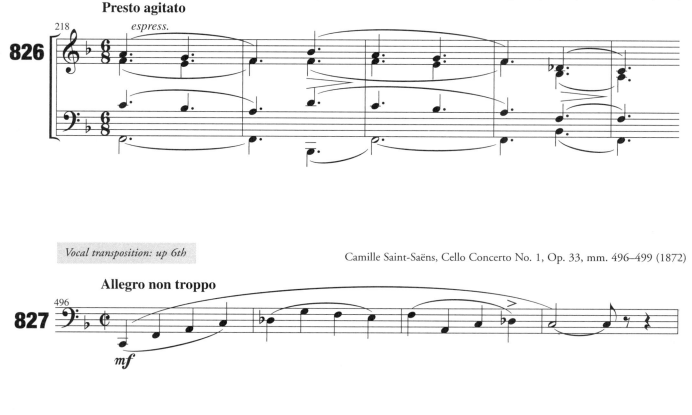

Vocal transposition: up 6th

Camille Saint-Saëns, Cello Concerto No. 1, Op. 33, mm. 496–499 (1872)

Vocal transposition: down 3rd (men sing the lower two parts; many basses will have to sing the second note in m. 17 up an octave)

Johannes Brahms, Piano Quartet No. 3, Op. 60, mvt. 3, mm. 17–18 (1875)

Corresponding Chapter in *Manual for Ear Training and Sight Singing*: 61

J. S. Bach, Chorale No. 59, "Herzliebster Jesu, was hast du verbrochen," mm. 4–6

Vocal transposition: Basses may sing the second note in m. 2 up an octave if necessary.

J. S. Bach, Chorale No. 23, "Zeuch ein zu deinen Toren," mm. 1–4

Maurice Ravel, *Mother Goose Suite,* "Pavane of the Sleeping Beauty," mm. 1–4 (1911)

J. S. Bach, Cantata No. 175, "Er rufet seinen Schafen mit Namen," No. 2, Aria, mm. 1–3 (1725)

Corresponding Chapter in *Manual for Ear Training and Sight Singing:* 61

Vocal transposition: up 4th

J. S. Bach, Chorale No. 324, "Jesu, meine Freude," mm. 1–2

833

Johann Kuhnau, *Keyboard Studies,* Book II, No. 4, Ciacona, mm. 89–97 (1692)

834

Vocal transposition: down 2nd–6th

Ludwig van Beethoven, *Twelve Irish Songs,* WoO 154, No. 5,
"Oh! Who, My Dear Dermot," mm. 6–14 (1813)

Andante con espressione.

835

Oh! who, my dear Der - mot, has dar'd to de - ceive thee, and

what's the dis - hon - our this gold is to buy?

Corresponding Chapter in *Manual for Ear Training and Sight Singing:* 61

Vocal transposition: down 3rd–4th

Modest Mussorgsky, *Pictures at an Exhibition,* "Bydlo," mm. 1–10 (1874)

836

Corresponding Chapter in *Manual for Ear Training and Sight Singing:* 61

MELODIC SEQUENCE

Domenico Scarlatti, Sonata K. 271, mm. 4–7

837 **Vivo**

Vocal transposition: down 4th–7th

Pierre Francisque Caroubel, *Terpsichore,* No. 96, Courante, mm. 13–24 (1612)

838

Ludwig van Beethoven, String Quartet Op. 130, mvt. 2, mm. 1–8 (1826)

839 **Presto.**

pp

Arcangelo Corelli, Concerto Grosso Op. 6, No. 12, Giga, mm. 78–83

840 **Allegro**

p

Vocal transposition: The range of the following excerpt is rather wide. Transpose down a 3rd or 4th and use good support for the highest notes at the opening and in m. 4, and for the lowest note in m. 8.

Jean-Philippe Rameau, *Pièces de clavecin,* "La joyeuse" (Rondeau), mm. 1–8 (1724)

841

Corresponding Chapter in *Manual for Ear Training and Sight Singing:* 62

C. P. E. Bach, Sonata H. 510, mvt. 3, mm. 55–57 (1759)

Allegro assai

842

Vocal transposition: up 2nd

J. S. Bach, Orchestra Suite No. 3, BWV 1068, mvt. 2, Air, mm. 1–2 (c. 1739)

843

J. S. Bach, Organ Concerto BWV 593 [arrangement of Antonio Vivaldi, Concerto, Op. 3, No. 8, rv522], mvt. 2, mm. 1–5 (c. 1714)

Adagio

844

Vocal transposition: up 2nd–6th

George Frideric Handel, Concerto Grosso Op. 6, No. 7, HWV 325, mvt. 1, mm. 1–4 (1739)

Largo.

845

Corresponding Chapter in *Manual for Ear Training and Sight Singing*: 62

Vocal transposition: down 2nd–5th

Bianca Maria Meda, "Cari musici" (Motet), mm. 162–174 (1591)

Tempo di Minuetto

William Boyce, Symphony No. 3 (Op. 2, No. 3), mvt. 3, mm. 1–8

Vocal transposition: down 4th–7th

W. A. Mozart, Variations on "Lison dormait" from N. Dezède:
Julie, K. 264 (315ᵈ) Variation 9, mm. 1–8 (1778)

Vocal transposition: down 2nd–7th

J. S. Bach, Cantata No. 212, "Mer hahn en neue Oberkeet"
("Peasant Cantata"), No. 1, mm. 16–23 (1742)

Corresponding Chapter in *Manual for Ear Training and Sight Singing*: 62

"Ding! Dong! Merrily on High," English Christmas carol [after a 16th-century French branle]

Vocal transposition: down 3rd–5th

Domenico Scarlatti, Sonata K. 73, mm. 50–61

Minuetto

C. P. E. Bach, Keyboard Sonata No. 147, H. 189, mvt. 3, mm. 1–5 (1765)

Presto

Corresponding Chapter in *Manual for Ear Training and Sight Singing*: 62

Vocal transposition: down 2nd–3rd   Johann Caspar Ferdinand Fischer, *Musikalischer Parnassus,* "Melpomene," Bourée, mm 1–4

853

J. S. Bach, Invention No. 5, BWV 776, mm. 1–4 (c. 1720)

854

Vocal transposition: down 3rd–6th   J. S. Bach, Chorale Prelude "Nun freut euch, lieben Christen gmein," BWV 734, mm. 1–2

855

George Frideric Handel, *Samson,* HWV 57, Act I, "Why Does the God of Israel Sleep?" mm. 4–5 (1742)

Allegro

856

p

Vocal transposition: down 3rd–5th   George Frideric Handel, *Israel in Egypt,* HWV 54, Part III, "Thou Did'st Blow," mm. 1–2 (1738)

Andante larghetto

857

f

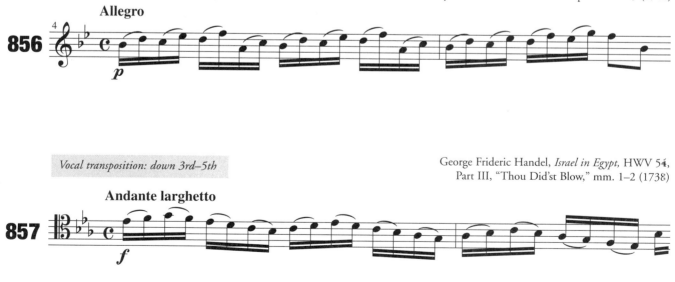

Corresponding Chapter in *Manual for Ear Training and Sight Singing*: 62

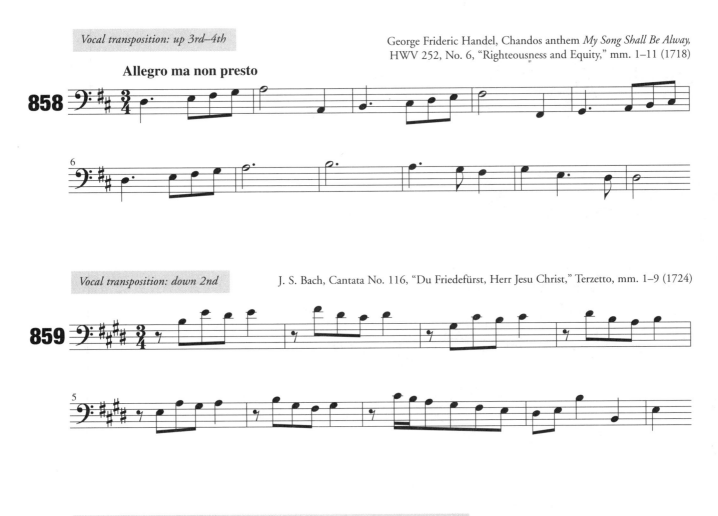

Vocal transposition: up 3rd–4th

George Frideric Handel, Chandos anthem *My Song Shall Be Alway*, HWV 252, No. 6, "Righteousness and Equity," mm. 1–11 (1718)

Allegro ma non presto

858

Vocal transposition: down 2nd

J. S. Bach, Cantata No. 116, "Du Friedefürst, Herr Jesu Christ," Terzetto, mm. 1–9 (1724)

859

Vocal transposition: The range of the following excerpt is a bit wide. Transpose it up a step if necessary to fit your vocal range. Watch out for the octave leap in m. 24.

Joseph Haydn, Symphony No. 44, mvt. 1, mm. 21–25 (c. 1771)

Allegro con brio

860

ff

Joseph Haydn, Symphony No. 28, mvt. 4, mm. 1–4 (1765)

Presto assai

861

p

Corresponding Chapter in *Manual for Ear Training and Sight Singing*: 62

862 Andante grazioso
W. A. Mozart, Piano Sonata K. 331 (300^i), mvt. 1, mm. 1–8 (1783)

Vocal transposition: up 2nd–7th

863 Andante molto cantabile e con dolore.   *poco espr.*
Modest Mussorgsky, *Pictures at an Exhibition,* "The Old Castle," mm. 1–7 (1874)

864 Immer sehr gemächlich
Gustav Mahler, Symphony No. 1, mvt. 1, mm. 62–74 (1838)

Nicht eilen

Corresponding Chapter in *Manual for Ear Training and Sight Singing*: 62

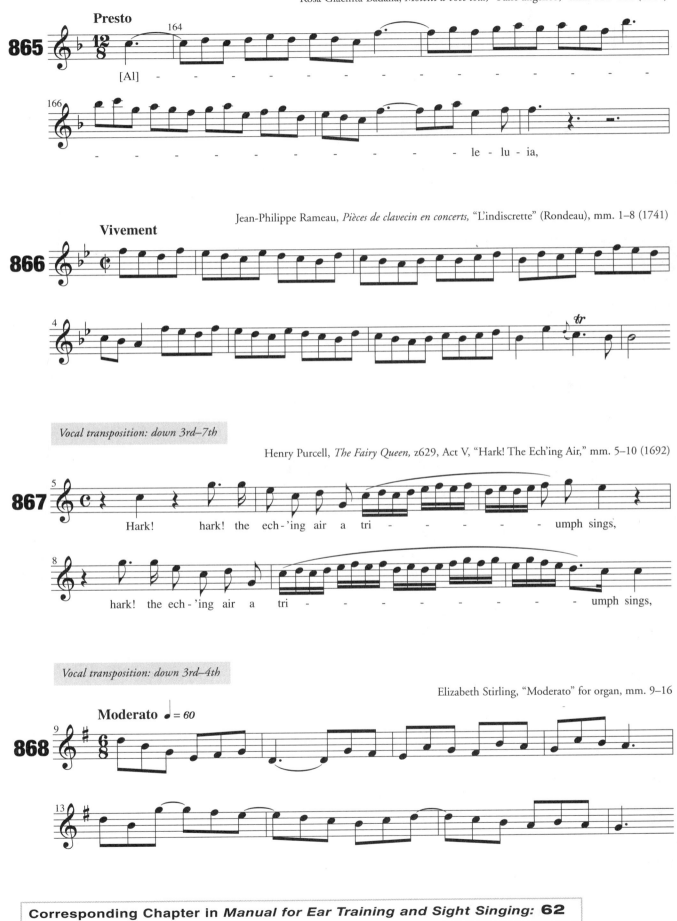

Rosa Giacinta Badalla, *Motetti a voce sola*, "Pane angelico," mm. 164–168 (1684)

865

Presto

[Al] - - - - - - - - - - -

- - - - - - - - - le - lu - ia,

Jean-Philippe Rameau, *Pièces de clavecin en concerts*, "L'indiscrette" (Rondeau), mm. 1–8 (1741)

866

Vivement

Vocal transposition: down 3rd–7th

Henry Purcell, *The Fairy Queen*, z629, Act V, "Hark! The Ech'ing Air," mm. 5–10 (1692)

867

Hark! hark! the ech-'ing air a tri - - - - umph sings,

hark! the ech-'ing air a tri - - - - - - umph sings,

Vocal transposition: down 3rd–4th

Elizabeth Stirling, "Moderato" for organ, mm. 9–16

868

Moderato ♩ = 60

Corresponding Chapter in *Manual for Ear Training and Sight Singing*: 62

Allegro

Antonio Vivaldi, *L'estro armonico,* Op. 3, Concerto No. 6, RV 356, mvt. 1, mm. 1–7 (1711)

869

Vocal transposition: down 2nd–5th

Allegro moderato

George Frideric Handel, Chandos anthem *O Come Let Us Sing,* HWV 253, No. 5, "Tell It out among the Heathen," mm. 1–21 (1718)

870

Tell it, tell it out a - mong the hea - then____

that the Lord is King, tell it, tell it,

tell it, tell it out a - mong the hea - then, tell it out a - mong the

hea - - - - - - then that the Lord is King.

George Frideric Handel, Chandos anthem *Let God Arise,* HWV 256ª,
No. 5, "O Sing unto God," mm. 11–22 (1718)

871

O sing ———— un - to God, sing ——— un - to God and sing prai ———————————— ses, and sing prai ———————————————————————— ses un - to his name,

Vocal transposition: down 5th

Georg Philipp Telemann, Sonata for Two Flutes or Two Violins,
Op. 2, No. 5, mvt. 4, mm. 1–18 (1727)

872

Vocal transposition: up 2nd–3rd

Johann Ernst Eberlin, *Magnificat,* mm. 1–8

873

Vocal transposition: down 5th

Joseph Haydn, String Quartet Op. 20, No. 6 (Hob. III:36), mvt. 4, mm. 1–5 (1772)

Allegro

sempre sotto voce

874

Vocal transposition: down 4th–7th

J. S. Bach, Sonata for Viola da Gamba BWV 1028, mvt. 4, mm. 65–69

Allegro

875

Vocal transposition: down 5th–7th

J. S. Bach, Flute Sonata BWV 1031, mvt. 3, mm. 108–112 (1734)

Allegro

876

Corresponding Chapter in *Manual for Ear Training and Sight Singing:* 62

George Frideric Handel, Chandos anthem *In the Lord Put I My Trust,*
HWV 247, No. 2, "In the Lord Put I My Trust," mm. 27–37 (1718)

Vocal transposition: If the range of the following excerpt is too wide, sing the final two notes up an octave.

Ludwig van Beethoven, Symphony No. 9, Op. 125, mvt. 3, mm. 25–32 (1824)

Corresponding Chapter in *Manual for Ear Training and Sight Singing*: 62

Vocal transposition: down 2nd–5th

Johannes Brahms, *Romanzen und Lieder,* Op. 84, No. 4,
"Vergebliches Ständchen," mm. 2–20 (1882)

Lebhaft und gut gelaunt

880

(Er) Gu - ten A - bend, mein Schatz, gu - ten A - bend, mein

Kind,   gu - ten A - bend, mein Kind!

Ich komm aus Lieb zu dir, ach, mach mir auf die Tür, mach mir auf die

Tür,   mach mir auf,   mach mir auf,   mach mir auf die Tür!

Vocal transposition: down 3rd–5th

Johann Strauss, Jr., *Künstler-Leben (Artist's Life),* Op. 316, mm. 2–10 (1867)

Andante moderato

881

p espr.

pp

Corresponding Chapter in *Manual for Ear Training and Sight Singing:* 62

OTHER CLEFS

J. S. Bach, *Art of Fugue,* "Canon alla Ottava," BWV 1080/15, mm. 1–5 (1749)

882

Andrea Gabrieli, "A caso un giorno mi guidò la sorte," mm. 1–8 (1575)

883

A ca-so_un gior-no mi gui-dò la sor - te, mi gui-dò la sor - te,

A ca-so_un gior-no mi gui-dò la sor - te, mi gui-dò la sor-te,

A ca-so_un gior - no mi gui-dò la sor - te,

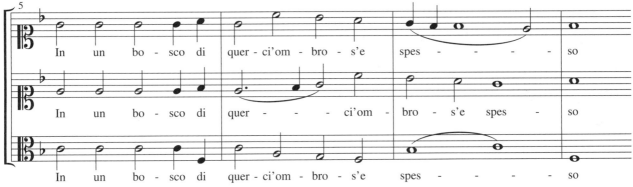

In un bo-sco di quer-ci'om-bro-s'e spes - - - so

In un bo-sco di quer - - -ci'om - bro-s'e spes - so

In un bo-sco di quer-ci'om-bro-s'e spes - - - so

Vocal transposition: down 2nd

Felix Mendelssohn, Symphony No. 2 ("Lobgesang"),
Op. 52, No. 2, mm. 17–21 (1840)

Allegro moderato maestoso. M.M. = *100*.

884

In the following two excerpts, what is fitting about the clefs Handel used for the voice parts?

George Frideric Handel, *Hercules,* HWV 60, Act I, "Oh Filial Piety," mm. 1–6 (1744)

Largo

885

Corresponding Chapter in *Manual for Ear Training and Sight Singing: 64*

Vocal transposition: Men with lower ranges should sing the low G in m. 9; others should take that note up an octave.

George Frideric Handel, *Hercules,* HWV 60, Act III, "Tyrants Now No More Shall Dread," mm. 5–9 (1744)

886

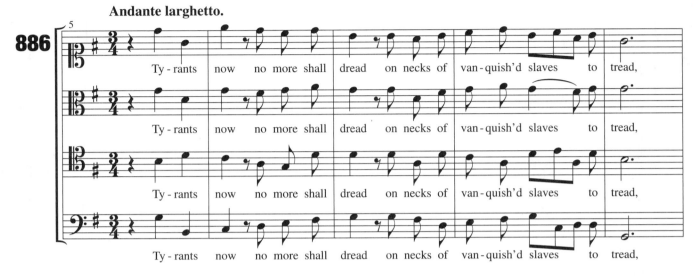

Andante larghetto.

Ty - rants now no more shall dread on necks of van-quish'd slaves to tread,

Ty - rants now no more shall dread on necks of van-quish'd slaves to tread,

Ty - rants now no more shall dread on necks of van-quish'd slaves to tread,

Ty - rants now no more shall dread on necks of van-quish'd slaves to tread,

Corresponding Chapter in *Manual for Ear Training and Sight Singing:* 64

Johann Rudolf Ahles, "Bedenke, liebe Seele, doch" (1664)

887

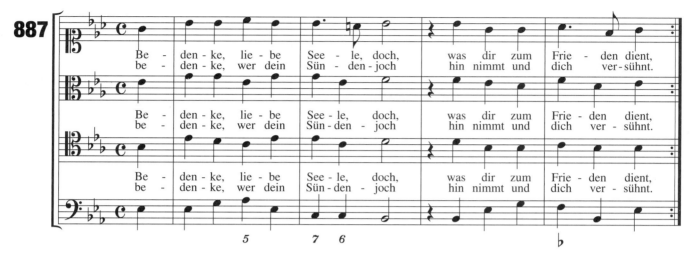

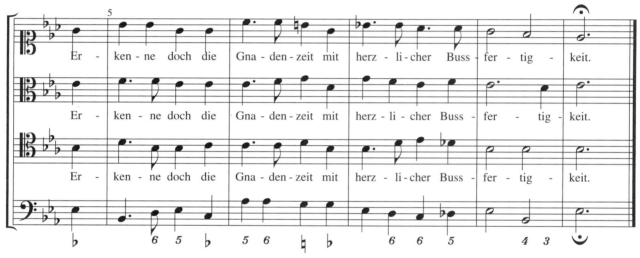

Heinrich Isaac, "Quis dabit capiti meo aquam?," secunda pars, mm. 30–37

888

nym - pha - - - - - - rum cho - -

Lau - - rus

et re - qui -

ris, cho - - ris.

ia - cet im - pe - tu ful - mi - nis.

e - sca - mus in pa - - ce.

John Dunstable, "Salve regina misericordie," No. 1, mm. 110–118

889

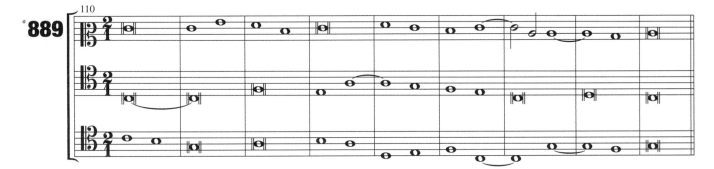

Corresponding Chapter in *Manual for Ear Training and Sight Singing:* 64

Antonio Lotti, *Missa II,* Gloria, mm. 1–5

890

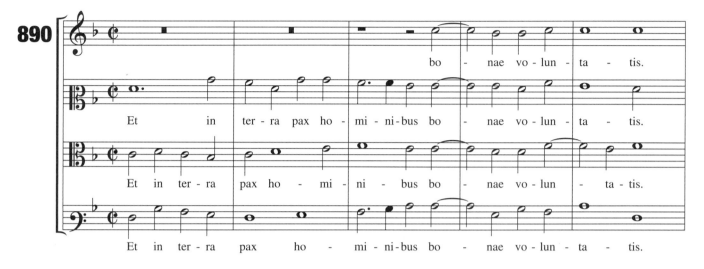

Heinrich Isaac, "Ne piu bella de queste," mm. 20–23

891

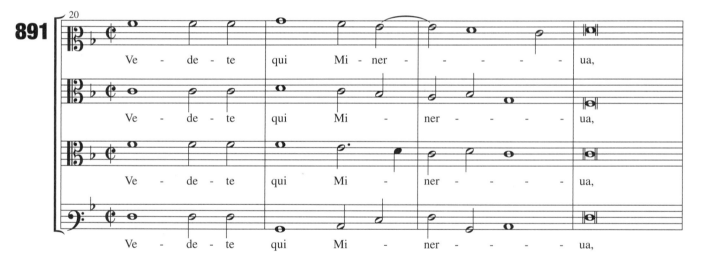

Corresponding Chapter in *Manual for Ear Training and Sight Singing: 64*

Vocal transposition: up 3rd

Heinrich Isaac, "Al mein mut," mm. 1–12

892

Corresponding Chapter in *Manual for Ear Training and Sight Singing*: 64

The following excerpt is the original notation for a four-voice canon by J. S. Bach. Each voice is derived by reading the music in each of the clefs printed successively at the beginning of the staff. Voice 1 begins first, and reads in the bass clef. Voice 2 reads in the tenor clef and begins when voice 1 reaches the first *segno* mark. Voice 3 reads in the mezzo-soprano clef and begins when voice 1 reaches the second *segno* mark. Voice 4 reads in the treble clef and begins when voice 1 reaches the third *segno* mark. Bach labeled this canon *perpetuus*. What did he mean by this?

Vocal transposition: Only the part in mezzo-soprano clef lies completely within the practical sight-singing range; altos should sing this part. Basses with somewhat lower ranges (down to G2) should sing the bass-clef part. Tenors with higher ranges (up to G4) should sing the tenor-clef part. Sopranos with the highest ranges (up to A5) should sing the treble-clef part.

J. S. Bach, Canon for Four Voices, BWV 1073 (1713)

Corresponding Chapter in *Manual for Ear Training and Sight Singing*: 64

HEMIOLA

"Pajaritos que vevis cantando," Spanish folk song, mm. 1–16

894

Vocal transposition: down 5th–7th

Peter Ilich Tchaikovsky, *Sleeping Beauty*, Op. 66, No. 6, Waltz, mm. 41–71 (1889)

Allegro (Tempo di valse)

895

p cantabile

più f

f

p

cresc.

f

Corresponding Chapter in *Manual for Ear Training and Sight Singing*: 65

Vocal transposition: When singing the top part alone from the following excerpt, transpose it down a 2nd or 3rd. When singing all parts together, transpose down a 2nd and women with the highest ranges should sing the top part while men on the lowest part should take the last two notes up an octave.

George Frideric Handel, *Giulio Cesare,* HWV 17, Act III, scene 4, "Aure, deh, per pietà spirate," mm. 143–148 (1724)

896

Vocal transposition: For most men, the low E that appears three times in the lowest
bass part of the following excerpt will be much too low to sing. If necessary, take this
E up an octave.

John Blow, anthem, "O Give Thanks unto the Lord, and Call upon His Name," mm. 177–186

897

Corresponding Chapter in *Manual for Ear Training and Sight Singing*: 65

"Mañanas, mañanitas," Spanish folk song

898

"Macario romero," Mexican folk song, mm. 1–8

899

"Las chaparreras," Mexican folk song, mm. 1–8

900

"Ashishito y su comparsa," Spanish folk song, mm. 1–8

901

Corresponding Chapter in *Manual for Ear Training and Sight Singing*: 65

"El sapo," Honduran folk song, mm. 1–8

El sa-po_es un a-ni mal   Que no tie-ne buen ta-lan_te, Chi-mi-chi-mi-

ni-que, chi-mi-chi-mi - ni - que,   ¡Que no tie-ne buen ta - lan - te!

"Launako," Basque folk dance, mm. 1–16

Vocal transposition: The outer voices in the following excerpt should be sung by women with the highest and men with the lowest ranges.

Jean-Baptiste Lully, *Le bourgeois gentilhomme,* Act IV,
"Ti non star furba?," mm. 11–21 (1670)

"Banako," Basque folk dance

What has happened to the meter in the following excerpt?

Emmanuel Chabrier, *España*, mm. 29–45 (1883)

Allegro con fuoco

Which parts in the following excerpt exhibit characteristics of hemiola? Which do not? Why do you think some musicians use the term "metric dissonance" to refer to this type of situation?

Vocal transposition: To sing all parts together, sing the top two parts down an octave, sing the last note in the alto-clef part up an octave, and basses sing mm. 1 and 4 down an octave.

W. A. Mozart, Symphony No. 40, K. 550, mvt. 3, mm. 1–6 (1788)

907

From what you have learned about hemiola, can you find a spot in this excerpt that can be performed as one?

Vocal transposition: up 5th. You might also try singing the voice part while realizing the unfigured bass on the piano (do this at concert pitch and take the low E in m. 61 up an octave). What criteria do you use in selecting chords?

George Frideric Handel, *Messiah*, HWV 56, "Thou Shalt Break Them," mm. 59–65 (1741)

908

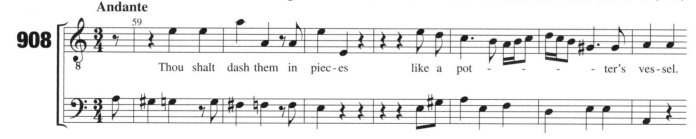

Thou shalt dash them in piec-es   like a pot- - - - - ter's ves-sel.

Corresponding Chapter in *Manual for Ear Training and Sight Singing*: 65

Are there any places in this excerpt that you might perform as hemiola? Are there any places that *could* be performed as hemiola but you would not? If so, why not?

Vocal transposition: down 3rd–5th

George Frideric Handel, *Messiah,* HWV 56, "I Know That My Redeemer Liveth," mm. 54–66 (1741)

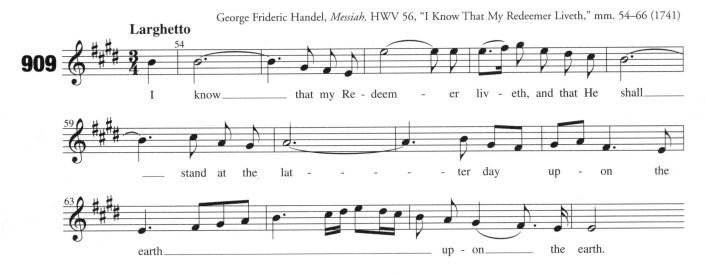

909

STEPWISE CHROMATIC ALTERATIONS

Calixa Lavallée, "O Canada!" national anthem of Canada (1880)

910

O Can - a - da! Our home and na - tive land! True pa - triot
O Can - a - da! Ter - re de nos aï - eux, Ton front est

love in all thy sons com - mand. With glow - ing hearts we
ceint de fleur - ons glo - ri - eux! Car ton bras sait por - ter l'é -

see thee rise, The True North strong and free! From far and wide, O
pé - e, Il sait por - ter la Croix! Ton his - toire est une é - po -

Can - a - da! We stand on guard for thee. God keep our
pé - e Des plus bril - lants ex - ploits. Et ta va -

land glo - rious and free! O Can - a - da! We stand on
leur, de foi trem - pée, Pro - té - ge - ra nos foy - ers

guard for thee, O Can - a - da! We stand on guard for thee.
et nos droits, Pro - té - ge - ra nos foy - ers et nos droits.

J. S. Bach, *Well-Tempered Clavier,* Book II, Fugue in E major (No. 9), BWV 878, mm. 1–5 (c. 1740)

911

Corresponding Chapter in *Manual for Ear Training and Sight Singing*: 66

Vocal transposition: up 2nd–3rd

Edward Elgar, *Pomp and Circumstance Military March,* Op. 39, No. 1, Trio, mm. 1–40 (1901)

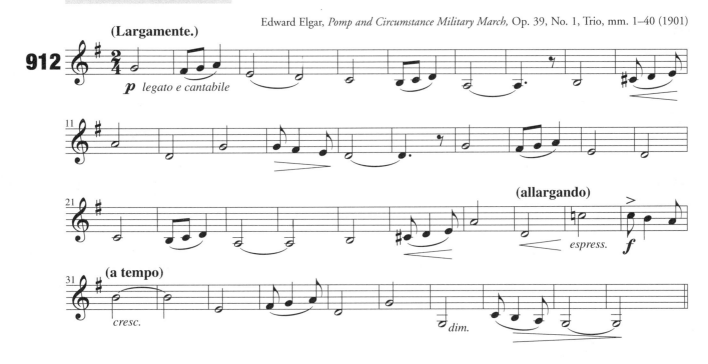

Vocal transposition: down 4th–6th

Louis Moreau Gottschalk, *Union, Paraphrase de Concert,* Op. 48, mm. 43–50 (1862)

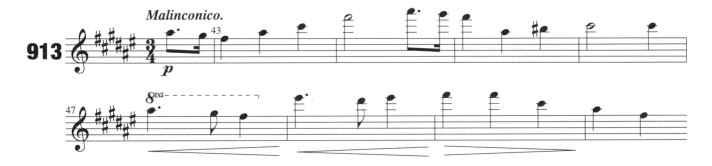

Michael Haydn, *Menuetti,* No. 2, mm. 1–8 (1772)

Corresponding Chapter in *Manual for Ear Training and Sight Singing:* 66

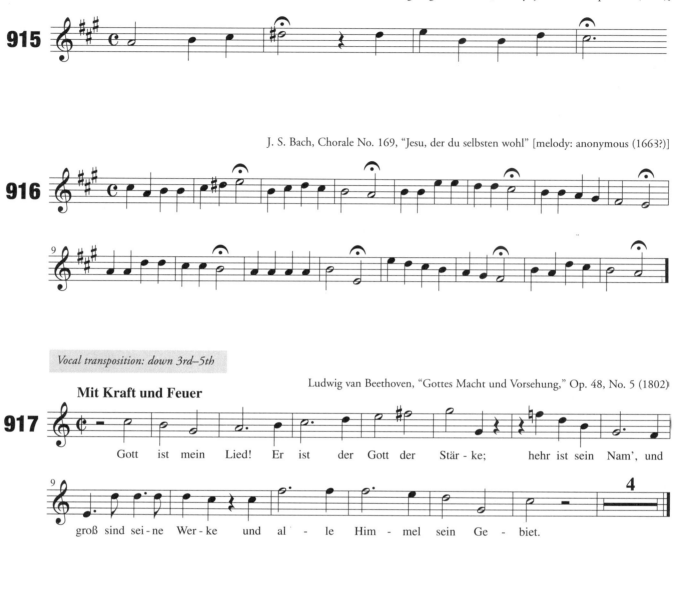

915 J. S. Bach, Chorale No. 216, "Es ist genug," mm. 1–4 [melody: Johann Rodolph Ahle (1662)]

916 J. S. Bach, Chorale No. 169, "Jesu, der du selbsten wohl" [melody: anonymous (1663?)]

Vocal transposition: down 3rd–5th

Mit Kraft und Feuer

917 Ludwig van Beethoven, "Gottes Macht und Vorsehung," Op. 48, No. 5 (1802)

Gott ist mein Lied! Er ist der Gott der Stär-ke; hehr ist sein Nam', und

groß sind sei-ne Wer-ke und al - le Him - mel sein Ge - biet.

Adagio (♩ = 76)
dolce

918 Gabriel Fauré, Nocturne No. 6, Op. 63, mm. 1–3 (1894)

p

Corresponding Chapter in *Manual for Ear Training and Sight Singing*: 66

Vocal transposition: 4th–5th

George Frideric Handel, *Serse*, HWV 40, Act I, "Nè men con l'ombre" (1738)

Vocal transposition: When singing the top part of the following excerpt alone, transpose down a 2nd. When singing all parts together, perform at concert pitch using sopranos with higher ranges for the top part.

Franz Schubert, Symphony No. 4, D. 417, mvt. 2, mm. 1–20 (1816)

Corresponding Chapter in *Manual for Ear Training and Sight Singing*: 66

Vocal transposition: The range of the following excerpt is a bit wide. Try transposing up a 2nd or 3rd and use good support for the high and low notes in mm. 30 and 32, respectively.

J. S. Bach, Invention No. 8, BWV 779, mm. 30–34 (c. 1720)

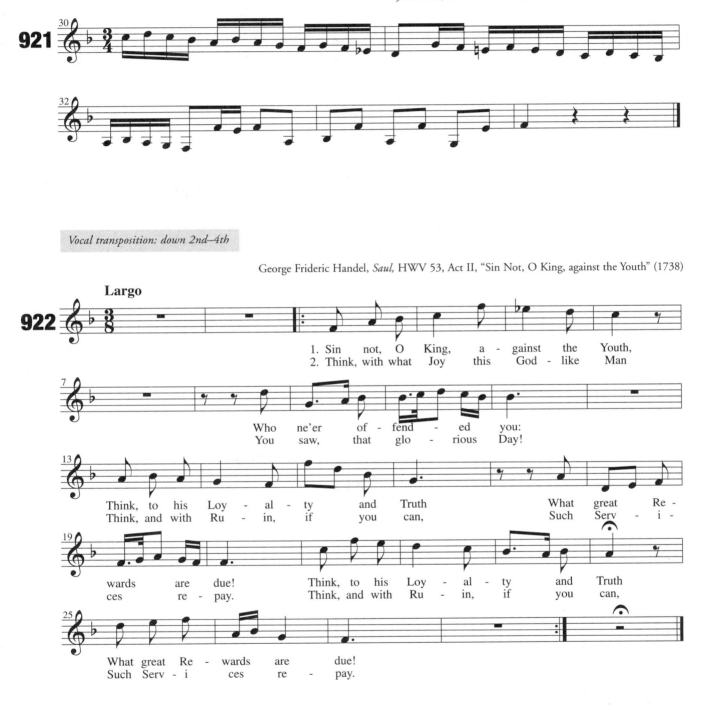

Vocal transposition: down 2nd–4th

George Frideric Handel, *Saul,* HWV 53, Act II, "Sin Not, O King, against the Youth" (1738)

Allegro moderato

Franz Schubert, Symphony No. 8 ("Unfinished"), D. 759, mvt. 1, mm. 258–267 (1822)

923

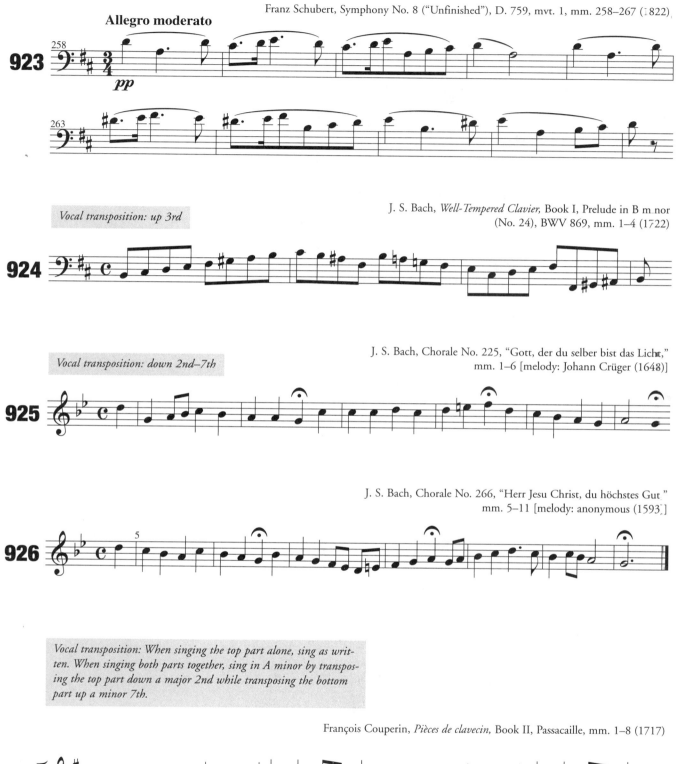

Vocal transposition: up 3rd

J. S. Bach, *Well-Tempered Clavier,* Book I, Prelude in B minor (No. 24), BWV 869, mm. 1–4 (1722)

924

Vocal transposition: down 2nd–7th

J. S. Bach, Chorale No. 225, "Gott, der du selber bist das Licht," mm. 1–6 [melody: Johann Crüger (1648)]

925

J. S. Bach, Chorale No. 266, "Herr Jesu Christ, du höchstes Gut," mm. 5–11 [melody: anonymous (1593)]

926

Vocal transposition: When singing the top part alone, sing as written. When singing both parts together, sing in A minor by transposing the top part down a major 2nd while transposing the bottom part up a minor 7th.

François Couperin, *Pièces de clavecin,* Book II, Passacaille, mm. 1–8 (1717)

927

Corresponding Chapter in *Manual for Ear Training and Sight Singing*: 66

Carl Maria von Weber, Piano Sonata No. 2, Op. 39, mvt. 2, mm. 1–8 (1816)

Vocal transposition: up 2nd–6th

J. S. Bach, *Well-Tempered Clavier,* Book II, Fugue in C minor
(No. 2), BWV 871, mm. 1–5 (c. 1740)

J. S. Bach, Chorale No. 145, "Warum betrübst du dich," [melody: anonymous (1565)]

Corresponding Chapter in *Manual for Ear Training and Sight Singing*: 66

Vocal transposition: down 3rd–6th

Larghetto

Henry Purcell, *Dido and Aeneas*, z626, Act III, "When I Am Laid in Earth," mm. 6–38 (1639?)

931

George Frideric Handel, Anthem for the Royal Chapel HWV 251ᵃ, "As Pants the Hart," mm. 2–9 (1714)

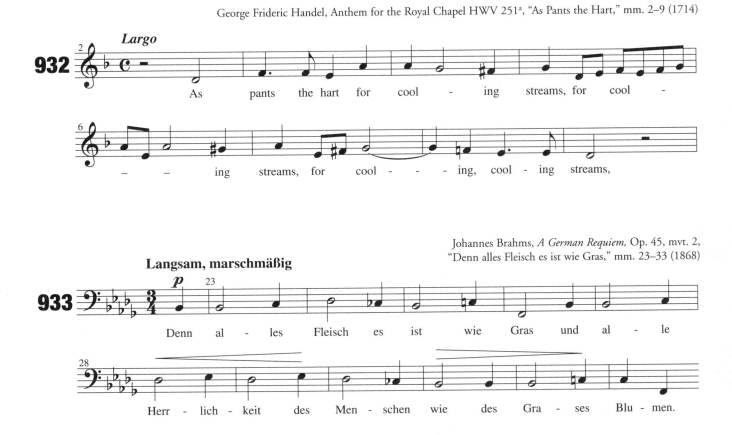

932

Largo

As pants the hart for cool - ing streams, for cool -

- - ing streams, for cool - - - ing, cool - ing streams,

Johannes Brahms, *A German Requiem,* Op. 45, mvt. 2,
"Denn alles Fleisch es ist wie Gras," mm. 23–33 (1868)

Langsam, marschmäßig

933

Denn al - les Fleisch es ist wie Gras und al - le

Herr - lich - keit des Men - schen wie des Gra - ses Blu - men.

J. S. Bach, *Well-Tempered Clavier,* Book I, Fugue in F♯ minor
(No. 14), BWV 859, mm. 1–4 (1722)

934

Corresponding Chapter in *Manual for Ear Training and Sight Singing:* 66

Béla Bartók, *For Children*, Part I, No. 27, "My Sheep Are Lost," mm. 5–16 (1909)

935 Allegramente

David Del Tredici, *Final Alice*, mm. 1456–1463 (1975)

936 Presto, con fuoco e bravura (♩ = 108)

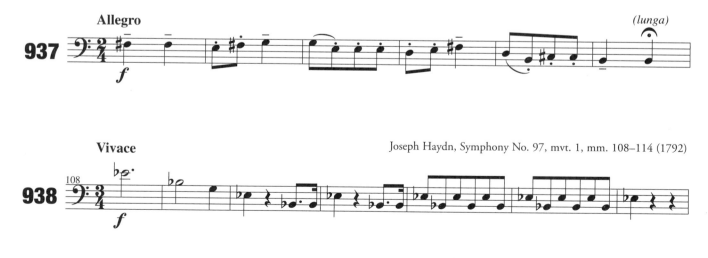

Béla Bartók, *For Children*, Part I, No. 29, "Oh! Hey! What Do You Say?" mm. 1–6 (1909)

937 Allegro

Joseph Haydn, Symphony No. 97, mvt. 1, mm. 108–114 (1792)

938 Vivace

Corresponding Chapter in *Manual for Ear Training and Sight Singing*: 67

Béla Bartók, *For Children*, Part I, No. 26, "Go Round, Sweetheart, Go Round" (1909)

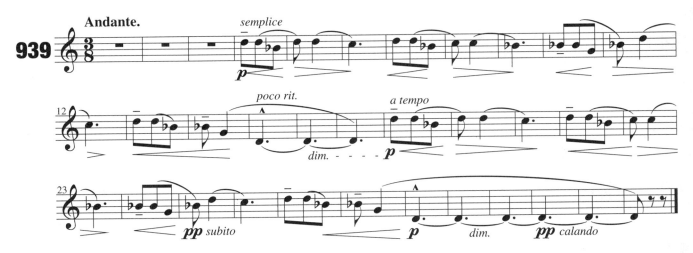

Franz Schubert, "Gruppe aus dem Tartarus," D. 583 [Op. 24, No. 1], mm. 40–46 (1817)

Arcangelo Corelli, Sonata da camera Op. 2, No. 2, Corrente, mm. 1–9

Arcangelo Corelli, Sonata da camera Op. 4, No. 2, Preludio, mm. 1–5

Corresponding Chapter in *Manual for Ear Training and Sight Singing*: 67

George Frideric Handel, Concerto HWV 287 [Oboe Concerto No. 3], mvt. 2, mm. 1–4

Allegro

943

Chiara Margarita Cozzolani, "O dulcis Jesu," mm. 1–6 (1642)

944

O_____ dul - cis,   dul - cis Je - su,

George Frideric Handel, Chandos anthem *Have Mercy upon Me O God,* HWV 248, No. 8, "Then Shall I Teach thy Ways unto the Wicked," mm. 1–5 (1718)

Allegro

945

J. S. Bach, Suite No. 3 for Unaccompanied Cello, BWV 1009, mvt. 6, Bourée II, mm. 1–4 (c. 1720)

946

Corresponding Chapter in *Manual for Ear Training and Sight Singing:* 67

Vocal transposition: down 4th–7th

George Frideric Handel, Chandos anthem *O Praise the Lord with One Consent*,
HWV 254, No. 2, "Praise Him All Ye," mm. 1–8 (1718)

947

Larghetto

Praise him all ye, all ye
that in_____ his house at - tend_____
with con - stant care,

Pietro Antonio Locatelli, Concerto Grosso Op. 1, No. 2, mvt. 2, mm. 1–6 (1721)

Allegro

948

Vocal transposition: down 3rd–7th

Rosa Giacinta Badalla, *Motetti a voce sola*, "Pane angelico," mm. 73–86 (1684)

949

Tan - to pro - di - gio tan - to pro - di - gi - o tri - um - pha
a - mor, tan - to, tan - to, tan - to pro - di - gi - o tri - um - - - - pha,

Corresponding Chapter in *Manual for Ear Training and Sight Singing:* **67**

*Vocal transposition: The range of the following excerpt is slightly large.
Transpose down a 5th or 6th and use good support for the high note in
m. 1 and the low note in m. 4.*

Pietro Antonio Locatelli, Concerto Grosso Op. 1,
No. 11, mvt. 3, Sarabanda, mm. 1–4 (1721)

Pietro Antonio Locatelli, Concerto Grosso Op. 1, No. 6, mvt. 3, mm. 1–6 (1721)

Pietro Antonio Locatelli, Violin Concerto Op. 7, No. 2, mvt. 2, mm. 1–3 (1741)

Vocal transposition: down 3rd–6th

Maria Margherita Grimani, *La decollazione di San Giovanni Battista,*
"Anche col piede," mm. 9–25 (1715)

Corresponding Chapter in *Manual for Ear Training and Sight Singing*: 67

George Frideric Handel, Chandos anthem *Have Mercy upon Me O God,* HWV 248,
No. 2, "Wash Me Throughly from My Wickedness," mm. 1–13 (1718)

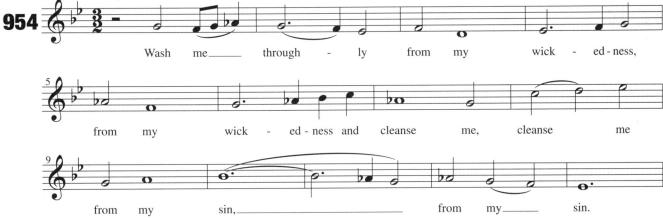

Wash me_____ through - ly from my wick - ed - ness,

from my wick - ed - ness and cleanse me, cleanse me

from my sin,_____ from my_____ sin.

Arcangelo Corelli, Sonata da camera Op. 2, No. 10, Sarabanda, mm. 1–4

J. S. Bach, Invention No. 8, BWV 779, mm. 12–14 (c. 1720)

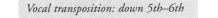
Vocal transposition: down 5th–6th

Joseph Haydn, Symphony No. 29, mvt. 4, mm. 74–81 (1765)

Corresponding Chapter in *Manual for Ear Training and Sight Singing*: 67

George Frideric Handel, Chandos anthem *I Will Magnify Thee,*
HWV 250a, No. 3, Air, mm. 91–95 (1718)

and   praise_____

Joseph Haydn, Symphony No. 104, mvt. 4, mm. 55–64 (1795)

George Frideric Handel, Trio Sonata Op. 2, No. 5, HWV 390a, mvt. 4, mm. 27–33

J. S. Bach, Sonata for Viola da Gamba BWV 1027, mvt. 2, mm. 5–10

J. S. Bach, *Well-Tempered Clavier,* Book I, Fugue in A minor (No. 20), BWV 865, mm. 11–14 (1722)

Corresponding Chapter in *Manual for Ear Training and Sight Singing:* **67**

Vocal transposition: down 3rd–6th

J. S. Bach, *Well-Tempered Clavier,* Book I, Fugue in A♭ major
(No. 17), BWV 862, mm. 17–21 (1722)

963

J. S. Bach, *Well-Tempered Clavier,* Book II, Fugue in C♯ minor
(No. 4), BWV 873, mm. 2–4 (c. 1740)

964

W. A. Mozart, Piano Sonata K. 545, mvt. 2, mm. 17–24

Andante

965

W. A. Mozart, Symphony No. 41, K. 551 ("Jupiter"), mvt. 1, mm. 56–62 (1788)

Allegro vivace

966

Franz Schubert, Symphony No. 8 ("Unfinished"), D. 759, mvt. 1, mm. 44–53 (1822)

Allegro moderato

967

Corresponding Chapter in *Manual for Ear Training and Sight Singing*: 67

Richard Wagner, *Rienzi*, Overture, mm. 155–158 (1840)

968

Gustav Mahler, *Das Lied von der Erde,* No. 1, "Das Trinklied vom
Jammer der Erde," mm. 335–343 (1909)

969

Dun - kel   ist   das   Le - ben,   ist   der   Tod!

Vocal transposition: down 4th–7th

Maurice Ravel, *Don Quichotte à Dulcinée,* No. 3,
"Chanson à boire," mm. 7–30 (1933)

970

Foin du bâ - tard,   il - lus - tre Da - me,——   Qui   pour me perdre à vos doux

yeux   Dit que l'a - mour   et   le vin vieux   Met - tent en deuil mon

coeur—— mon   â - me!———— Ah!————   ah!

ah!————

Corresponding Chapter in *Manual for Ear Training and Sight Singing*: 67

Vocal transposition: down 3rd–6th

Ludwig van Beethoven, Piano Sonata No. 16, Op. 31, No. 1, mvt. 1, mm. 66–73 (1802)

Allegro vivace

971

Franz Schubert, Piano Sonata D. 625, mvt. 4, mm. 147–158 (1818)

Allegro

972

Ludwig van Beethoven, Symphony No. 9,
Op. 125, mvt. 3, mm. 91–96 (1824)

Adagio molto e cantabile ♩ = *60*

973

Richard Strauss, *Alpine Symphony*, Op. 64, rehearsal 144, mm. 3–9 (1915)

Lento

974

Gustav Mahler, Symphony No. 9, mvt. 4, mm. 11–13 (1909)

Sehr langsam und noch zurückhaltend.

975

Corresponding Chapter in *Manual for Ear Training and Sight Singing*: 67

Robert Schumann, *Liederkreis* Op. 24, No. 9, "Mit Myrthen und Rosen," mm. 37–40 (1840)

Vocal transposition: down 2nd–5th

Franz Schubert, "Leichenfantasie," D. 7, mm. 245–249 (1811?)

Corresponding Chapter in *Manual for Ear Training and Sight Singing*: 67

CLOSELY RELATED MODULATION
FROM THE MAJOR MODE

Robert Schumann, *Carnaval,* Op. 9, No. 21, "Marche des Davidsbündler contre les Philistins," mm. 1–8 (1835)

978

Vocal transposition: up 2nd–5th

Johannes Schenck, *Scherzi musicali,* Op. 6, Suite in A minor, mvt. 8, mm. 9–24 (1698)

Menuet II

979

Vocal transposition: down 4th–7th

Bernardo Pasquini, Bizzarria in C major, mm. 1–8

980

Corresponding Chapter in *Manual for Ear Training and Sight Singing:* 69

Vocal transposition: down 5th–7th

Domenico Zipoli, *Sonate d'intavolatura,* Partita in A minor, mm. 5–8 (1716)

981

Vocal transposition: When singing the top part alone, transpose down 4th–7th. When singing all parts together, sing at concert pitch using only sopranos with the highest ranges on the top part.

George Frideric Handel, Concerto Grosso Op. 3, No. 4, HWV 315, mvt. 4, mm. 9–16

982

Jean Baptiste Loeillet (de Gant), Sonata, Op. 3, No. 4, mvt. 4, mm. 1–22 (1715)

983

Corresponding Chapter in *Manual for Ear Training and Sight Singing:* **69**

George Frideric Handel, Psalm *Laudate pueri Dominum* No. 2,
HWV 237, "Suscitans a terra inopem," mm. 13–30 (1707)

984

Su - sci - tans a ter - ra   in - o - pem, a terra in - o - pem,   su - sci - tans a ter - ra

in - o - pem, - a ter - ra in - o - pem,   a   ter - ra,   et de ster - - - co - re

e - - - - - - - ri - gens   pau - pe - rem,

Vocal transposition: up 2nd–3rd   J. S. Bach, Concerto for Three Harpsichords, BWV 1064, mvt. 1, mm. 1–4 (c. 1730)

985

Corresponding Chapter in *Manual for Ear Training and Sight Singing:* 69

Vocal transposition: down 2nd–5th

986 **Etwas Kokett.**

Robert Schumann, "Der Hidalgo," Op. 30, No. 3, mm. 2–18 (1840)

Es ist so süss, zu scher-zen mit Lie-dern und mit Her-zen

und mit dem ernst-en Streit! Er-glänzt des Mon-des Schim-mer da

treibt's mich fort vom Zim-mer durch Platz und Gass-en weit; da

bin zur Lieb' ich im-mer wie sum Ge-fecht, wie zum Ge-fecht be-reit!

Carl Maria von Weber, "Invitation to the Dance," Op. 65, mm. 98–129 (1819)

987 **Allegro vivace.**

p wiegend

cresc.

dim.

Vocal transposition: Sing all parts beginning in the key of C major by transposing the two upper parts down a perfect 4th while transposing the bass part up a perfect 5th.

Arcangelo Corelli, Sonata da chiesa Op. 1, No. 1, mvt. 2, mm. 1–5

988

Allegro

Vocal transposition: Only singers with the widest ranges should sing this excerpt as written. Others should transpose up a 2nd and omit the octave leaps in mm. 10–15 by singing the middle note in each of these measures up an octave.

Antonio Caldara, Cantata *Titano all' inferno,* Aria "Intatto sol resti quel core," mm. 9–30

989

In - tat - to sol re - sti quel co - re in - u - ma - no da

me si cal - pe - sti e chie - da ma in - va - no pie - ta - de e mer -

cè, pie - ta - - - - - - - - - - - de, pie - ta - de e mer - cè.

Vocal transposition: up 3rd–4th

W. A. Mozart, *The Magic Flute,* K. 620, Act II, "O Isis und Osiris," mm. 4–24 (1791)

990

O I - sis und O - si - ris, schen - ket der Weis - heit Geist dem

neu - en Paar! Die ihr der Wand - rer Schrit - te len - ket, stärkt mit Ge -

duld sie in Ge - fahr, stärkt mit Ge - duld sie in Ge - fahr.

Corresponding Chapter in *Manual for Ear Training and Sight Singing:* 69

Vocal transposition: down 2nd–5th

Franz Schubert, "Geheimnis," D. 491, mm. 3–12 (1816)

991 **Mäßig geschwind**

Sag an, wer lehrt dich Lie - der, so schmeich - elnd und so zart?____

Sie ru - fen ei - nen Him - mel aus trü - ber Ge - gen - wart.

George Frideric Handel, *Giulio Cesare*, HWV 17, Act I,
"Son nato a sospirar, e il dolce," mm. 32–38 (1724)

992 *Largo.*

Se il fa - to ci tra - di,   se - re—no e lie - to di___ mai

Se il fa - to ci tra - di,   se - re—no e lie - to di___ mai

più spe - rar po - trò,   mai più,____   mai più,____   mai più spe - rar___ po - trò.

più spe - rar po - trò,   mai più,____   mai più,____   mai più spe - rar___ po - trò.

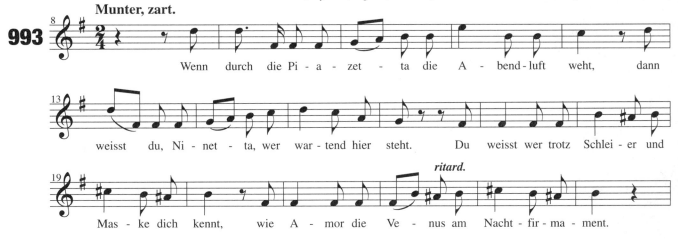

Robert Schumann, *Myrthen*, Op. 25, No. 18 ["Zwei Venetianische Lieder," II],   mm. 8–24 (1840)

993 **Munter, zart.**

Wenn durch die Pi - a - zet - ta die A - bend - luft weht,   dann

weisst du, Ni - net - ta, wer war - tend hier steht.   Du weisst wer trotz Schlei - er und

ritard.

Mas - ke dich kennt,   wie A - mor die Ve - nus am Nacht - fir - ma - ment.

Corresponding Chapter in *Manual for Ear Training and Sight Singing: 69*

Allegretto

dolce

Antonio Salieri, *Mass in B Minor,* Credo, mm. 1–11 (1809)

994

Cre - do in u - num De - um, Pa - trem o - mni - po - ten - tem, fa - cto - rem coe - li et

Cre - do in u - num De - um, Pa - trem o - mni - po - ten - tem, fa - cto - rem coe - li et

Cre - do in u - num De - um, Pa - trem o - mni - po - ten - tem, fa - cto - rem coe - li et

Cre - do in u - num De - um, Pa - trem o - mni - po - ten - tem, fa - cto - rem coe - li et

ter - rae, vi - si - bi - li - um o - mni - um et in - vi - si - bi - li - um.

ter - rae, vi - si - bi - li - um o - mni - um et in - vi - si - bi - li - um.

ter - rae, vi - si - bi - li - um o - mni - um et in - vi - si - bi - li - um.

ter - rae, vi - si - bi - li - um o - mni - um et in - vi - si - bi - li - um.

Vocal transposition: down 3rd–7th

Johannes Brahms, *Lieder und Gesänge,* Op. 57, No. 2,
"Wenn du nur zuweilen lächelst," mm. 1–7 (c. 1871)

Poco Andante

995

Wenn du nur zu - wei - len lä - chelst, nur zu - wei - len Küh - le fä - chelst

die - ser un - ge - mess - nen Glut, die - ser un - ge mess - nen Glut.

Corresponding Chapter in *Manual for Ear Training and Sight Singing:* 69

Vocal transposition: When singing any of the upper three parts without the bass part, sing at concert pitch. When singing all parts together, only basses with the lowest ranges should sing the bass part.

Hector Berlioz, *L'enfance du Christ,* Op. 25, "L'adieu des bergers à la sainte famille," mm. 5–20 (1854)

Giacomo Carissimi, Cantata "Vittoria, mio core," mm. 1–7 (1653)

Corresponding Chapter in *Manual for Ear Training and Sight Singing:* 69

Vocal transposition: down 2nd–7th

Robert Schumann, *Dichterliebe,* Op. 48, No. 4,
"Wenn ich in deine Augen seh," mm. 1–8 (1840)

Joseph Haydn, *Theresienmesse,* Gloria, mm. 135–147 (1799)

Vocal transposition: down 3rd–7th

Henry Purcell, *King Arthur*, z628, Act III, "Thou Doting Fool," mm. 17–32 (1691)

1000

Thou dot - ing fool, for - bear, for - bear! What dost thou mean by freez - ing here?

Win - ter sub - du - ing, And Spring re - new - ing, My beams cre - ate a more glo - rious year.

Vocal transposition: up 2nd–4th

Johann Joseph Fux, Sonata (Canon) for Two Violas da Gamba, mvt. 2, mm. 1–21

1001

CLOSELY RELATED MODULATION
FROM THE MINOR MODE

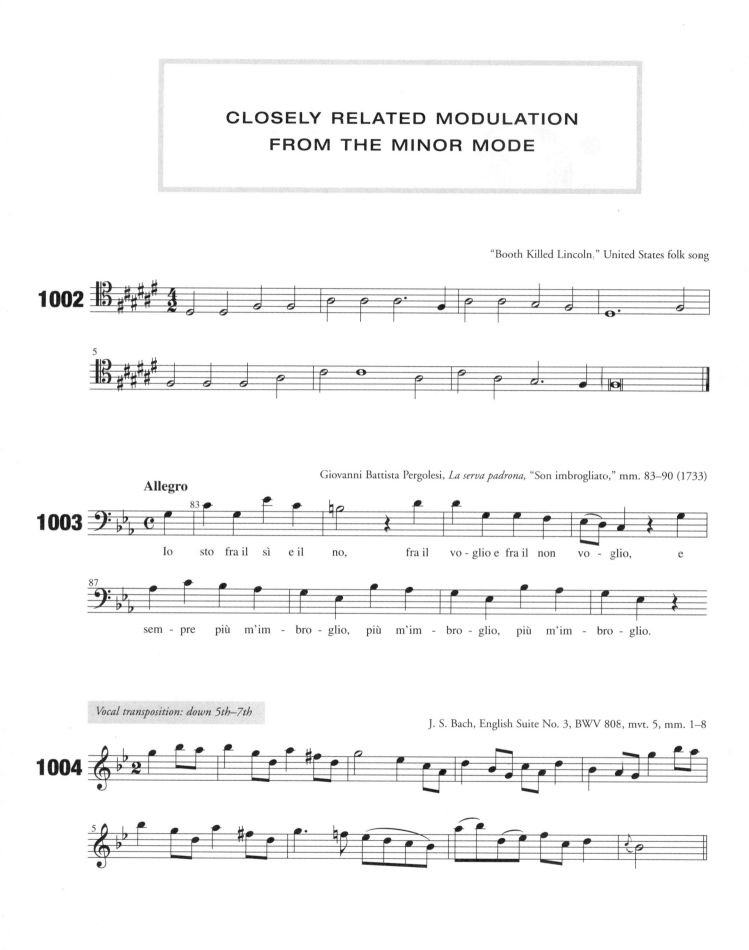

"Booth Killed Lincoln." United States folk song

1002

Giovanni Battista Pergolesi, *La serva padrona,* "Son imbrogliato," mm. 83–90 (1733)

Allegro

1003

Io sto fra il sì e il no, fra il vo - glio e fra il non vo - glio, e

sem - pre più m'im - bro - glio, più m'im - bro - glio, più m'im - bro - glio.

Vocal transposition: down 5th–7th

J. S. Bach, English Suite No. 3, BWV 808, mvt. 5, mm. 1–8

1004

Corresponding Chapter in *Manual for Ear Training and Sight Singing:* 70

George Frideric Handel, *Saul*, HWV 53, Part I, "With Rage I Shall Burst His Praises to Hear!," mm. 12–24 (1738)

With Rage I shall burst his___ Prai - ses to hear! Oh! how I both hate the

Strip - ling, and fear! What Mor - tal a Ri - val in Glo - ry can bear?

Vocal transposition: down 4th–6th

Richard Wagner, *Die Walküre*, Act III, scene 1, mm. 36-40 (1856)

Franz Schubert, Ecossaise D. 781, No. 7 (1823)

Corresponding Chapter in *Manual for Ear Training and Sight Singing*: 70

George Frideric Handel, *Acis and Galatea*, HWV 49, "Mourn, All Ye Muses!," mm. 1–14 (1718)

Vocal transposition: down 6th–7th

Joseph Haydn, Piano Sonata in E minor (Hob. XVI:34), mvt. 3, mm. 1–8 (c. 1784)

Corresponding Chapter in *Manual for Ear Training and Sight Singing*: 70

Franz Schubert, *Winterreise*, D. 911, No. 10, "Rast," mm. 37–45 (1827)

Mäßig

1010

In ei - nes Köh - lers en - gem Haus hab Ob - dach ich ge - fun - den;

doch mei - ne Glie - der ruhn nicht aus; so bren - nen ih - re Wun - den.

Vocal transposition: down 2nd–5th

Felix Mendelssohn, "Romanze," Op. 8, No. 10, mm. 1–11 (1827)

Andante. *p*

1011

Ein - mal aus sei - nen Bli - cken, von sei - nem sü - ssen Mund, soll Gruss und Kuss er -

qui - cken des Her - zens trü - ben Grund. Ich kann ihn nicht ver - gess - en ich kann es nicht be -

reu'n, ich sünd' - ge nicht ver - mes - sen, der Him - mel wird ver - zeih'n,

der Him - mel wird ver - zeih'n!

Corresponding Chapter in *Manual for Ear Training and Sight Singing: 70*

Franz Schubert, *Drei Klavierstücke,* D. 946, No. 2, mm. 122–138 (1828)

J. S. Bach, Suite No. 3 for Unaccompanied Cello, BWV 1009, mvt. 6, mm. 1–8 (c. 1720)

Franz Schubert, Ecossaise D. 977, No. 8, mm. 1–8 (1816)

Vocal transposition: down 4th–7th

W. A. Mozart, String Quartet K. 406 (516ᵇ), mvt. 4, mm. 1–8 (1788)

Corresponding Chapter in *Manual for Ear Training and Sight Singing: 70*

Vocal transposition: down 4th

Felix Mendelssohn, *Songs Without Words* Op. 19b,
No. 6, "Venetian Boat Song," mm. 7–17 (1830)

1016 Andante sostenuto.

Robert Schumann, Symphony No. 4, Op. 120, mvt. 2, mm. 2–12 (1851)

1017 Ziemlich langsam. (♩ = 66.)

Vocal transposition: down 2nd–5th

Franz Schubert, *Die schöne Müllerin*, D. 795 [Op. 25],
No. 5, "Am Feierabend," mm. 7–15 (1823)

1018 Ziemlich geschwind.

Hätt ich tau-send Ar-me zu rüh-ren, könnt ich brau-send die Rä-der füh-ren, könnt ich

we-hen durch al - le Hai - ne, könnt ich dre-hen al - le Stei - ne,

J. S. Bach, Sinfonia No. 13, BWV 799, mm. 1–8 (c. 1720)

1019

Corresponding Chapter in *Manual for Ear Training and Sight Singing*: 70

Vocal transposition: down 2nd–4th

Fanny Mendelssohn, *Schwanenlied*, Op. 1, No. 1, mm. 1–9 (1846)

1020

Es Fällt ein Stern Her - un - ter   aus sei - ner funk - eln - den

Höh,   das ist der Stern der Lie - be,   den ich dort fal - len seh.

J. S. Bach, Chorale No. 120, "Was mein Gott will, das g'scheh' allzeit," mm. 3–6

1021

Vocal transposition: up 2nd

J. S. Bach, Chorale No. 297, "Jesu, der du meine Seele," mm. 5–10

1022

Corresponding Chapter in *Manual for Ear Training and Sight Singing*: 70

Vocal transposition: down 2nd–6th

Franz Schubert, "Gretchen am Spinnrade," D. 118 [Op. 2], mm. 2–11 (1814)

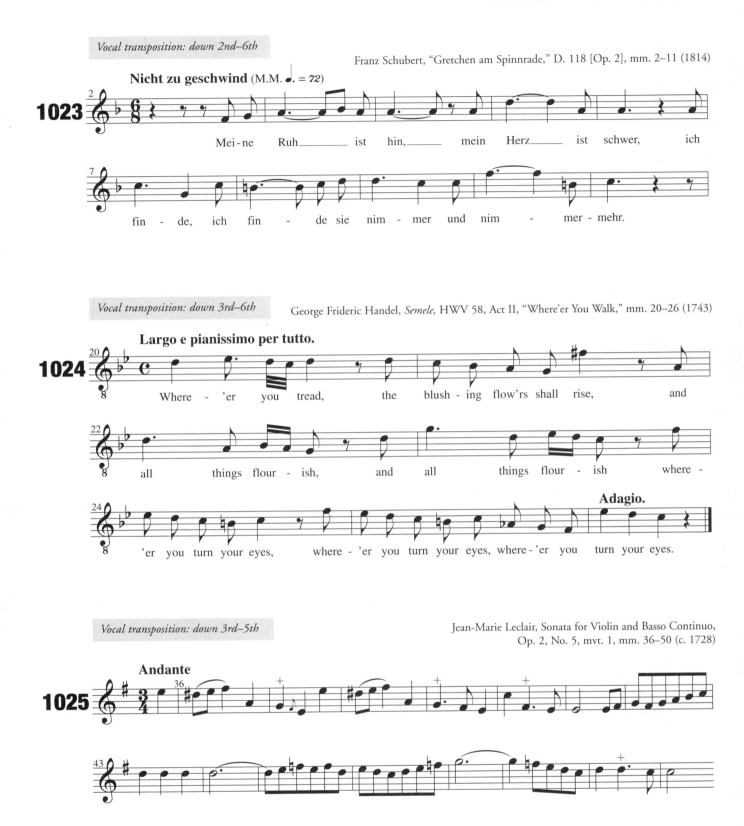

Nicht zu geschwind (M.M. ♩. = 72)

1023

Mei - ne Ruh_____ ist hin,_____ mein Herz_____ ist schwer, ich

fin - de, ich fin - de sie nim - mer und nim - mer - mehr.

Vocal transposition: down 3rd–6th

George Frideric Handel, *Semele*, HWV 58, Act II, "Where'er You Walk," mm. 20–26 (1743)

Largo e pianissimo per tutto.

1024

Where - 'er you tread, the blush - ing flow'rs shall rise, and

all things flour - ish, and all things flour - ish where -

Adagio.

'er you turn your eyes, where - 'er you turn your eyes, where - 'er you turn your eyes.

Vocal transposition: down 3rd–5th

Jean-Marie Leclair, Sonata for Violin and Basso Continuo, Op. 2, No. 5, mvt. 1, mm. 36–50 (c. 1728)

Andante

1025

Corresponding Chapter in *Manual for Ear Training and Sight Singing*: 70

Joseph Haydn, String Quartet Op. 74, No. 3 (Hob. III:74), mvt. 2, mm. 23–30 (1793)

1026

Vocal transposition: down 3rd–4th

Ludwig van Beethoven, Bagatelle Op. 119, No. 1, mm. 1–24 (1822)

1027

Corresponding Chapter in *Manual for Ear Training and Sight Singing*: 70

DISTANT MODULATIONS

Vocal transposition: down 2nd–6th

Franz Schubert, German Dance D. 365, No. 33, mm. 1–16 (1821)

1028

Vocal transposition: down 2nd–4th

Franz Schubert, German Dance D. 790 [Op. 171], mm. 1–26 (1823)

1029

Corresponding Chapter in *Manual for Ear Training and Sight Singing*: 71

Vocal transposition: down 3rd–6th

Allegro spiritoso (♩. = 96)   Hector Berlioz, *Les nuits d'été*, Op. 7, No. 6, "L'île inconnue," mm. 5–12 (1841)

1030

Di - tes,   la   jeu - ne   belle, Où vou - lez - vous al - ler?   La

Voi - le en - fle son   ai - le,   La bri - se va   souf - fler!

Vocal transposition: down 3rd–4th

Robert Schumann, "Wanderlust" ["Wanderlied"], Op. 35, No. 3, mm. 22–40 (1840)

Sehr lebhaft.

1031

Mit ei - len - den Wol - ken der Vo - gel dort zieht und singt in der Fer - ne ein

ritard.

hei - math - lich Lied. So treibt es den Bur - schen durch Wäld - er und Feld, zu gleich - chen der Mut - ter, der

Etwas langsamer.

wan - dern - den Welt!___   Da grüss - en ihn Vö - gel be - kannt ü - berm Meer, sie

flo - gen von Flu - ren der Hei - math hie - her,   da duf - ten die Blu - men ver -

trau - lich um ihn,   sie trie - ben vom Lan - de die Lüf - te da - hin.

Corresponding Chapter in *Manual for Ear Training and Sight Singing*: 71

Robert Schumann, "Mein Wagen rollet langsam," Op. 142, No. 4, mm. 8–23 (1840)

Nach dem Sinn des Gedichts.

1032

Mein Wa - gen rol - let lang - sam durch lu - sti - ges Wal - des -
grün, durch blu - mi - ge Thä - ler, die zau - brisch im Son - nen -
glan - ze blüh'n. Ich si - tze und sin - ne und sin - ne und
träu - me und denk' an die Lieb - - ste mein.

Sergei Prokofiev, Symphony No. 1 ("Classical"), Op. 25, mvt. 3, mm. 1–4 (1935)

Non troppo allegro ♩ = 144

1033

f pesante   *f*   *< f*

Vocal transposition: down 3rd–5th

Franz Schubert, "Kennst du das Land," D. 321, mm. 1–11 (1815)

Mässig.

1034

Kennst du das Land, wo die Ci - tro - nen blühn, im dun - klen Laub die
Gold - O - ran - gen glühn, ein sanf - ter Wind vom blau - en Him - mel weht,

Corresponding Chapter in *Manual for Ear Training and Sight Singing*: 71

Camille Saint-Saëns, *The Carnival of the Animals,* "The Elephant," mm. 21–30 (1886)

Allegretto pomposo

1035

Vocal transposition: down 2nd–6th

Joseph Haydn, String Quartet Op. 76, No. 6 (Hob III:80), mvt. 2, mm. 31–39 (c. 1797)

Adagio

1036

Vocal transposition: down 2nd–4th

Claude Debussy, *Fêtes galantes,* No. 2, "Fantoches," mm. 6–16 (1891)

Allegro scherzando

1037

Sca - ra - mouche et Pul - ci - nel - la Qu'un mau - vais des -

sein ras - semb - la Ges - ti - cu - lent noirs sous la lu - ne, la la la la la

la la la la la la la la la

Corresponding Chapter in *Manual for Ear Training and Sight Singing:* 71

Vocal transposition: up 2nd–4th

Mike Masser, "Do You Know Where You're Going To?"
(Theme from *Mahogany*), mm. 10–17 (1973) [words by Gerry Goffin]

1038

Do you get___ what you're Hop-ing for? When you look be-hind you there's no

o-pen door.___ What are you hop-ing for,___ do you

know? Once we were stand - ing still in time,

chas - ing the fan - ta - sies___ that filled our minds.___

Antonín Dvořák, Slavonic Dance Op. 46, No. 3, mm. 125–150 (1878)

1039

Corresponding Chapter in *Manual for Ear Training and Sight Singing:* **71**

Vocal transposition: down 3rd–5th

Andante con moto (♪ = 92)

Ludwig van Beethoven, Symphony No. 5, Op. 67, mvt. 2, mm. 23–31 (1808)

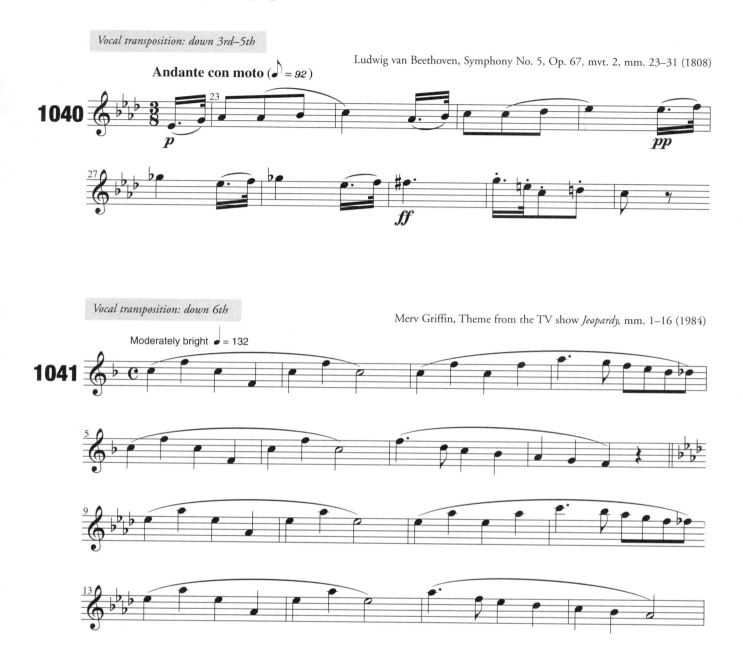

Vocal transposition: down 6th

Merv Griffin, Theme from the TV show *Jeopardy*, mm. 1–16 (1984)

Moderately bright ♩ = 132

Corresponding Chapter in *Manual for Ear Training and Sight Singing*: 71

Vocal transposition: The range of this excerpt is a bit wide. Sing it at concert pitch and use good support for the low G♯ at the beginning and the high E♯s in mm. 7–10 and 13–14.

Franz Schubert, German Dance D. 139, mm. 1–32 (1815)

Although the following excerpt frequently touches on F♯, Mendelssohn's setting treats the opening of this passage unequivocally in A major. As you sing this excerpt, think of it in A major until you must make a modulation towards the end.

Felix Mendelssohn, "Keine von der Erde Schönen," mm. 5–39 (1833)

1043

Andante con moto.

Kei - ne von der Er - de Schö - nen wal - tet zaub - ernd gleich dir; auf der Fluth ein Sil - ber - tö - nen dünkt dei - ne Stim - me mir,___ dünkt dei - ne Stim - me mir. Lei - ser wird des Mee - res Rau - schen, ent - zückt dir zu lau - schen, legt sich der Wo - gen Schäu - men,___ al - le die Win - de träu - men, al - le die Win - de träu - men. Gol - den webt der Mond auf Wel - len sein Netz, sanft scheint der Fluth die vol - le Brust zu schwel - len, wie ein Kind schlum - mernd ruht,

Corresponding Chapter in *Manual for Ear Training and Sight Singing:* **71**

Vocal transposition: down 3rd

Franz Schubert, *Schwanengesang,* D. 957, No. 10,
"Das Fischermädchen," mm. 7–44 (1828)

1044

Etwas geschwind

Du schö - nes Fi - scher - mäd - chen, trei - be den Kahn ans

Land___ komm zu mir und set - ze dich nie - der, wir

ko - sen Hand in Hand, komm zu mir und set - ze dich nie - der, wir

ko - sen Hand in Hand,___ wir ko - sen Hand in Hand.

leg an mein Herz dein Köpf - chen und fürch - te dich nicht zu

sehr,___ ver - traust du dich doch sorg - los

täg - lich dem wil - den Meer, ver - traust du dich doch sorg - los

täg - lich dem wil - den Meer,___ täg - lich dem wil - den Meer.

Corresponding Chapter in *Manual for Ear Training and Sight Singing*: 71

"Mon père m'a marieé," French folk song

1045

Franz Schubert, "Der Flug der Zeit," D. 515 [Op. 7, No. 2], mm. 4–11 (1821)

1046

Etwas geschwind (M. M. ♩· = *112*)

Es floh   die   Zeit   im Wir - bel - flu - ge

und   trug   des   Le - bens Plan   mit   sich.

Vocal transposition: down 3rd–5th

Franz Schubert, "Marche caractéristique," D. 968b [Op. 121], No. 2, mm. 2–12 (1826?)

Allegro vivace

1047

pp   *cresc.*   *pp*

cresc.   *f*

Corresponding Chapter in *Manual for Ear Training and Sight Singing*: 71

Vocal transposition: down 3rd–7th

Antonín Dvořák, Slavonic Dance Op. 46, No. 8, mm. 1–8 (1878)

1048

Vocal transposition: down 2nd–3rd

Amy Beach, Ariette, Op. 1, No. 4, mm. 59–87 (1886)

1049

Though the sound o-ver-powers, Sing a - gain,

Though the sound o-ver-powers, Sing a - gain,

with thy sweet voice re - veal - ing a tone of some world

far from ours, Where mu - sic and moon - light

— e - nu — to al fine. and feel - - - - ing Are one.

SUCCESSIVE MODULATIONS

W. A. Mozart, "Das Kinderspiel," K. 598 (1791)

1050

Wir Kin - der, wir schmek - ken _ der Freu - den recht viel! Wir
schä - kern und nek - ken (ver - steht sich, im _ Spiel!) Wir lär - men _ und
sin - gen und ren - nen uns um und hüp - fen und
sprin - gen _ im _ Gra - se _ her - um!

W. A. Mozart, "O Gotteslamm," K. 343 (336ᶜ), No. 1 (1787)

1051

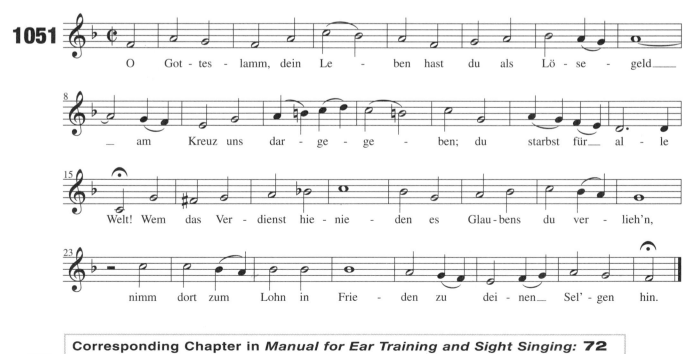

O Got - tes - lamm, dein Le - ben hast du als Lö - se - geld _
_ am Kreuz uns dar - ge - ge - ben; du starbst für _ al - le
Welt! Wem das Ver - dienst hie - nie - den es Glau - bens du ver - lieh'n,
nimm dort zum Lohn in Frie - den zu dei - nen _ Sel' - gen hin.

Corresponding Chapter in *Manual for Ear Training and Sight Singing:* **72**

Vocal transposition: down 3rd–6th

Antonia Bembo, *Produzioni armoniche,* No. 20, "Affettuoso" ["Amor mio"], mm. 1–16

1052

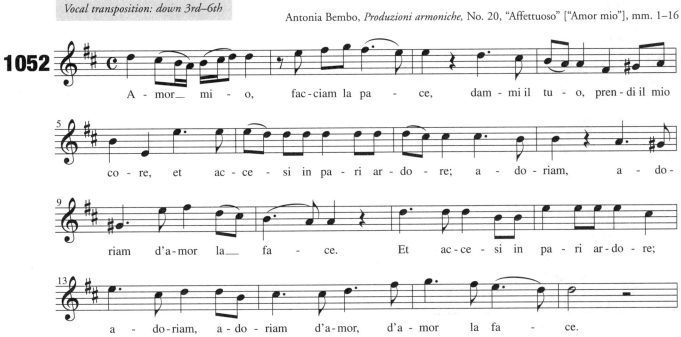

A - mor__ mi - o, fac-ciam la pa - ce, dam - mi il tu - o, pren-di il mio

co - re, et ac-ce-si in pa-ri ar-do-re; a - do-riam, a - do-

riam d'a-mor la__ fa - ce. Et ac-ce-si in pa-ri ar-do-re;

a - do-riam, a-do-riam d'a-mor, d'a-mor la fa - ce.

Corresponding Chapter in *Manual for Ear Training and Sight Singing:* **72**

Vocal transposition: down 3rd–4th

Jean-Philippe Rameau, *Pièces de clavecin,* "Menuet en Rondeau" (1724)

1053

Vocal transposition: down 4th–5th

W. A. Mozart, Minuet K. 104 (61ᵉ), No. 4 (1772)

1054

Corresponding Chapter in *Manual for Ear Training and Sight Singing*: 72

Vocal transposition: down 3rd–7th

Franz Schubert, "Heidenröslein," D. 257 [Op. 3, No. 3] (1815)

1055

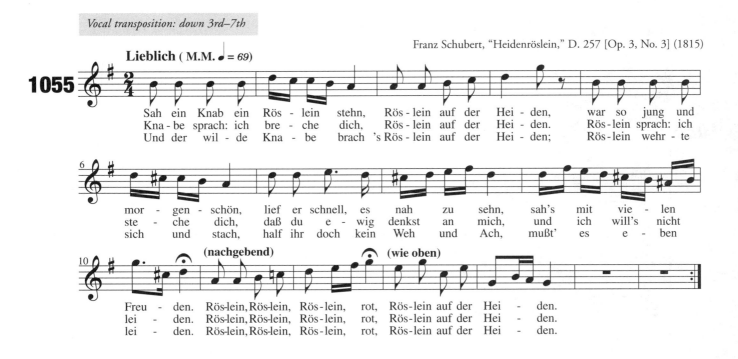

Sah ein Knab ein Rös - lein stehn, Rös - lein auf der Hei - den, war so jung und
Kna - be sprach: ich bre - che dich, Rös - lein auf der Hei - den. Rös - lein sprach: ich
Und der wil - de Kna - be brach 's Rös - lein auf der Hei - den; Rös - lein wehr - te

mor - gen - schön, lief er schnell, es nah zu sehn, sah's mit vie - len
ste - che dich, daß du e - wig denkst an mich, und ich will's nicht
sich und stach, half ihr doch kein Weh und Ach, mußt' es e - ben

Freu - den. Rös-lein, Rös-lein, Rös - lein, rot, Rös - lein auf der Hei - den.
lei - den. Rös-lein, Rös-lein, Rös - lein, rot, Rös - lein auf der Hei - den.
lei - den. Rös-lein, Rös-lein, Rös - lein, rot, Rös - lein auf der Hei - den.

Corresponding Chapter in *Manual for Ear Training and Sight Singing:* 72

Vocal transposition: What octave transpositions can you make in which measures of the following excerpt in order to accommodate vocal ranges?

George Frideric Handel, Chandos anthem *O Come Let Us Sing,*
HWV 253, No. 1, Symphony, mm. 42–66 (1718)

1056

Corresponding Chapter in *Manual for Ear Training and Sight Singing*: 72

"A Geneyve," Yiddish folk melody

Johannes Brahms, *49 deutsche Volkslieder,* WoO 33, No. 15, "Schwesterlein," mm. 1–12 (1894)

Nicht zu langsam und mit inniger Teilnahme

Schwes - ter - lein,   Schwes - ter - lein,   wann   gehn   wir   nach   Haus?

"Mor - gen wenn   die   Hah - nen   krähn,   wolln   wir   nach   Hau - se   gehn,

Brü - der - lein,   Brü - der - lein,   dann gehn   wir   nach   Haus."

Corresponding Chapter in *Manual for Ear Training and Sight Singing:* 72

Vocal transposition: down 3rd–4th

George Frideric Handel, *Almira, Königen von Kastilien,*
HWV 1, Act III, "Edle Sinnen," mm. 17–43 (1704)

1059

Ed - le Sin - nen schaf-fen von hin-nen, was Un-mut und Scha-den zu-fügt, ed - le Sin - nen schaf-fen von hin-nen, was Un-mut und Scha-den zu - fügt, was Un-mut und Scha-den zu-fügt, ed - le Sin - nen schaf-fen von hin-nen, was Un-mut und Scha-den, und Scha-den zu - fügt,

"Play the New Song for Me," Yiddish folk song

1060

Vocal transposition: To sing the following excerpt in four parts, use sopranos with higher ranges on the top part and basses with lower ranges on the lowest part.

Henry Purcell, *Dido and Aeneas*, z626, Act I, "When Monarchs Unite," mm. 1–13 (1689?)

1061

Johannes Brahms, *Lieder und Gesänge,* Op. 32, No. 3, "Ich schleich umher," mm. 1–20 (1864)

Vocal transposition: down 3rd–4th

Johannes Brahms, *Fünf Lieder,* Op. 49, No. 2, "An ein Veilchen," mm. 3–16 (c. 1868)

Corresponding Chapter in *Manual for Ear Training and Sight Singing*: 72

Ludwig van Beethoven, *Alla ingharese quasi un capriccio* [also known as *Rage Over a Lost Penny*], Op. 129, mm. 1–24 (1795)

Vocal transposition: down 2nd–4th

Felix Mendelssohn, *Songs Without Words* Op. 102, No. 2, mm. 1–16 (1845)

Corresponding Chapter in *Manual for Ear Training and Sight Singing*: 72

Tomaso Albinoni, Cantata Op. 4, No. 8, "Mi dà pena quando spira," mm. 80–124 (1702)

1066

Larghetto

Pren - de sem - pre più for - za il mio gran fo - co, il

mio gran fo - co, il mi - o gran fo - co, pren - de

sem - pre più for - za il mio gran fo - co, il mio gran fo - -

- - co, pren - de sem - pre più for - za il

mio gran fo - - - - - - - -

- - - - - - - - co, pren - de sem - - - pre più

for - za il mio gran fo - - - - - - co,

pren - de sem - pre più for - za il mio gran fo - - co.

Corresponding Chapter in *Manual for Ear Training and Sight Singing*: 72

Bettine von Arnim (Bettine Brentano), *Spontini Songbook*, No. 6, "Abendstille öffnet Thüren" (1842)

Robert Schumann, Piano Concerto Op. 54, mvt. 1, mm. 19–32 (1841)

Allegro affettuoso. (♩ = 84.)

1068

Vocal transposition: down 3rd–5th

Franz Liszt, "Du bist wie ein Blume" (1843)

Lento con fervore

mezza voce

1069

Du___ bist wie ei-ne Blu - me, so

hold___ und schön und rein; ich___ schau'dich an, und Weh -

mut schleicht mir ins Herz hin - ein.

sotto voce

Mir ist, als ob ich die Hän - de aufs Haupt dir le - gen

poco rit. *poco più lento*

sollt', be - tent, daß dich Gott er - hal - te

so rein und schön___ und hold.

Corresponding Chapter in *Manual for Ear Training and Sight Singing*: 72

Robert Schumann, *Myrthen,* Op. 25, No. 17
["Zwei Venetianische Lieder," I], mm. 5–32 (1840)

Heimlich, streng im Takt.

1070

Leis' ru - dern hier, mein Gon - do - lier, leis', leis'! Die
Fluth vom Ru - der sprüh'n so lei - se lass, dass sie uns nur ver - nimmt, zu der wir
zieh'n. O könn - te wie er schau-en kann, der Him - mel re - den, traun, er sprä - che vie-les
wohl von dem, was Nachts die Ster - ne schau'n. Leis', leis', leis', leis'!

Vocal transposition: down 3rd–7th

Antonia Bembo, *Produzioni armoniche,* No. 39, "Tota pulcra es," mm. 1–9

1071

To - ta pul - cra es, a - mi - ca me - a, a - mi - ca me - a, et ma - cu - la non
est in te. Ve - ni, ve - ni de Li - ba - no, de Li - ba no, spon - sa me - a.

Corresponding Chapter in *Manual for Ear Training and Sight Singing:* 72

Vocal transposition: down 5th

Felix Mendelssohn, *Songs Without Words* Op. 53, No. 5, "Volkslied," mm. 20–42 (1341)

Vocal transposition: The range of the following excerpt is wider than the practical vocal range. Try transposing down a 2nd and use good support for the low note in m. 13 and the highest notes in mm. 19 and 46–47.

Robert Schumann, "Sonntags am Rhein," Op. 36, No. 1 (1840)

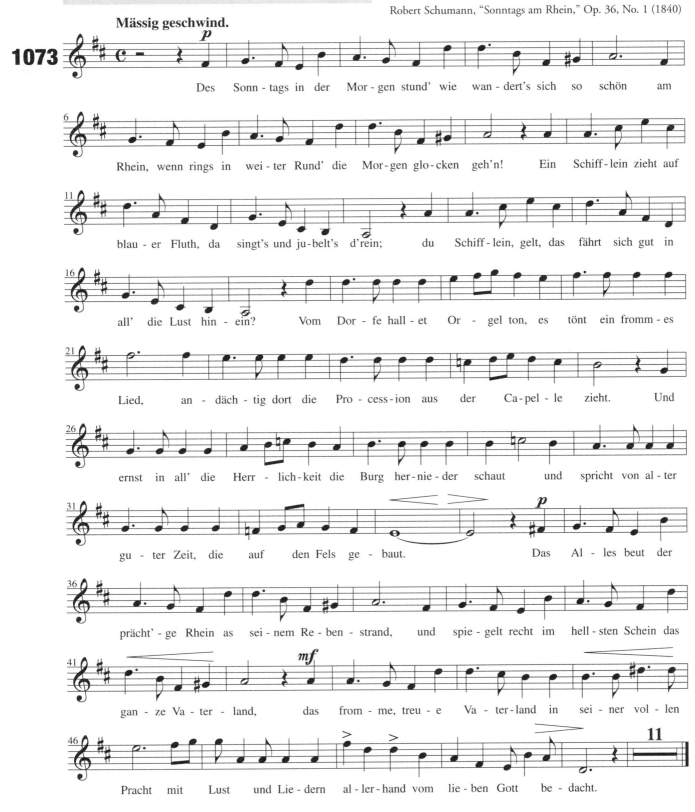

1073

Des Sonn-tags in der Mor-gen stund' wie wan-dert's sich so schön am

Rhein, wenn rings in wei-ter Rund' die Mor-gen glo-cken geh'n! Ein Schiff-lein zieht auf

blau-er Fluth, da singt's und ju-belt's d'rein; du Schiff-lein, gelt, das fährt sich gut in

all' die Lust hin-ein? Vom Dor-fe hall-et Or-gel ton, es tönt ein fromm-es

Lied, an-däch-tig dort die Pro-cess-ion aus der Ca-pel-le zieht. Und

ernst in all' die Herr-lich-keit die Burg her-nie-der schaut und spricht von al-ter

gu-ter Zeit, die auf den Fels ge-baut. Das Al-les beut der

prächt'-ge Rhein as sei-nem Re-ben-strand, und spie-gelt recht im hell-sten Schein das

gan-ze Va-ter-land, das from-me, treu-e Va-ter-land in sei-ner vol-len

Pracht mit Lust und Lie-dern al-ler-hand vom lie-ben Gott be-dacht.

Corresponding Chapter in *Manual for Ear Training and Sight Singing: 72*

Ernesto de Curtis, "Come Back to Sorrento"

1074

Slowly

Vocal transposition: down 3rd–7th

Antonín Dvořák, Slavonic Dance Op. 46, No. 8, mm. 65–72 (1878)

1075

Presto
grandioso

Franz Schubert, German Dance D. 365, No. 36 (1821)

1076

Corresponding Chapter in *Manual for Ear Training and Sight Singing*: 72

Jaime Nunó, national anthem of Mexico (1854)
[Lyrics by Francisco González Bocanegra]

1077

Moderately

Me - xi - ca - nos, al gri - to de gue - rra El a - cer - o_a - pres - tad y_el bri -

dón, Y re - tiem - ble_en sus cen - tros la tie - rra Al so - no - ro ru - gir del ca -

ñón; Y re - tiem - ble_en sus cen - tros la tie - rra Al so - no - ro ru - gir del ca -

ñón. Ci - ña_¡oh Pa - tria! tus sie - nes de_o - li - va De la paz el ar - cán - gel di -

vi - no, Que_en el cie - lo tu_e - ter - no des - ti - no, Por el de - do de Dios se_es - cri -

bió; Mas si_o - sa - re_un ex - tra - ño_e - ne - mi - go, Pro - fa - nar con su plan - ta tu

sue - lo, Pien - sa_¡oh Pa - tria que - ri - da!, que_el cie - lo Un sol - da - do_en ca - da hi - jo te

dió; Un sol - da - do_en ca - da hi - jo te dió. Me - xi -

no - ro ru - gir del ca - ñón.

To Coda

D.C. al Coda

Corresponding Chapter in *Manual for Ear Training and Sight Singing:* **72**

Vocal transposition: down 2nd

Franz Schubert, "Der Alpenjäger," D. 524 [Op. 13, No. 3] (1822)

Frisch, doch nicht zu schnell

1078

Auf ho - hen Ber - ges-rü - cken, wo

fri - scher al - les grünt, ins Land hin-ab zu bli - cken, das

ne - bel-leicht zer - rinnt, er - freut den Al - pen-jä - ger, er -

freut den Al - pen-jä - ger. Je stei - ler und__ je schrä - ger die

Pfa - de sich__ ver - win - den, je mehr Ge - fahr aus Schlün - den, so

frei - er schlägt die Brust, so frei - er schlägt die Brust.

Er ist. der fer - nen Lie - ben, die

inm da-deim ge - blie - ben, sich se - li ger__ be - wußt, sich

se - li - ger be - wußt. Und ist er nun am

Zie - le, so drängt sich in__ der Stil - le ein sü - - ßes

Bild_____ ihm vor; der Son - ne gold - ne Strah - len, sie
we - ben und___ sie ma - len, die er___ im Tal___ er - kor,_____ die
er___ im Tal___ er - kor._____

Wie oben

Auf ho - hen Ber - ges - rü - cken, wo fri - scher al - les grünt, ins
Land hin - ab zu bli - cken, das ne - bel - leicht zer - rinnt, er - freut den Al - pen -
jä - ger, er - freut den Al - pen - jä - ger. Je stei - ler und___ je
schrä - ger die Pfa - de sich ver - win - den, je mehr Ge - fahr aus Schlün - den, so
frei - er schlägt die Brust, so frei - er schlägt die Brust.

Corresponding Chapter in *Manual for Ear Training and Sight Singing:* **72**

Billy Joel, "She's Always a Woman," bridge (1977)

1079

Moderately

Oh_____ she takes care of her - self_____ she can wait if she

wants, she's a-head of her time._____ Oh_____ and she nev - er gives

out_____ and she nev - er gives in, she just chang - es her mind.

Corresponding Chapter in *Manual for Ear Training and Sight Singing:* **72**

Vocal transposition: down 2nd–3rd

Robert Schumann, *Myrthen,* Op. 25, No. 7, "Die Lotosblume" (1840)

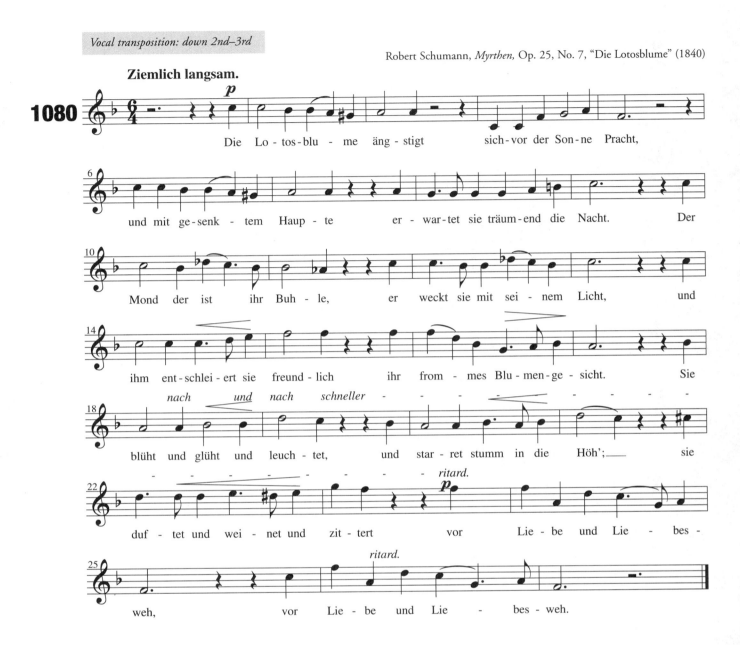

Vocal transposition: The range of this excerpt is slightly wider than the practical vocal range. Try transposing down a 2nd or 3rd and use good support for the high note in mm. 8–9 and the low note in mm. 17 and 21.

Robert Schumann, *Myrthen,* Op. 25, No. 1, "Widmung" (1840)

Vocal transposition: down 4th–6th

Richard Strauss, "Der Stern," Op. 69, No. 1 (1918)

1082

Freundlich bewegt

Ich se - he ihn wie - der den lieb - li - chen Stern; er win - ket her - nie - der, er

nah - te mir gern; er wär - met und fun - kelt, je nä - her er kömmt,

poco calando

_ die an - dern ver - dun - kelt, die Her - zen be - klemmt. Die

a tempo

Haa - re im Flie - gen er ei - let mir zu, das Volk träumt von Sie - gen,

ruhiger *poco rit.* *tempo primo*

ich träu - - me von Ruh. Die an - dern sich deu - ten die

poco cal. *sehr ruhig*

Zu - kunft dar - aus, ver - gan - ge - ne Zei - ten mir leuch - - - ten ins

a tempo, etwas breit

Haus.

Corresponding Chapter in *Manual for Ear Training and Sight Singing*: 72

Franz Liszt, *Les Préludes, Symphonic Poem after Lamartine*, mm. 370–385 (1855)

Hugo Wolf, *Italienisches Liederbuch,* No. 34,
"Und steht Ihr früh am Morgen auf," mm. 2–21 (1896)

1084

Und steht Ihr früh am Mor-gen auf vom Bet - te, scheucht Ihr vom Him-mel al - le Wol - ken fort, die Son-ne lockt Ihr auf die Ber-ge dort, und En-ge-lein er-schei - nen um die Wet - te und brin-gen Schuh und Klei - der Euch so-fort. Dann, wenn Ihr aus-geht in die heil' - ge Met-te, so weit Ihr al - le Men - schen mit Euch fort, und wenn Ihr naht der be-ne-dei-ten Stät - te, so zün-det Eu - er Blick die Lam - pen an.

Corresponding Chapter in *Manual for Ear Training and Sight Singing:* 72

Norman Petty and Charles Hardin [pseudonym for Buddy Holly], "Everyday" (1957)

1085

Very brightly

Ev - 'ry day   it's a - get-tin' clos - er,   Go - ing   fast - er

than a roll-er-coast-er,   Love like yours will   tru - ly come my   way.____

____   Ev - 'ry   day   it's a - get-tin' fast - er,   Ev - 'ry

one   said,   "Go on up and   ask   her,"   Love   like   yours   will   tru - ly

come   my   way.____   Ev - 'ry   day

seems a lit - tle long - er,   Ev - 'ry way   love's a lit - tle strong - er,

Come   what   may,   do   you   ev - er   long   for   true   love   from

me?____   Ev - 'ry   day   it's a - get-tin' clos - er,   Go - ing

fast - er   than a roll-er-coast - er,   Love   like   yours   will   tru - ly

1.
come my   way.____

2.
way.____

FRAGMENTS OF TONALITY

George Frideric Handel, *Flavio, Re de' Langobardi*, HWV 16,
Act II "Privarmi ancora dell'amata beltà?" (1723)

1086

W. A. Mozart, Cantata "Wo bin ich, bittrer Schmerz" (Grabmusik), K. 42 (35a), recitative (1767)

1087

W. A. Mozart, *Ascanio in Alba*, K. 111, Part II, "Cerco di loco in loco" (1771)

(continues)

Vocal transposition: down 2nd–7th

Ludwig van Beethoven, Symphony No. 8, Op. 93, mvt. 3, mm. 52–61 (1812)

1089

Vocal transposition: down 6th–7th

Joseph Haydn, String Quartet Op. 50, No. 4 (Hob. III:47), mvt. 1, mm. 91–100 (1787)

1090

Corresponding Chapter in *Manual for Ear Training and Sight Singing*: 73

Vocal transposition: down 4th–5th

Franz Schubert, Symphony No. 1, D. 82, mvt. 1, mm. 212–227 (1813)

1091

Hector Berlioz, *La damnation de Faust,* Part II, scene 6, "Certain rat, dans une cuisine" (Brander's Song), mm. 7–57 (1846)

1092

Cer - tain rat, dans u - ne cui - sine E - ta - bli, comme un vrai fra -

ter, S'y trai - tait si bien que sa mine Eût fait en -

vie au gros Lu - ther. Mais un beau jour le pau - vre dia - ble, Em - poi -

son - né, sau - ta de - hors Aus - si triste, aus - si mi -

sé - ra - ble Que s'il eût eu l'a - mour au corps!

Corresponding Chapter in *Manual for Ear Training and Sight Singing*: 73

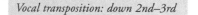
Vocal transposition: down 2nd–3rd

Samuel Barber, "In the Dark Pinewood," mm. 1–8 (1937)

Charles Ives, *Pictures,* mm. 23–30, [The Moor] (1906)

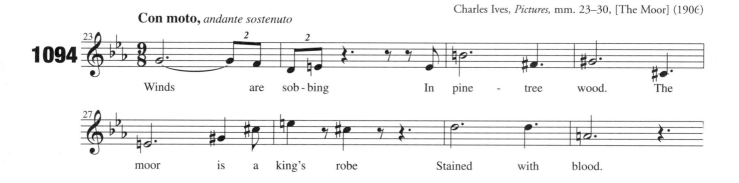

Corresponding Chapter in *Manual for Ear Training and Sight Singing:* **73**

Arthur Honegger, *Six poemes de Guillaume Apollinaire*, "Adieu" (1917)

1095

Pas trop lent. ♩ = 80   *p*

J'ai cueil - li   ce   brin de bru - yè - re   L'au - tomne est

mor - te   sou - viens t'en   Nous ne nous ver - rons plus sur ter - re

O - deur du temps   brin de bru - yè - - re

Et sou - viens toi que je t'at - tends____

Arthur Honegger, *Six poésies de Jean Cocteau*, No. 4, "Ex-Voto" (1923)

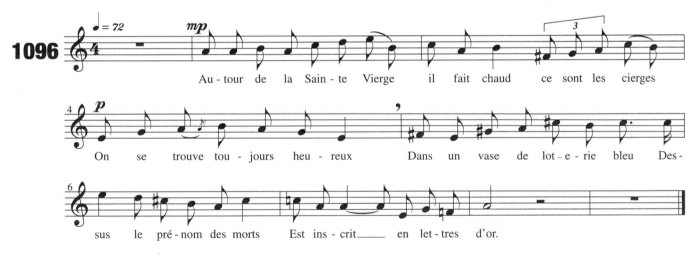

1096

♩ = 72   *mp*

Au - tour de la Sain - te Vierge   il fait chaud   ce sont les cierges

p

On se trouve tou - jours heu - reux   Dans un vase de lot - e - rie bleu Des -

sus le pré - nom des morts   Est ins - crit____ en let - tres d'or.

Corresponding Chapter in *Manual for Ear Training and Sight Singing*: 73

Vocal transposition: down 2nd–4th

Non vite

Erik Satie, *Aperçus désagréables,* "Fugue," mm. 4–10 (1912)

1097

p **Souriez**

Paul Hindemith, *Sing und Spielmusik für Liebhaber und Musikfreunde*
Op. 45, No. 1, "Frau Musica," first piece, mm. 29–42 (1928)

Mäßig schnell

1098

Hie kann nicht sein ein bö - ser Mut,_____ wo da sin - gen Ge -

sel - len gut; hie bleibt kein Zorn_____ noch Neid, wei - chen muß

Her - ze - leid; Geiz, Sorg und was sonst hart an - leit, fährt hin, fährt

hin mit al - ler, al - - ler Trau - rig - keit.

Vocal transposition: up 4th

Erik Satie, *Douze petits chorales,* No. 4 (1906)

Modéré sans lenteur

1099

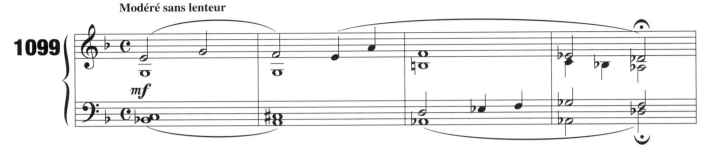

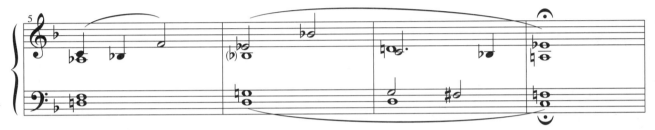

Corresponding Chapter in *Manual for Ear Training and Sight Singing:* 73

Vocal transposition: down 2nd–3rd

Hugo Wolf, "Heimweh" (1888)

1100

An - ders wird die Welt mit je - dem Schritt, den ich wei - ter von der Lieb - sten ma - che; mein Herz, das will nicht wei - ter mit.

Hier ____ scheint die Son - ne kalt ins Land, ____ ____ hier däucht mir al - les un - be - kannt, so - gar die Blu - men am Ba - che! Hat je - de Sa - che so fremd ei - ne Mie - ne, so falsch ein Ge - sicht.

Das Bäch - lein mur - melt wohl und spricht: ar - mer Kna - be, komm bei mir vor - ü - ber, siehst auch hier Ver - giss - mein - nicht! Ja die sind schön an je - dem Ort, a - ber nicht wie dort.

Fort, ____ nur fort! Die Au - gen geh'n ____ mir ü - ber!

Vocal transposition: down 2nd–3rd

Claude Debussy, "Beau soir" (1880)

1101

Andante ma non troppo.

Lorsque au so-leil cou-chant les ri - viè - res sont

ro - ses, Et qu'un tiè - de fris-son court sur les champs de blé,

Un con - seil d'être heu - reux sem - ble sor - tir des cho - ses

Et mon - ter vers le cœur trou - blé Un con -

seil de goû-ter le char - me d'être au mon - de Ce-pen-dant qu'on est

jeune et que le soir est beau, Car nous nous en al - lons,

Com-me s'en va cette on - de Elle a la mer,

Nous au tom - beau.

Vocal transposition: up 2nd

Carl Nielsen, Symphony No. 2, Op. 16, mvt. 3, mm. 2–14 (1902)

Vocal transposition: down 3rd–4th

Hugo Wolf, *Italienisches Liederbuch,* No. 36, "Wenn du, mein Liebster, steigst zum Himmel auf" (1896)

The following excerpt may tax your ability to think in terms of tonal fragments.
Why is this the case? How else might you approach this kind of music?

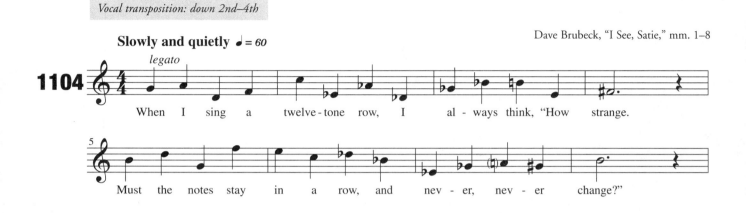

Vocal transposition: down 2nd–4th

Slowly and quietly ♩ = 60

Dave Brubeck, "I See, Satie," mm. 1–8

1104

legato

When I sing a twelve-tone row, I al - ways think, "How strange.

Must the notes stay in a row, and nev - er, nev - er change?"

Corresponding Chapter in *Manual for Ear Training and Sight Singing: 73*

ADVANCED METER

"Prinz Eugen, der edle Ritter," German folk song

1105

Vocal transposition: down 5th–6th

Peter Ilich Tchaikovsky, Symphony No. 6, Op. 74 ("Pathétique"), mvt. 2, mm. 1–9 (1893)

Allegro con grazia (♩ = 144)

1106

Vocal transposition: down 2nd–6th

Benjamin Britten, *War Requiem*, Op. 66, "Agnus Dei," mm. 3–18 (1962)

Slow ♪ = 80
(*Lento*)

1107

One e-ver hangs___ where shelled roads part.___ In this

war___ He too lost a limb, But His di-sci-ples

hide a-part;___ And now the Sol-diers bear with Him.

Corresponding Chapter in *Manual for Ear Training and Sight Singing*: 74

Nicolai Rimsky-Korsakov, *Russian Easter Festival Overture,* Op. 36, mm. 1–3 (1888)

Benjamin Britten, *Peter Grimes,* Op. 33, Act II, "O All Ye Works of the Lord," rehearsal 12, mm. 1–8 (1945)

Vocal transposition: down 3rd–5th

Edward Elgar, *Caractacus,* Op. 35, scene 4, "Lament," mm. 1–6 (1898)

* This division is made for convenience only: there should be no accent, however, on the fourth crochet.

Corresponding Chapter in *Manual for Ear Training and Sight Singing:* 74

"Koledo," Bulgarian folk song

"Ej, sama moma tsrny ochy," Macedonian folk song

"Urrundik," Basque folk song

Corresponding Chapter in *Manual for Ear Training and Sight Singing*: 74

"Zortziko," Basque folk dance

"Ishala mashala," Bulgarian folk song

"Lemperino maloj mome," Macedonian folk song

The following excerpt may be performed as a round with up to six voices, each entering at four-measure intervals.

Benjamin Britten, *Peter Grimes,* Act I, "Ned Keene Starts a Round," mm. 2–25 (1945)

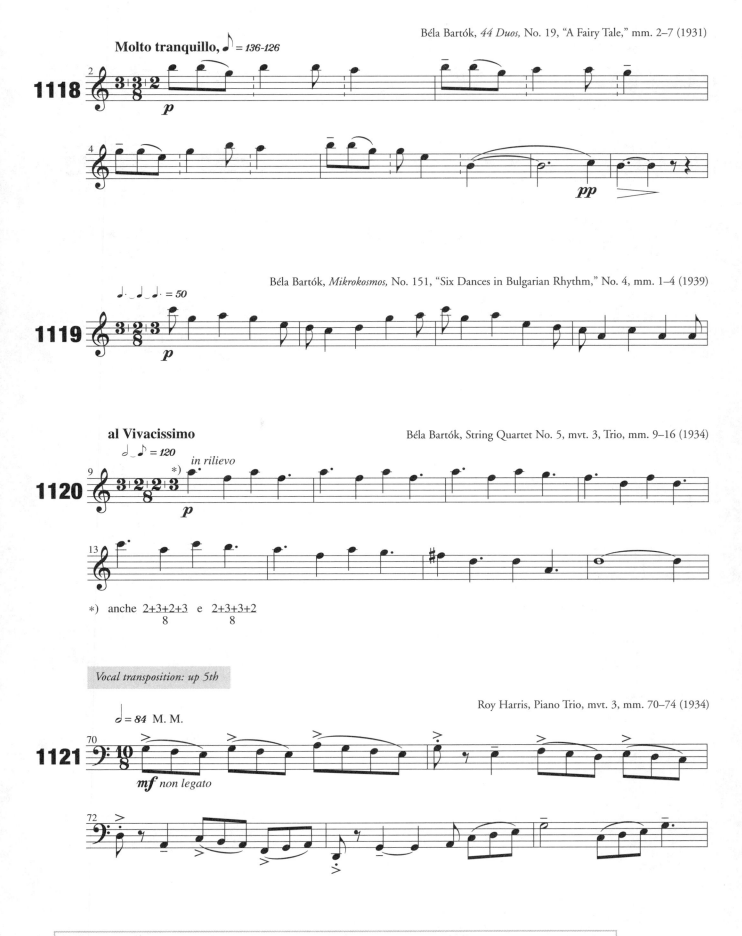

*) anche 2+3+2+3 e 2+3+3+2
          8   8

Vocal transposition: up 5th

Roy Harris, Symphony No. 7, rehearsal 32, mm. 8–14 (1955)

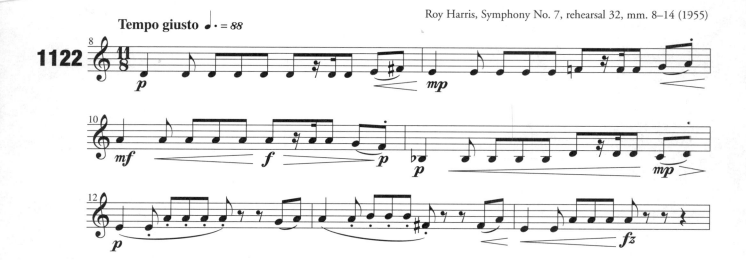

Nicolai Rimsky-Korsakov, *The Snow Maiden,* final chorus,
Hymn to the Sun-God Yarilo, mm. 4–9 (1881)

Corresponding Chapter in *Manual for Ear Training and Sight Singing*: 74

Igor Stravinsky, *Le cinq doigts,* No. 1, mm. 1–11 (1921)

Andantino

1124

"Là-haut, à la montagne," French folk song, mm. 1–9

1125

"Quand mon père il m'a mariée," French folk song

1126

André Previn, Theme from *Valley of the Dolls,* mm. 1–20 (1967)
[lyrics by Dory Previn]

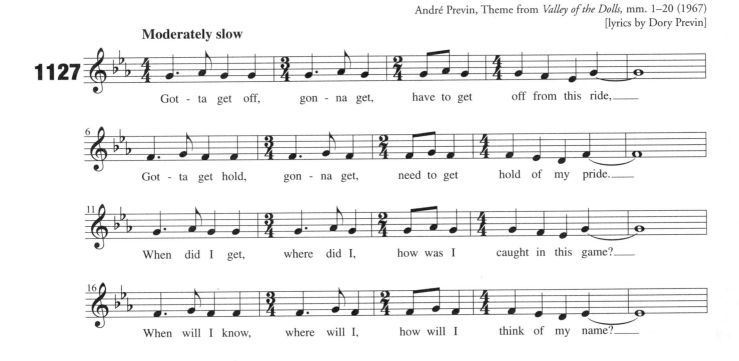

1127

Got - ta get off, gon - na get, have to get off from this ride,____

Got - ta get hold, gon - na get, need to get hold of my pride.____

When did I get, where did I, how was I caught in this game?____

When will I know, where will I, how will I think of my name?____

Alexander Borodin, Symphony No. 2, mvt. 3, mm. 91–96 (1887)

1128

William Schuman, *Concerto on Old English Rounds,* mvt. 1,
"Amaryllis—Introduction & Variations," mm. 1–5 (1974)

1129

TURN AM - A - RYL - LIS TO THY SWAIN, THY

DA - MON CALLS THEE BACK A - - - GAIN

Corresponding Chapter in *Manual for Ear Training and Sight Singing: 74*

Nicolai Rimsky-Korsakov, *Russian Easter Festival Overture,* Op. 36, rehearsal L, mm. 2–13 (1888)

Poco più sostenuto e tranquillo.

1130

Vocal transposition: up 2nd–7th

Nicolai Rimsky-Korsakov, *Russian Easter Festival Overture,* Op. 36, rehearsal Y, mm. 16–28 (1888)

Maestoso

1131

Vocal transposition: down 3rd–4th

Charles Gounod, *Mireille,* Act I, "Chanson de Magali," mm. 5–19 (1864)

Allegretto.

1132

La brise est douce et par-fu - mée   L'oi-seau s'en-dort sous la ra -

mé - e   Au   fond du bois si - len - ci - eux___   Au   fond du bois si - len - ci -

eux___   La   nuit sur nous é-tend son   voi - le   Et   dans les cieux   Je

vois   une a - mou-reuse é-toi - le   Luire   à   mes   yeux!___

Corresponding Chapter in *Manual for Ear Training and Sight Singing:* 74

"Ah! Que les femmes sont bêtes," French folk song

1133

Vocal transposition: down 2nd–5th

Johannes Brahms, *Lieder und Gesänge,* Op. 63, No. 8, "Heimweh," II, mm. 4–13 (1874)

Etwas langsam

1134

O wüßt ich doch den Weg zu - rück, den

lie - ben Weg __ zum Kin - der - land! O war - um sucht ich

nach dem Glück und ließ der Mut - ter

Hand, der Mut - - - - ter Hand?

Corresponding Chapter in *Manual for Ear Training and Sight Singing:* 74

Vocal transposition: down 2nd–4th

In a moderate waltz time

Charles Ives, "The Side Show" (1921)

1135

"Is__ that Mis - ter Ri - ley, who keeps the ho -

tel?" is the tune that ac - comp'-nies the trott - ing track bell; An

old horse un - sound, turns the mer - ry - go - round, mak - ing

poor Mis - ter Ri - ley look a bit like a Rus - sian dance,__

__ Some speak of so high - ly, as they do of Ri - ley!

Molto moderato e pesante

Alexander Borodin, "Song of the Dark Forest," mm. 4–16 (1868)

1136

Tyom - ny lyes shu - myel, tyom - ny lyes gu - dyel, pyes - nyu pyel, pyes - nyu

sta - ru - yu, byl' by - va - lu - yu, ska - zy - val: kak zhi -

va - la tam vo - lya - vo - lyush - ka, vol' - na - ya; kak sbi -

ra - las' tam si - la - si - lush - ka, sil' - na - ya.

Corresponding Chapter in *Manual for Ear Training and Sight Singing*: 74

"Jetzt fängt das schöne Früjahr an," German folk song

Paul Hindemith, Sonata for Viola and Piano,
Op. 11, No. 4, mvt. 2, mm. 1–12 (1919)

Ruhig und einfach, wie ein Volkslied

Vocal transposition: down 2nd–7th

Johannes Brahms, *Lieder und Gesänge,* Op. 59, No. 5, "Agnes," mm. 3–17 (1873)

Corresponding Chapter in *Manual for Ear Training and Sight Singing*: 74

Vocal transposition: down 2nd–6th

Johannes Brahms, *Sieben Lieder,* Op. 95, No. 1, "Das Mädchen," mm. 1–8 (1883)

Munter, mit freiem Vortrag

1140

Stand das Mäd - chen, stand am Ber - ges - ab - hang,

wi - der - schien der Berg von - ih - rem Ant - litz, und das Mäd - chen

sprach zu ih - rem Ant - litz: "Wahr - lich, Ant - litz, o du mei - ne Sor - ge,"

Hindemith notated the following excerpt without a meter sign. What do you suppose this means? Compare with No. 1185.

Paul Hindemith, Sonata for Viola and Piano, Op. 11, No. 4, mvt. 3, mm. 45–54 (1919)

Breit

1141

Manuel de Falla, *El retablo de maese Pedro,* scene 2, "Melisendra, mm. 1–12 (1923)

Molto lento e sostenuto

1142

dolce marc. il canto

Corresponding Chapter in *Manual for Ear Training and Sight Singing*: 74

"Tus ojos," Spanish folk song

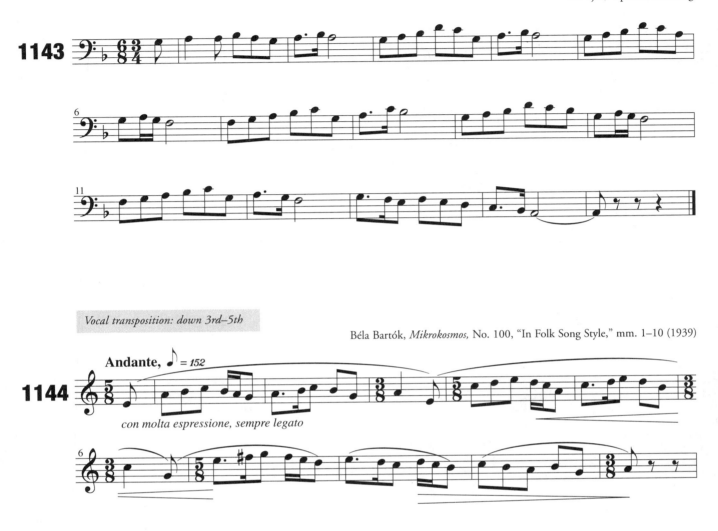

Vocal transposition: down 3rd–5th

Béla Bartók, *Mikrokosmos,* No. 100, "In Folk Song Style," mm. 1–10 (1939)

Andante, ♪ = 152

con molta espressione, sempre legato

Vocal transposition: down 4th–5th

George Frideric Handel, *Rinaldo,* HWV 7, Act III, "Bel piacere," mm. 9–40 (1711)

1145

Vocal transposition: down 2nd–5th

Germaine Tailleferre, "Pastorale," mm. 1–8 (1919)

1146

Charles Ives, "1, 2, 3," mm. 19–31 (1921)

1147

Why   does-n't   one, two, three   seem   to   ap - peal

to   a   Yan - kee   as   much   as   one,   two!

Corresponding Chapter in *Manual for Ear Training and Sight Singing: 74*

MORE ADVANCED RHYTHMS

George Frideric Handel, Keyboard Suite HWV 430, mvt. 4,
Air ("Harmonious Blacksmith"), mm. 35–39 [Double 5] (1720)

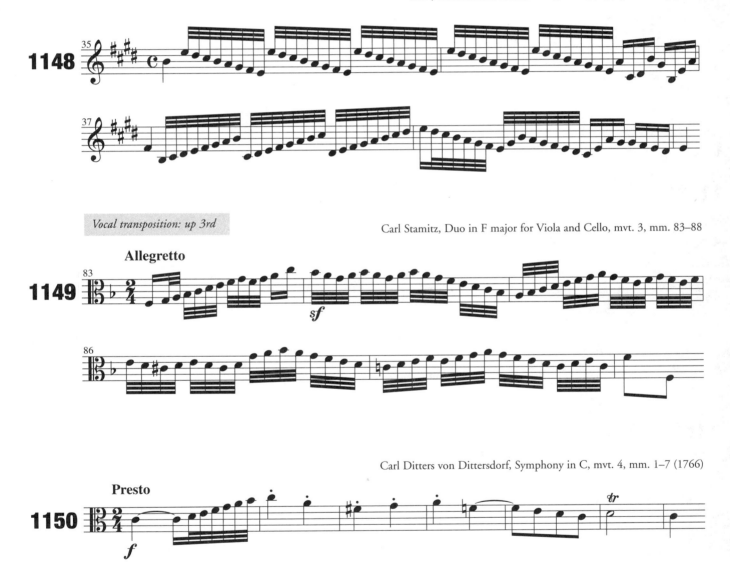

Vocal transposition: up 3rd

Carl Stamitz, Duo in F major for Viola and Cello, mvt. 3, mm. 83–88

Carl Ditters von Dittersdorf, Symphony in C, mvt. 4, mm. 1–7 (1766)

J. S. Bach, Flute Sonata BWV 1030, mvt. 1, mm. 1–2 (c. 1736)

Corresponding Chapter in *Manual for Ear Training and Sight Singing*: 75

Vocal transposition: down 3rd–4th

Hélène Riese Liebmann, *Grande sonate,* Op. 15, mvt. 3, mm. 1–8 (1815)

Rondo alla Polacca

1152

Allegro spiritoso

W. A. Mozart, Symphony No. 28, K. 200 (189ᵏ), mvt. 1, mm. 3–7 (c. 1774)

1153

J. S. Bach, *Well-Tempered Clavier,* Book I, Fugue in D major (No. 5), BWV 850, mm. 1–5 (1722)

1154

*This dot is worth only a 32nd note

Corresponding Chapter in *Manual for Ear Training and Sight Singing:* 75

W. A. Mozart, *The Magic Flute,* K. 620, Act II, "Ein Mädchen oder Weibchen wünscht Papageno sich!," mm. 9–20 (1791)

1155 Ein Mäd-chen o-der Weib - chen wünscht Pa-pa-ge-no sich! O

so ein sanf-tes Täub - chen wär' Se-lig-keit für mich! wär'

Se-lig-keit für mich! wär' Se-lig-keit für mich!

Vocal transposition: down 2nd–3rd

Robert Schumann, Piano Sonata No. 1, Op. 11, mvt. 1, mm. 7–13 (1835)

1156

Joseph Haydn, Symphony No. 67, mvt. 2, mm. 1–10 (c. 1776?)

1157

Corresponding Chapter in *Manual for Ear Training and Sight Singing:* 75

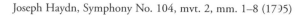

Joseph Haydn, Symphony No. 104, mvt. 2, mm. 1–8 (1795)

Vocal transposition: down 6th

Joseph Haydn, Symphony No. 101, mvt. 2, mm. 2–10 (1794)

Corresponding Chapter in *Manual for Ear Training and Sight Singing*: 75

Joseph Haydn, Symphony No. 55, mvt. 2, mm. 1–24 (1774)

Adagio ma semplicemente

1160

J. S. Bach, Orchestra Suite No. 2, BWV 1067, Overture, mm. 1–11 (c. 1739)

Overture

1161

C. P. E. Bach, *Kurze und leichte Clavierstücke mit veränderten Reprisen*, No. 8, "Allegretto," mm. 1–4 (1766)

Vocal transposition: down 2nd–7th

1162

Corresponding Chapter in *Manual for Ear Training and Sight Singing*: 75

C. P. E. Bach, *Kurze und leichte Clavierstücke mit veränderten Reprisen,* No. 22, "Poco allegro," mm. 1–4 (1766)

W. A. Mozart, *The Marriage of Figaro,* K. 492, Sinfonia, mm. 221–228 (1786)

J. S. Bach, *Well-Tempered Clavier,* Book II, Fugue in D minor (No. 6), BWV 875, mm. 1–3 (c. 1740)

J. S. Bach, Flute Sonata BWV 1030, mvt. 1, mm. 100–103 (c. 1736)

Corresponding Chapter in *Manual for Ear Training and Sight Singing:* 75

Gioachino Rossini, *L'Italiana in Algeri,* Act II, "Per lui che adoro," mm. 41–52 (1813)

1167

Tu sai se l'a - mo, pia - - - - cer gli io

bra - mo: Gra - - - - zie, pre - - - -

sta - te - mi vez - zi e splen - - dor,

vez - zi, vez - zi, gra - zie, gra - zie, vez - zi e splen - dor.

Vocal transposition: down 4th–6th

Antonín Dvořák, Cello Concerto Op. 104, mvt. 3, mm. 33–40 (1895)

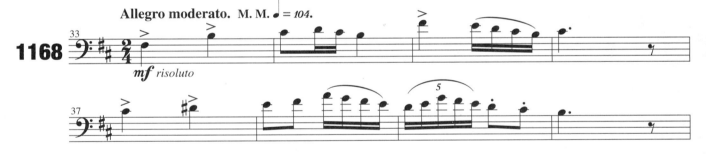

1168

Johannes Brahms, Symphony No. 3, Op. 90, mvt. 3, mm. 1–12 (1883)

1169

Corresponding Chapter in *Manual for Ear Training and Sight Singing*: 75

Vocal transposition: The range of this excerpt is a bit too wide to fit the practical sight-singing range. Transpose down a 3rd or 4th and use good support for the low notes in mm. 815–818 and the high note at the end.

Béla Bartók, Suite No. 1 for Orchestra, Op. 3, mvt. 3, mm. 815–831 (1905)

1170

Frédéric Chopin, Prelude Op. 28, No. 15, mm. 1–8 (1839)

1171

Frédéric Chopin, Nocturne Op. 15, No. 2, mm. 1–4 (1832)

1172

Corresponding Chapter in *Manual for Ear Training and Sight Singing*: 75

Gian Carlo Menotti, *Amahl and the Night Visitors,* mm. 557–572 (1951)

Corresponding Chapter in *Manual for Ear Training and Sight Singing:* 75

Sempre molto vivace

(♩ = *110-120*)

Béla Bartók, Suite No. 1 for Orchestra, Op. 3, mvt. 3, mm. 279–285 (1905)

1174

Charles Ives, *Three Places in New England,* No. 3,
"The Housatonic at Stockbridge," mm. 8–12 (1921)

Adagio molto (*Very slowly*) (about *50* = ♩)

1175

Corresponding Chapter in *Manual for Ear Training and Sight Singing:* **75**

SOME COMMON NON-DIATONIC PITCH COLLECTIONS

Mikhail Glinka, *Ruslan and Lyudmila*, Overture, mm. 349–360 (1842)

1176

Perform the following excerpt at a slower, more singable tempo.

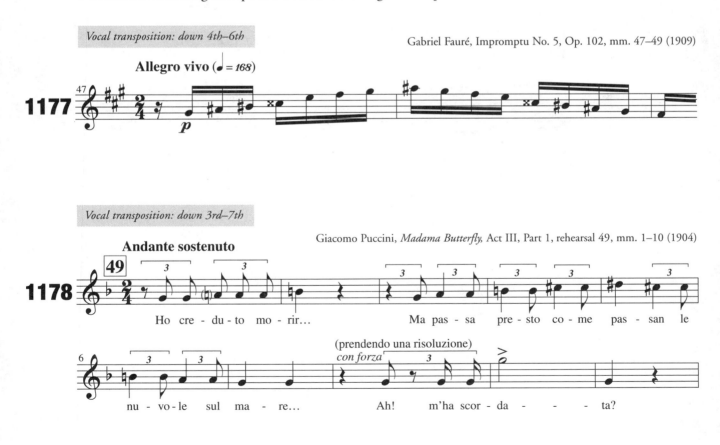

Vocal transposition: down 4th–6th

Gabriel Fauré, Impromptu No. 5, Op. 102, mm. 47–49 (1909)

Allegro vivo (♩ = 168)

1177

Vocal transposition: down 3rd–7th

Giacomo Puccini, *Madama Butterfly*, Act III, Part 1, rehearsal 49, mm. 1–10 (1904)

Andante sostenuto

1178

Ho cre-du-to mo-rir...   Ma pas-sa pre-sto co-me pas-san le

nu-vo-le sul ma-re...   Ah!   m'ha scor-da---ta?

Claude Debussy, *Estampes,* No. 2, "La soirée dans Grenade," mm. 61–66 (1903)

Mouvement de Habanera
tempo rubato

1179

p expressif

retenu - - - - -

dim. - - - - p

Vocal transposition: down 3rd–6th

Claude Debussy, "L'isle joyeuse," mm. 117–120 (1904)

Tempo: Modéré et très souple

Un peu cédé. Molto rubato

1180

p expressif et en dehors

Vocal transposition: down 4th–5th

Claude Debussy, *Six épigraphes antiques,* No. 2, "Pour un tombeau sans nom," mm. 8–11 (1915)

Triste et lent ♩ = *60*

1181

p

più p

Corresponding Chapter in *Manual for Ear Training and Sight Singing:* 76

George Rochberg, "Psalm 23," mm. 1–6 (1954)

Corresponding Chapter in *Manual for Ear Training and Sight Singing*: 76

The following excerpt is from the right-hand part of a work for piano. Sing it as a duet.

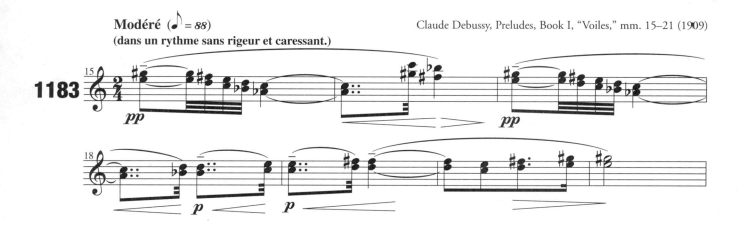

Claude Debussy, Preludes, Book I, "Voiles," mm. 15–21 (1909)

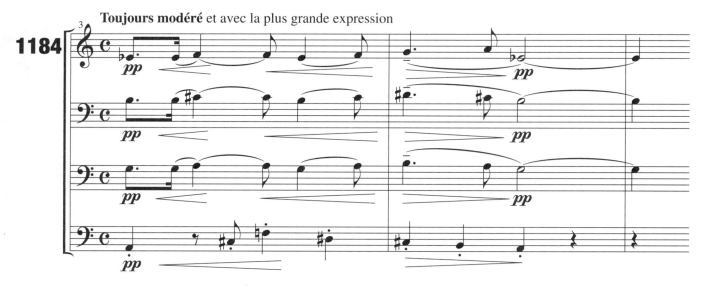

Claude Debussy, *Pelléas et Mélisande,* Act IV, scene 2, rehearsal B, mm. 3–5 (1902)

What do you make of the rhythm and meter in the following excerpt? How does the use of non-diatonic pitch collections reflect the text?

Charles Ives, "The Cage" (1906)

NOTE: All notes not marked with sharp or flat are natural.

Perform the following excerpt at a slower, more singable tempo.

Béla Bartók, Suite, Op. 14, No. 3, mm. 27–33 (1916)

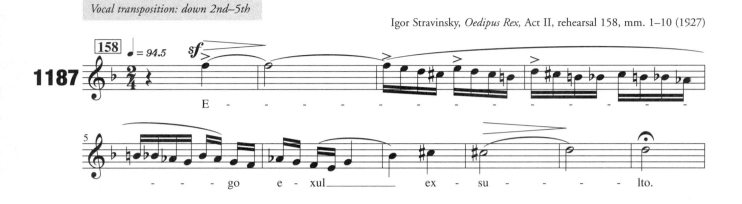

Vocal transposition: down 2nd–5th

Igor Stravinsky, *Oedipus Rex,* Act II, rehearsal 158, mm. 1–10 (1927)

E - - - - - - - - - - - - - - - go e - xul___ ex - su - - - lto.

Perform the following excerpt at a slower, more singable tempo.

Benjamin Britten, Sonata Op. 65, mvt. 5 ("Moto perpetuo"), mm. 1–7 (1961)

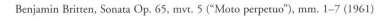

Vocal transposition: up 4th–5th

Alexander Scriabin, Prelude Op. 74, No. 3, mm. 21–26 (1914)

Béla Bartók, *Mikrokosmos,* No. 101, "Diminished Fifth," mm. 1–5 (1939)

Béla Bartók, *44 Duos,* No. 33, "Song of the Harvest," mm. 1–5 (1931)

Corresponding Chapter in *Manual for Ear Training and Sight Singing*: 76

Only those with the widest ranges can sing the top part in the following excerpt.

Charles Ives, "Psalm XXIV," mm. 22–27 (c. 1913)

Béla Bartók, *Mikrokosmos,* No. 131, "Fourths," mm. 1–8 (1939)

The top two parts of the following excerpts should be sung by sopranos with very high ranges (or, alternatively, played on an instrument). The lowest part should be sung by basses with lower ranges, taking the last measure up an octave.

Dave Brubeck, *Nocturnes,* "Study in Fourths," mm. 1–8

Vocal transposition: down 2nd–4th

Alban Berg, *Wozzeck,* Op. 7, Act I, scene 2, mm. 12–16 (1922)

Das ist die schö - ne Jä - ge - rei, Schie - ßen steht Je - dem frei!

Corresponding Chapter in *Manual for Ear Training and Sight Singing:* 76

HYPERMETER

What are the hypermetric implications of Beethoven's performance indications in the following excerpt?

Più presto quasi prestissimo ♩. = *100*
Si ha s'immaginar la battuta di 𝄴

Ludwig van Beethoven, String Quartet Op. 74, mvt. 3, mm. 78–95 (1809)

1196

Sing the following excerpt at concert pitch.

Ludwig van Beethoven, Symphony No. 6, Op. 68
("Pastoral"), mvt. 3, mm. 133–161 (1808)

1197

Sing the following excerpt at concert pitch.

George Frideric Handel, *Water Music* Suite No. 1, HWV 348, mvt. 5, mm. 1–46 (1717)

Vocal transposition: The range of the following excerpt is a bit large, but try to accommodate the low Gs and high Fs (in your own octave, of course).

Hector Berlioz, *Symphonie fantastique*, Op. 14, mvt. 2, "Un bal," mm. 120–160 (1830)

Robert Schumann, *Kinderscenen*, Op. 15, No. 1,
"Von fremden Ländern und Menschen" (1838)

Vocal transposition: down 3rd–5th

Corresponding Chapter in *Manual for Ear Training and Sight Singing*: 77

"Gift Song," Chippewa Native American song, mm. 1–13

Vocal transposition: down 2nd–6th

Johannes Brahms, Variations on a Theme by Joseph Haydn, Op. 56ᵃ, mm. 1–29 (1873)

"Amsterdam," English psalm-tune (1742)

1203

(continues)

Corresponding Chapter in *Manual for Ear Training and Sight Singing*: 77

Rise my soul and haste a - way, To seats pre - par'd a - bove.

Rise my soul and haste a - way, To seats pre - par'd a - bove.

Rise my soul and haste a - way, To seats pre - par'd a - bove.

Rise my soul and haste a - way, To seats pre - par'd a - bove.

Corresponding Chapter in *Manual for Ear Training and Sight Singing:* 77

Vocal transposition: down 2nd

Nicolai Rimsky-Korsakov, *Two Choruses for Children's Voices*, No. 2, "Kitty" (1884)

1204

Once there was a kit - ty cat   Who was such a

Once there was a kit - ty cat   Who was such a

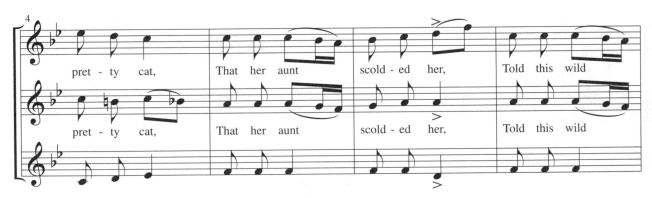

pret - ty cat,   That her aunt   scold - ed her,   Told this wild

pret - ty cat,   That her aunt   scold - ed her,   Told this wild

gid - dy cat,   Ah!   "Don't you wan - der too

gid - dy cat,   To this wild   gid - dy cat: "Don't you wan - der too

far from home,   Though I know you would   like to roam,   Don't you wan - der

far from home,   Though I know you would   like to roam,   Don't you wan - der

(continues)

Corresponding Chapter in *Manual for Ear Training and Sight Singing*: 77

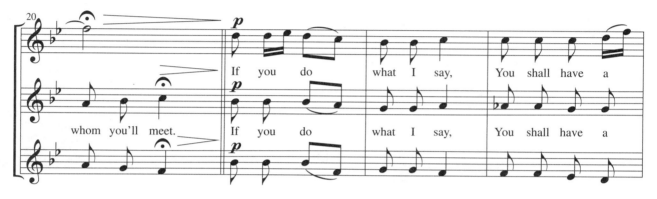

Corresponding Chapter in *Manual for Ear Training and Sight Singing: 77*

Is the following excerpt tonal or modal? Why? How will the solmization of a tonal interpretation differ from a modal one? How does the text interact with the hyper-metric structure?

Nicolai Rimsky-Korsakov, *One Hundred Folk Songs,* Op. 24, No. 12, "There upon the Field, See the Fog So Dense Descend" (1876)

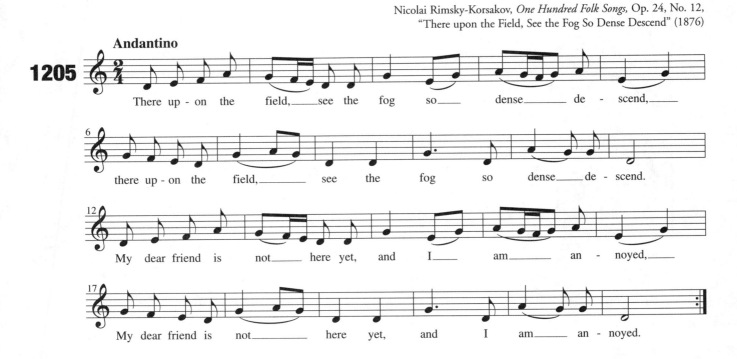

2. My dear friend has left, but for just a little while, *(2 times)*
   My dear friend has promised me—I'll return quite soon *(2 times)*

3. If when you return, wave your hand to welcome me, *(2 times)*
   But, he never waved to me, as the good Lord knows! *(2 times)*

4. So all by myself, I remained alone at home. *(2 times)*
   I shall go to my own room, waiting on the bench! *(2 times)*

5. On the bench I'll sit, by the new oak table there! *(2 times)*
   My dear friend is not here yet, and I am annoyed! *(2 times)*

Corresponding Chapter in *Manual for Ear Training and Sight Singing:* **77**

Vocal transposition: down 2nd

Joseph Haydn, Canon, "Vixi" (Hob. XXVIIb:10) (c. 1799)

1206

The following excerpt is an example of a "teasing song," a humorous musico-poetic form that has a long tradition. How does the hypermetric structure of this song contribute to its humor?

"Miss Susie," teasing song

1207

Miss Sus-ie had a steam-boat, the steam-boat had a bell, Miss Su-sie went to - heav-en, the

steam-boat went to Hell-o Op-er - a-tor, please give me num-ber nine, and if you dis-con-

nect me, I'll kick you from be-hind the 'fridg-er - a-tor, there was a piece of glass, Miss

Sus-ie sat up - on it, and cut her lit-tle Ask me no more ques-tions, I'll tell you no more

lies, the boys are in the bath-room, zip-ping up their flies are in the mead-ow,

bees are in the park, Miss Sus-ie and her boy-friend, are kiss-ing in the dark.

Corresponding Chapter in *Manual for Ear Training and Sight Singing:* **77**

ADDITIONAL EXCERPTS
FOR SIGHT SINGING

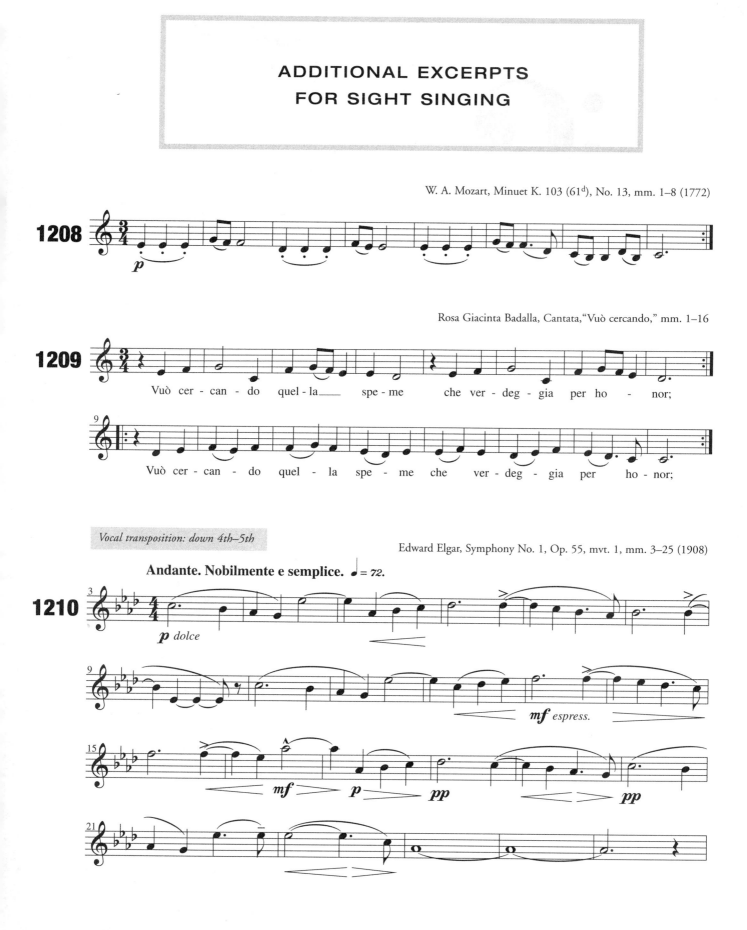

W. A. Mozart, Minuet K. 103 (61^d), No. 13, mm. 1–8 (1772)

1208

Rosa Giacinta Badalla, Cantata, "Vuò cercando," mm. 1–16

1209

Vuò cer - can - do quel - la____ spe - me che ver - deg - gia per ho - nor;

Vuò cer - can - do quel - la spe - me che ver - deg - gia per ho - nor;

Vocal transposition: down 4th–5th

Edward Elgar, Symphony No. 1, Op. 55, mvt. 1, mm. 3–25 (1908)

Andante. Nobilmente e semplice. ♩ = 72.

1210

p dolce

mf espress.

mf   *p*   *pp*   *pp*

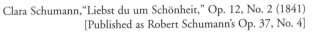

Clara Schumann, "Liebst du um Schönheit," Op. 12, No. 2 (1841)
[Published as Robert Schumann's Op. 37, No. 4]

1211

Nicht zu langsam.

Liebst du um Schön-heit, o nicht mich lie-be! Lie-be die Son-ne, sie trägt ein gold'-nes Haar!___ Liebst du um Ju-gend, o nicht_ mich lie-be! Lie-be den Früh-ling, der jung ist je-des Jahr! Liebst du um Schä-tze, o nicht_ mich lie-be! Lie-be die Meer-frau, sie hat viel Per-len klar. Liebst du um Lie-be, o ja_ mich lie-be! Liebst du um Lie-be, o ja mich lie-be, lie-be mich im-mer, dich lieb ich im-mer-dar!___

"Ah ree rahng," Korean folk song

1212

Franz Liszt, *Les Préludes, Symphonic Poem after Lamartine*, mm. 47–50 (1855)

1213

Vocal transposition: down 2nd–3rd

Peter Ilich Tchaikovsky, *1812, Festival Overture*, Op. 49, mm. 165–176 (1880)

1214

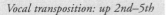

Vocal transposition: up 2nd–5th

Johannes Brahms, Symphony No. 1, Op. 68, mvt. 4, mm. 62–78 (1876)

Allegro non troppo, ma con brio

1215

Christoph Willibald von Gluck, *Ezio,* Act I, "Pensa a serbarmi," mm. 13–22 (1750)

Moderato

1216

Pen - sa a ser - bar - mi, o ca - ra, i dol - ci af - fet - ti

tuo - i, i dol - ci af - fet - ti_ tuo - - i:

Vocal transposition: up 3rd–4th

Béla Bartók, *First Term at the Piano,* No. 14, mm. 1–4 (1913)

Andante. (♩ = *69*)

1217

p sempre legato

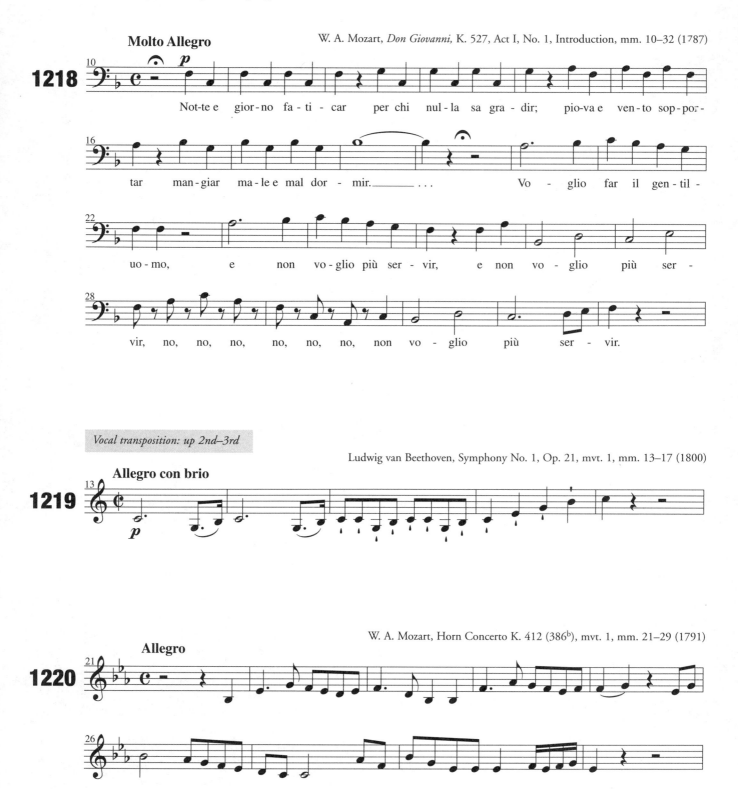

Molto Allegro

W. A. Mozart, *Don Giovanni,* K. 527, Act I, No. 1, Introduction, mm. 10–32 (1787)

1218

Not-te e gior-no fa-ti-car per chi nul-la sa gra-dir; pio-va e ven-to sop-por-

tar man-giar ma-le e mal dor - mir._____ ... Vo - glio far il gen-til-

uo - mo, e non vo-glio più ser - vir, e non vo - glio più ser-

vir, no, no, no, no, no, no, non vo - glio più ser - vir.

Vocal transposition: up 2nd–3rd

Ludwig van Beethoven, Symphony No. 1, Op. 21, mvt. 1, mm. 13–17 (1800)

Allegro con brio

1219

W. A. Mozart, Horn Concerto K. 412 (386ᵇ), mvt. 1, mm. 21–29 (1791)

Allegro

1220

Vocal transposition: down 3rd–4th

Clara Schumann, Piano Trio Op. 17, mvt. 1, mm. 1–8 (1846)

1221

Vocal transposition: down 3rd–5th

Johannes Brahms, *Sechs Gesänge,* Op. 3, No. 4,
"Lied aus dem Gedicht 'Ivan'," mm. 1–4 (1853)

1222

Mit feurigem Schwung

Weit üb - er das Feld durch die Lüf - - te hoch nach

Beu - - te ein mäch - ti - ger Gei - er___ flog.

J. S. Bach, Cantata No. 147, "Herz und Mund und Tat und Leben,"
No. 10, "Jesus bleibet meine Freude," mm. 1–9 (1723)

Vocal transposition: down 3rd–4th

1223

J. S. Bach, *Well-Tempered Clavier*, Book II, Prelude in B♭ major
(No. 21), BWV 890, mm. 1–6 (c. 1740)

1224

Vocal transposition: This excerpt is a bit wider than the practical vocal range. Transpose down a 3rd or 4th and use good support for the low note in m. 14 and the high note in m. 18.

Rosa Giacinta Badalla, *Motetti a voce sola*, "Pane angelico," mm. 9–19 (1684)

1225

De coe - lo ra - pi - di, o— cho - ri an - ge - li - ci, ve - ni - te vo -

la - - - - - - - - - - - - te,

Vocal transposition: down 2nd–6th

W. A. Mozart, Bassoon Concerto K. 191 (186ᵉ), mvt. 3, Rondo, mm. 89–96 (1774)

Tempo di Minuetto

1226

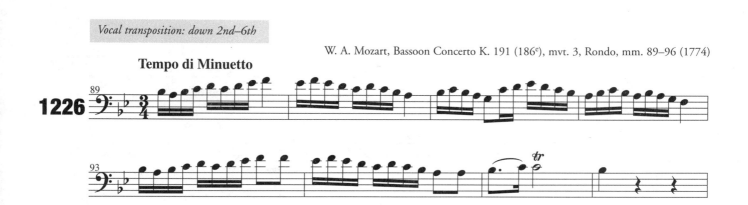

Vocal transposition: down 3rd–7th

Ludwig van Beethoven, Symphony No. 1, Op. 21, mvt. 4, mm. 7–22 (1800)

Allegro molto e vivace

1227

Vocal transposition: This excerpt is a bit wider than the practical vocal range. Transpose down a 2nd or 3rd and use good support for the low note in m. 16 and the high note in mm. 21–22.

W. A. Mozart, Six-Voice Canon K. 231 (382ᶜ) (c. 1782)

1228

Laßt froh uns sein! Laßt uns froh sein! Mur - ren

ist ver - ge - bens! Knur - ren, Brum - men ist ver - ge - bens, ist das

wah - re Kreuz des Le - bens, das Brum - men ist ver - ge - bens,

Knur - ren, Brum - men ist ver - ge - bens, ver - ge - bens!

Drum laßt uns froh und fröh - lich, froh sein! Laßt uns froh und fröh - lich, froh sein!

W. A. Mozart, *Vier Rätselkanons,* K. 89ªII (73ʳ), No. 3 (1770)
[canon at the 12th; second voice begins at *]

1229

Con - fi - te - bor ti - bi___ Do - mi - ne   in gen - - ti - bus,

et no - mi - ni   tu - o can - ta - - - - - - - - - - - bo.___

Joseph Haydn, Symphony No. 104, mvt. 3, mm. 1–16 (1795)

1230

Vocal transposition: up 2nd–6th

Johannes Brahms, Symphony No. 1, Op. 68, mvt. 4, mm. 30–38 (1876)

1231

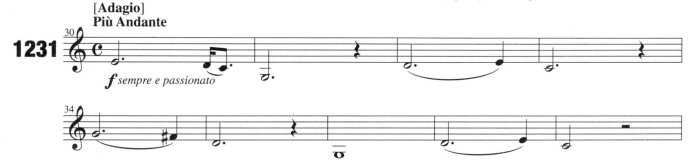

Vocal transposition: down 5th–6th

Giuseppi Verdi, *La traviata,* Act II, No. 6, mm. 81–98 (1853)

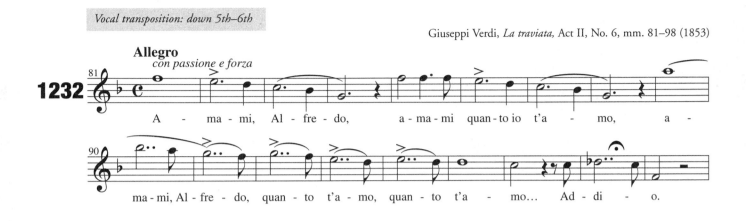

1232

A - ma - mi, Al - fre - do, a - ma - mi quan - to io t'a - mo, a -

ma - mi, Al - fre - do, quan - to t'a - mo, quan - to t'a - mo... Ad - di - o.

Antonín Dvořák, Slavonic Dance Op. 46, No. 4, mm. 71–85 (1878)

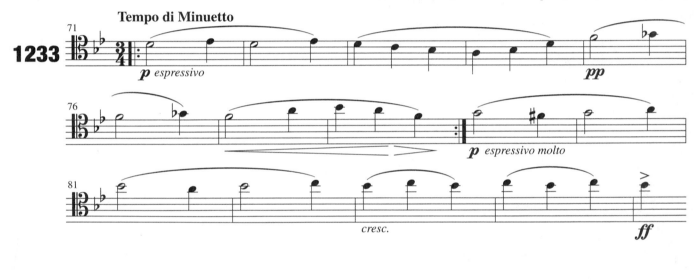

1233

Vocal transposition: up 3rd–5th

Johannes Brahms, Symphony No. 3, Op. 90, mvt. 4, mm. 1–4 (1883)

1234

Vocal transposition: down 3rd–4th

Richard Wagner, *Lohengrin,* Act III, Prelude, mm. 16–49 (1848)

1235

Vocal transposition: down 2nd–6th

Arthur Sullivan, *The Yeomen of the Guard,* Act I,
"This the Autumn of Our Life," mm. 27–43 (1888)

1236

USEFUL LISTS

These lists organize excerpts by motion, range, number of parts, and genre.
Excerpt numbers are given.

Stepwise Excerpts

1	153	649 (Part 1)
2	164	680 (Parts 3 and 4)
3	165	701 (Part 2)
4	166	703
5	167	704
16	170	747 (Part 2)
17	171	787 (Part 4)
20 (Part 2)	174	815 (Part 3)
21 (Parts 2 and 3)	175	816 (Parts 2 and 3)
23 (Part 1)	176	818 (Part 3)
28	178	823 (Parts 2 and 3)
29 (Part 1)	182	833 (Part 1)
34	189	834 (Part 3)
46	194	874 (Part 2)
49 (Parts 1 and 3)	199	885 (Part 4)
50	202	890 (Part 1)
51	243	891 (Parts 1 and 3)
57	255 (Parts 2 and 3)	892 (Part 3)
58	256 (Part 2)	958
59	258	960
60	314 (Parts 1 and 2)	974
61	318	988 (Part 1)
64	329	994 (Part 2)
65	376	1099 (Part 3)
66 (Part 1)	421 (Part 1)	1112
71	427 (Part 3)	1130
100	428 (Part 3)	1131
106	429 (Part 2)	1153 (Parts 1 and 2)
109	484 (Part 2)	1177
116	525 (Parts 2 and 3)	1184 (Parts 2 and 3)
138	526 (Part 1)	1196
141	615 (Parts 1 and 3)	
150	618	

Excerpts with a Range of a Fifth or Smaller

2	249	730 (Part 3)
3	254 (Part 2)	738
7	255 (Parts 2 and 4)	747 (Parts 1, 2, and 3)
13 (Part 1)	256 (Parts 1, 2, and 3)	762 (Part 2)
17	258	779 (Part 2)
20 (Part 2)	267	784 (Part 1)
21 (Parts 2 and 3)	272	787 (Parts 2, 4, and 5)
23 (Part 1)	277 (Part 2)	789 (Part 2)
28	285 (Parts 2 and 3)	807 (Part 2)
29 (Part 1)	300	809 (Part 1)
37	305	815 (Parts 1, 2, 3, 4, and 5)
47	307	816 (Part 2)
49 (Parts 1, 3, 5, and 6)	314 (Part 2)	817 (Part 1)
50	322 (Parts 3, 5, and 6)	818 (Parts 1, 2, 3, and 4)
51	324	823 (Parts 1, 2, 3, 4, and 5)
57	327	828 (Part 3)
60	364 (Parts 2 and 3)	829 (Parts 1 and 2)
66 (Parts 1, 2, and 3)	365 (Part 3)	830 (Parts 1 and 2)
80	367	833 (Part 1)
81	411	834 (Parts 1, 2, 3, and 4)
82	421 (Parts 1, 2, 3, and 4)	862
83	427 (Parts 2 and 3)	883 (Part 3)
104a, b, and c	428 (Part 3)	885 (Parts 2 and 4)
106	429 (Parts 1, 2, 3, and 4)	886 (Part 2)
108 (Part 1)	430 (Part 2)	887 (Parts 2 and 3)
110	431 (Parts 2 and 3)	888 (Part 2)
113	457	890 (Parts 1, 2, 3, and 4)
114	484 (Parts 2 and 3)	891 (Parts 1, 3, and 4)
132 (Parts 1, 2, 3, and 4)	519 (Part 4)	892 (Part 3)
138	525 (Parts 2 and 3)	894
143 (Parts 1 and 2)	526 (Parts 1, 2, and 3)	897 (Parts 1, 2, and 3)
161	527 (Part 4)	904 (Parts 1 and 2)
163	566 (Part 2)	906
164	593 (Parts 2, 3, and 4)	915
174	615 (Parts 1, 3, and 6)	930
178	622	932
181 (Part 1)	630	934
186	631	994 (Parts 2 and 3)
189	641 (Parts 1 and 3)	1008 (Part 2)
195	642 (Parts 3 and 4)	1022 (Part 2)
211	645 (Part 1)	1061 (Parts 2 and 3)
212	647	1099 (Part 3)
217	649 (Parts 3 and 4)	1108
233 (Part 2)	654 (Parts 5, 6, and 7)	1111
234 (Part 2)	680 (Parts 2, 3, and 4)	1112
242	706	1115
243	715	1116

1124	1179	1192 (Parts 5 and 6)
1127	1182 (Parts 1, 2, 3, and 4)	1193 (Parts 1, 2, 3, and 4)
1130	1184 (Parts 1, 2, and 3)	1194 (Parts 7 and 8)
1142	1190 (Parts 1 and 2)	1205
1153 (Part 2)	1191 (Parts 1 and 2)	1209

Two-Part Excerpts

12	314	770
13	350	786
20	351	807
23	366	809
29	393	831
43	422	874
55	443	908
68	513	927
93	517	945
108	566	992
143	575	1001
173	604	1067
180	644	1086
183	645	1153
233	673	1173
235	674	1183
254	685	1190
290	701	1191
303	741	1217

Three-Part Excerpts

		853
21	417	883
66	455	888
256	650	889
277	766	892
285	779	988
364	789	999
365	816	1204
392	828	1206

Four-Part Excerpts

10	408	484
132	421	519
181	427	525
191	428	526
234	429	527
255	430	572
301 (canon)	431	641

Four-Part Excerpts (cont.)

642	830	982
649	833	994
680	834	996
688	884	1021
695 (canon)	885	1022
730	886	1056
747	887	1061
762	890	1099
784	891	1123
785	893 (canon)	1182
790 (canon)	896	1184
817	904	1193
826	907	1203
829	920	

Excerpts with Five or More Parts

49 (6 Parts)	654 (8 Parts)	897 (5 Parts)
322 (6 Parts)	787 (6 Parts)	1008 (5 Parts)
593 (5 Parts)	815 (5 Parts)	1192 (8 Parts)
594 (5 Parts)	818 (5 Parts)	1194 (8 Parts)
615 (6 Parts)	823 (5 Parts)	1228 (6 Parts—canon)

Excerpts from Folk Sources

3	105a, b, and c	302
5	111	306
27	113	309
31	117	316
32	118	320
35	119	323
36	120	325
37	126	328
38	133	329
39	135	330
60	145	331
72	146	332
77	156	336
82	158	337
83	219	338
85	220	341
88a and b	230	342
89a and b	231	345
90a and b	261	367
96a and b	280	375
97a and b	282	384
98a and b	289	411
103a, b, and c	292	459
104a, b, and c	297	506

576	794	1111
606	850	1112
619	894	1113
620	898	1114
621	899	1115
623	900	1116
627	901	1125
629	902	1126
632	903	1133
637	905	1137
638	1002	1143
639	1045	1201
672	1057	1207
748	1060	1212
761	1105	

Excerpts from Popular and Jazz Sources

225	564	1079
227	677	1085
379	683	1104
536	776	1127
556	1038	1194
557	1041	
558	1074	

CREDITS

INDEX OF COMPOSERS

Excerpt numbers are given.

INDEX OF WORKS

Excerpt numbers are given.